SOC...
Philosophy, Politics
and Practice

SOCIAL RESEARCH

Philosophy, Politics and Practice

edited by
MARTYN HAMMERSLEY

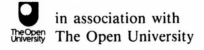 in association with
The Open University

 SAGE Publications
London • Thousand Oaks • New Delhi

Selection and arrangement. Introduction and Chapter 5
© The Open University 1993

First published 1993
Reprinted 1993 1994, 1996, 1997, 1999, 2004

SAGE Publications Ltd
6 Bonhill Street
London EC2A 4PU

SAGE Publications Inc
2455 Teller Road
Thousand Oaks, California 91320

SAGE Publications Ltd
32, M-Block Market
Greater Kailash – I
New Delhi 110 048

British Library Cataloguing in Publication Data

Social Research: Philosophy, Politics and Practice
  I. Hammersley, Martryn
  300.72

  ISBN 0–8039–8804–4
  ISBN 0–8039–8805–2 pbk

Library of Congress catalog card number 92–56439

Typeset by Mayhew Typesetting, Rhayader, Powys

Contents

Part 3   Practice

Introduction

The social sciences have been in recurrent crisis throughout their history, and these crises have often been methodological in character. Nevertheless, there can scarcely have been a time in the history of social research when it has been subject to such fundamental and diverse methodological criticism, from inside as well as outside, as it is today. Some of those outside the research community, while often willing to use research findings to support a point of view they already hold, nevertheless complain about: the obviousness of the findings of social research; its corrosive effects on social order and on religious and political beliefs; ideological bias among researchers etc. Within the research community, meanwhile, there are intense debates, for instance about what are and are not appropriate methods, especially concerning the superiority of quantitative or qualitative approaches; about whether research can realize its aim of producing accounts that correspond to the nature of social reality; about how research can and should be made more relevant to practice and policy-making; and even about whether its goal should be simply the production of knowledge or whether it must be committed to more practical and political goals.

This book cannot give a comprehensive account of *all* the methodological debates about social research, or all the views taken towards the issues involved. However, it includes articles, both classic statements and more recent contributions, that touch on many of these issues; and the views presented are diverse. The chapters are divided among the headings of philosophy, politics and practice; but this is no more than a rough and ready guide to their contents.

Part 1 begins with an introductory outline of positivist philosophy by Kolakowski. 'Positivism' is a term that is widely used by social researchers, in a variety of ways and often disparagingly. There are probably few social researchers today who would call themselves positivists, but the influence of positivism persists. Kolakowski focuses on the meaning of the term in philosophy where it is more clearly defined than in the social sciences. He identifies four features of positivism: phenomenalism, nominalism, denial of the possibility of knowledge of values, and commitment to the unity of scientific method.

All these features have had an important influence amongst social scientists from early in the twentieth century, both positively and negatively. Some social research has sought to apply positivist principles, notably in adopting what is taken to be the method of natural science and in restricting what is treated as knowledge to the results of research pursued on that basis. At the same time, there have been reactions against the influence of positivism in many areas, these becoming stronger over time. Interpretative critics have insisted that a natural science method is not appropriate to the study of the social world because the phenomena investigated by natural scientists are different in kind from those studied by social researchers: whereas physical phenomena and even animals simply react to stimuli, people interpret their surroundings and act on the basis of those interpretations, exercising free will. This anti-positivist response involves rejection both of the principle of the unity of scientific method and of phenomenalism, the idea that we must claim no knowledge beyond the data provided by science.

However, the situation has never been simple, nor has it remained static. By the middle of the twentieth century, many positivists in both philosophy and social science had modified their stance on these issues, recognizing other forms of inquiry outside of science and abandoning phenomenalism in favour of a modest realism. Meanwhile, more recently, some representatives of the interpretative tradition have come to place increased emphasis on differences between natural science and other forms of inquiry, and have rejected realism in favour of phenomenalism, idealism or relativism (Smith and Heshusius, 1986; Clifford and Marcus, 1986; Smith, 1989; Guba, 1990; Hammersley, 1992).

In the second chapter in the volume von Wright gives a brief outline of the historical basis of the reaction against positivism. He conceptualizes this reaction as an appeal to Aristotle's rather than Galileo's conception of science, and sees this as embodied in the ideas about understanding historical texts found in nineteenth century hermeneutics. This interpretation may seem misleading; after all, many anti-positivists simply reject the relevance of science to the study of human social life. However, in conceptualizing how human society should be studied they have often, wittingly or unwittingly, drawn on older ideas about science, including those of Aristotle. This way of thinking about anti-positivism also has the advantage of indicating that to oppose positivism does not mean that one must reject the natural sciences as a methodological model for social research. One may simply deny the validity of positivists' views of scientific method in favour of a different conception of that method (see, for example, Keat and Urry, 1975).

While positivist social scientists have themselves varied somewhat in their interpretations of science, in general they have taken quantitative measurement and the experimental or statistical manipulation of variables as its key elements. And it is against this conception of scientific method that anti-positivists in the social sciences have rebelled most strongly, often advocating instead the use of qualitative methods. In Chapter 3 Henwood and Pidgeon examine the debate about the relationship between qualitative and quantitative research with particular reference to psychology, where experimental research has long been and still remains the predominant method. They review the argument that qualitative research is based on a different epistemological paradigm to quantitative research, rejecting this but refusing to treat the difference between quantitative and qualitative as merely a technical matter concerning which method is most appropriate for the problem being investigated. They emphasize the qualitative researcher's concern with generating theory, and look in some detail at one of the most influential approaches to this: grounded theorizing. Finally, they consider the criteria that should be used for assessing qualitative research and how these differ from those characteristic of the quantitative tradition.

As significant as the anti-positivist rejection of the unity of science and of phenomenalism has been questioning of another of the elements of positivism identified by Kolakowski: the distinction between factual and value issues and the restriction of research to matters of fact. Important influences here have been the critical theory of the Frankfurt School, Marxism generally, and most recently feminism. Many critical researchers and feminists regard the distinction between facts and value as simply a device for disguising the role of conservative values in structuring much social research. In place of the idea that research should strive to be objective and neutral, they argue that it should be committed to the emancipation of oppressed groups, that it should be 'openly ideological' (Lather, 1986). In Chapter 4 Fay outlines the central elements of the sort of critical orientation that these approaches recommend, arguing that they must include: a critique of the self-understandings of the members of society and the provision of an empowering alternative; an explanation for the existence of false-consciousness; and an account of why and how this false-consciousness can be overcome. He argues that the viability of this sort of critical research depends on several important conditions: for example that the situation in which the research takes place is one of fundamental social structural conflict, and that one of the reasons why change has not occurred is the false-consciousness of the oppressed.

Jupp and Norris follow this up by looking at the influence and implications of the positivist, interpretative, and critical traditions in one particular field of research: documentary analysis. They trace the history of the influence of these approaches and examine the sorts of research thereby stimulated: the seminal interpretative analysis of personal documents, in the form of letters and life history material, carried out by Thomas and Znaniecki in their exploration of the experience of Polish immigrants to the United States; quantitative content analysis of newspapers; and critical analysis of the ideological assumptions generating official documents relating to crime. The authors give particular attention to the critical tradition, including the work of Foucault, noting its growing impact on the field in recent years.

Stavenhagen opens the section on the politics of research with a radical assessment of the theoretical assumptions he believes to be implicit in much applied social research, especially in the field of development studies in the Third World. In a classic article written in the early 1970s he argues that such research involves assumptions about the nature of society-at-large along with value judgements about it. He proposes that these assumptions be made explicit and subjected to scrutiny, with a view to making social research an effective challenge to the status quo. As part of this, the author recommends the study of elites and systems of domination, and the transformation of the social researcher into an activist seeking to bring about social change. Indeed, he argues that the social scientist cannot remain true to her or his scientific principles without doing this.

The next chapter, 'Towards a Methodology for Feminist Research', by Mies, is one of the most influential accounts of feminist methodology, and it highlights the differences between this and more conventional sorts of social research. She argues that feminism, as a critical approach to research, implies that the researcher must adopt a conscious partiality towards the people being studied, that the research should be geared towards bringing about the emancipation of women, and that its validity should be judged in terms of its contribution to this. She examines two examples of such research in which she has been involved, one concerned with a refuge for battered women in Cologne the other with landless female labourers in a rural part of India, both involving a life history approach.

Papadakis also discusses some examples of the application of a critical approach, in the form of interventionist research on new social movements. He looks first at the work of Touraine and his colleagues in relation to the French anti-nuclear movement, outlining Touraine's guiding theory of social movements and some of the consequences of his approach. A key issue here is the tension between Touraine's theory, used as a guiding evaluative framework for intervention, and the orientations of some of the anti-nuclear protesters. Later in the chapter Papadakis examines interventionist research by German sociologists in the Green Movement. Here too there emerge suspicions and dilemmas that throw important light on the nature and prospects of critical, interventionist research.

In the following chapter MacDonald focuses on evaluation studies in education. He points to the political character of the situation in which the evaluator finds her or himself, and emphasizes that it is impossible to avoid value issues. He argues that the evaluator can play different sorts of roles, and he outlines three that differ in political orientation: the bureaucratic, autocratic, and democratic models. As is clear from earlier chapters, these three models are applicable beyond the sphere of educational evaluation.

Ideas about the purposes of research and its political character have implications for judgements about the sort of methods that should be employed. For instance, some feminists have argued that the use of quantitative methods conflicts with the basic principles of feminism, especially if employed in the study of women. In Chapter 10 Jayaratne questions this argument. While she recognizes the validity of some of the criticisms of how those methods have been used, she claims that these defects are not essential to the method. And she outlines ways in which quantitative method may fulfil useful functions for feminists.

In the next chapter, Ahmad and Sheldon also address the political significance of a particular type of data. They examine one of the most controversial issues in social research in Britain in recent times: the debate concerning whether or not there should be questions about ethnic background in the census. They challenge the arguments in favour of this and point to some of the dangers. In particular, they are sceptical about the usefulness of the information such questions would provide for countering discrimination, and they fear that it would be misused.

In the first chapter of the section dealing with the practice of research, Hakim provides a detailed discussion of the uses that can be made of administrative records for research purposes. She points out that these are becoming more accessible through computerization, and argues that the assumption of some researchers that they are an irredeemably biased source of information is false. However, she underlines the problems involved in their use and the need for care in their interpretation.

This theme is continued in Chapter 13, which offers an inside view of the production of British Government statistics. The authors emphasize the scope for error, examining the various stages of the process of production of these statistics, and the threats to validity that may be involved in each. They also note the ways in which published statistics may be 'massaged' to give an impression that is seen as desirable by politicians and others. They recognize the usefulness of these statistics for research purposes, but they emphasize that the statistics must be interpreted with full awareness of the implications of their process of production for the likely validity of inferences drawn from them.

In the next chapter Finch provides a fascinating discussion of the issues that arise for feminists, and for others, in the process of interviewing. In particular, she examines the development of trust in the interview situation and the exploitative potential built into this. Indeed, she suggests that this potential may be even greater with unstructured than it is with structured interviewing. She illustrates her arguments from her own experience of research on clergy wives and playgroup mothers.

In Chapter 15 Punch presents an inside account of his experience in doing research on the police in an inner-city area of Amsterdam. He touches on many of the problems characteristic of participant observation research: negotiating initial access; building and maintaining relationships with the people observed; the selection of what to observe; the role of informants; and the extent to which participants may control the information that reaches the participant observer. Furthermore, his discussion of his role in the field highlights many of the ethical issues involved in this sort of research, and it provides a counterpoint to the arguments of those in the critical and feminist traditions.

Following this, Schofield looks at what many regard as the most serious problem with qualitative research: the uncertain generalizability of its findings. She considers several attempts to conceptualize this problem in the field of educational research. She also identifies the different sorts of generalization that can be involved in qualitative investigations, and examines some of the strategies that can be used to support general claims. Her argument is illustrated from her own experience working on several studies in applied educational research.

In the final chapter Gage addresses a widespread criticism of social research: that its findings are obvious. He examines a number of examples of this criticism, assessing their persuasiveness. He argues that very often social research findings are not the truisms they are claimed to be by critics. Furthermore, even when they are, research often provides us with information about when the truism does and does not apply to particular cases. In this way Gage shows that conventional forms of research are not always as vulnerable to criticism as they are sometimes taken to be.

The chapters in this book cover a wide variety of methodological issues. They illustrate the range and depth of thinking about these issues, both as regards principles and practice, to be found amongst social researchers today. Some very different approaches to social research are represented, based on conflicting philosophical, political, and practical assumptions. And the arguments marshalled to justify each approach often involve fundamental criticism of others. It is tempting to conclude from this that the field of social research is a war-zone in which competing paradigms based on quite different assumptions about the purposes and possibilities of social research must simply fight it out (for a review of this prospect in one field, see Gage, 1989). However, in my view, while we must recognize that there are some profound differences in approach, it is important to keep methodological discussions open. Only in that way can we hope to make progress towards resolving the problems that lie at the heart of the disagreements. One of the purposes of this book is precisely to facilitate and encourage such discussion.

References

Clifford, J. and Marcus, G. (eds) (1986) *Writing Culture: The Poetics and Politics of Ethnography*. Berkeley, CA: University of California Press.

Gage, N. (1989) 'The paradigm wars and their aftermath: a "historical" sketch of research on teaching since 1989', *Educational Researcher*, 18: 4–10.

Guba, E. (ed.) (1990) *The Paradigm Dialog*. Newbury Park, CA: Sage.

Hammersley, M. (1992) *What's Wrong with Ethnography?* London: Routledge.

Keat, R. and Urry, J. (1975) *Social Theory as Science*. London: Routledge & Kegan Paul.

Lather, P. (1986) 'Issues of validity in openly ideological research', *Interchange*, 17 (4): 63–84.

Smith, J.K. (1989) *The Nature of Social and Educational Inquiry*. Norwood, NJ: Ablex.

Smith, J.K. and Heshusius, L. (1986) 'Closing down the conversation: the end of the quantitative-qualitative debate among educational inquirers', *Educational Researcher*, 15 (1): 4–12.

Acknowledgements

The editor thanks other members of the DEH313 Course Team for their help in preparing this book. He would also like to thank Duncan Scott who, many years ago, introduced him to the article by Stavenhagen (reprinted as Chapter 6) and the issues it raises.

The editor and publishers wish to thank the following for permission to use copyright material: American Educational Research Association for material from N.L. Gage, 'The obviousness of social and educational research results', *Educational Researcher*, 20 (1), 1991. Copyright © 1991 by the American Educational Research Association; Basil Blackwell Ltd for material from B. Fay, 'The elements of critical social science', in *Critical Social Science: Liberation and its Limits*, Polity Press, 1987; British Psychological Society and the authors for material from K.L. Henwood and N.F. Pidgeon, 'Qualitative research and psychological theorizing', *British Journal of Psychology*, 83, 1992; Geisenheyner & Crone on behalf of the author for L. Kolakowski, 'An overall view of positivism', in *The Alienation of Reason*, Doubleday & Co.; Macmillan Publishers Ltd for material from M. Punch, 'Observation and the police: the research experience', in *Policing the Inner City: a study of Amsterdam Warmoesstraat*, 1979; Elim Papadakis and Sage Publications for 'Interventions in new social movements', in J. Gubrium and D. Silverman (eds), *The Politics of Field Research*, Sage, London, 1989; Pluto Press for material from Government Statisticians' Collective, 'How official statistics are produced: views from the inside', in J. Irvine, I. Miles and J. Evans (eds), *Demystifying Social Statistics*, 1979; Radical Statistics for W.I.V. Ahmad and T.A. Sheldon, '"Race" and statistics', *Radical Statistics*, 48 (Spring), 1991; Routledge for material from M. Mies, 'Towards a methodology for feminist research' and T.E. Jayaratne, 'The value of quantitative methodology for feminist research', in G. Bowles and R.D. Klein (eds), *Theories for Women's Studies*, 1983; C. Hakim, 'Research analysis of administrative records', in *Research Design*, Unwin Hyman, 1987; J. Finch, 'It's great to have someone to talk to: ethics and politics of interviewing women', in C. Bell and H. Roberts (eds), *Social Researching: Politics, Problems, Practice*, 1984; and G.H. von Wright, 'Two traditions', in *Explanation and Understanding*, 1971; The Society for Applied Anthropology for R. Stavenhagen, 'Decolonializing applied social sciences', *Human Organization*, 30 (4), 1971; Teachers College Press for J.W. Schofield, 'Increasing the generalizability of qualitative research', in E.W. Eisner and A. Peshkin (eds), *Qualitative Inquiry in Education: The Continuing Debate*, 1989. Copyright © 1989 by Teachers College, Columbia University.

Every effort has been made to trace all the copyright holders, but if any have been inadvertently overlooked the publishers will be pleased to make the necessary arrangement at the first opportunity.

PART 1

PHILOSOPHY

1

An Overall View of Positivism

Leszek Kolakowski

The term 'positive philosophy' was coined by Auguste Comte, and it has lasted down to the present time in the shorter form of 'positivism'. Not all, however, who according to historians or critics profess the positivist doctrine, would agree to be classified under this heading. As a rule these thinkers object because they are reluctant to admit that they profess a doctrine that has had a long and complex history. To respect these wishes, one would be obliged, in discussing each thinker, to single out those elements in positivism that are not to his taste, at the same time pointing out how much of the rest of it he none the less subscribes to. Also, many thinkers are conscious of the errors and oversimplifications that grow up around doctrinal labels, and for this reason hesitate to enrol themselves under any banner.

This means that setting boundaries to the current of thought positivism represents in nineteenth- and twentieth-century intellectual history requires a decision that is partly arbitrary. The same problem arises in many other cases (for example, when one discusses the history of existentialist or Marxist philosophy). A measure of arbitrariness, however, is unavoidable both for the historian and for the student of philosophical culture. One has to organize the material at hand according to some schema, disregarding differences in matters one looks upon as secondary, in order to bring out the continuity in primary contexts. Nor is this distinction between primary and secondary strains in philosophy entirely arbitrary. It is based on certain historical data that show, maybe

From *Positivist Philosophy*, Penguin, Harmondsworth, 1972, pp. 9–19.

with the aid of purely quantitative (though approximate) indices, that certain themes, propositions, or assertions held the attention of readers, polemicists, and adherents over a given period, while others went almost unnoticed. The classifier or historian who discerns a certain 'current' in the history of philosophy goes on to refer solely to historical, factual criteria in justifying his construction. Otherwise he might be suspected of ascertaining intellectual trends on the basis of arbitrarily chosen principles (though even this is permissible, provided he clearly formulates his criteria). Moreover he refers to a sense of continuity that actually was felt by successive generations of adherents, and given expression by them. There is room for error in interpreting such evidence, but it certainly merits being taken into account.

In the present instance, however, I am dealing with a matter that is scarcely controversial: the existence of a 'positivist current' in nineteenth- and twentieth-century philosophy is universally acknowledged. Doubts arise only when we try to define this current, and to formulate rigorous criteria setting it off from the other currents. This situation is as normal and inescapable in the history of philosophic thought as in the history of art: the interpenetration of ideas, the ways in which one current influences another or reacts against it, not to mention genuine ambiguities in the texts themselves, mean that there is always room for more than one interpretation; perfectly clear-cut divisions are ruled out by the facts of the case.

So let me try to characterize the positivist mode of thinking in the most schematic, overall terms.

Positivism stands for a certain philosophical attitude to human knowledge; strictly speaking, it does not prejudge questions about how men arrive at knowledge – neither the psychological nor the historical foundations of knowledge. But it is a collection of rules and evaluative criteria referring to human knowledge: it tells us what kind of contents in our statements about the world deserve the name of knowledge and supplies us with norms that make it possible to distinguish between that which may and that which may not reasonably be asked. Thus positivism is a normative attitude, regulating how we are to use such terms as 'knowledge', 'science', 'cognition', and 'information'. By the same token the positivist rules distinguish between philosophical and scientific disputes that may profitably be pursued and those that have no chance of being settled and hence deserve no consideration.

The most important of the rules that, according to the positivist doctrine, are to be observed in order, so to speak, to separate the wheat from the chaff in any statement about the world – i.e., to determine the questions worth considering and to discard questions that are falsely formulated or involve illegitimate concepts – are as follows.

1. *The rule of phenomenalism.* This may briefly be formulated as follows: there is no real difference between 'essence' and 'phenomenon'. Many traditional metaphysical doctrines assumed that various observed or observable phenomena are manifestations of a reality that we cannot get to know in the ordinary way; this assumption justified the use of such terms as 'substance', 'substantial form', 'occult quality', etc. According to positivism, the distinction between essence and phenomenon should be eliminated from science on the ground that it is misleading. We are entitled to record only that which is actually manifested in experience; opinions concerning occult entities of which experienced things are supposedly the manifestations are untrustworthy. Disagreements over questions that go beyond the domain of experience are purely verbal in character. It must be noted here that positivists do not reject every distinction between 'manifestation' and 'cause'. After all, it is well known that whooping cough *manifests* itself by characteristic fits of coughing, and once such a type of disease has been isolated, we are entitled to recognize the cough as a *manifestation* and to inquire into the specific 'hidden mechanism' of this manifestation. Discovery of *Bacillus pertussis* early in this century, as the causal agent of the infection, was not obviously incompatible with the assumptions of phenomenalism. For positivists do not object to inquiry into the immediately invisible causes of any observed phenomenon, they object only to any accounting for it in terms of occult entities that are by definition inaccessible to human knowledge. Classical examples of entities the positivists condemn as illegitimate interpolations lying beyond the domain of possible experience are 'matter' and 'spirit'. Since matter is supposed to be something different from the totality of the world's observed qualities, and since with this concept we do not account for observed phenomena more effectively than without it, there is no reason to make use of it at all. Similarly, if 'soul' is to denote a certain object different from the totality of the describable qualities of human mental life, it is a superfluous construct, for no one can tell us how the world without soul would differ from the world with soul.

Needless to say, the phenomenalist 'don't' so formulated can give rise to doubt, for it is hard to state it in such a form that it will settle once and for all, in every possible case, whether the question is a legitimate one, whether it represents the search for the mechanism behind the manifestation, or whether it is to be thrown into the dustbin as 'metaphysical'. In some extreme cases the decision is easy to make. For instance, if anyone maintained that absolutely unknowable objects exist, a positivist would consider him an incorrigible metaphysician on the ground that he has made a statement about a reality that is by definition not subject to experimental control. Conversely there can be no doubt about whether it makes sense to inquire into the possible existence and properties of a specific cancer-virus, for all that it is for the time being observable only through its manifestations. But there are many cases in which the decision is not so obvious. I mention this not as an objection to positivism but to call attention to the highly abstract way in which I have characterized the positivist programme, also to the fact that incompatible interpretations of this same overall rule are to be found within positivism itself. For the moment, however, I shall not go into the overall rules in greater detail but let them stand out starkly as a means of identifying one fairly important current in philosophical thought. This would appear more instructive than to restrict the designation 'positivism' to certain branches of this current only.

2. *The rule of nominalism.* Strictly speaking, this rule may be regarded as a consequence of the preceding one, but it is preferable to state it separately, in view of the fact that in philosophical controversy terminological ambiguities are such that additional distinctions allow us to affirm two judgements that seem incompatible at first glance. The rule of nominalism states that we may not assume that any insight formulated in general terms can have any real referents other than individual concrete objects. As is well known, attempts to define knowledge in this way were made from the very beginning of European thought. When Plato considered the question of what we are actually speaking about when, for instance, we speak about the triangle or about justice, he formulated a question that has not lost its vitality down to our own day, though it is often posed in different words. We say that the sum of the angles in any triangle is equal to two right angles. But what does the statement actually refer to? Not to this or that triangular body, since there is no absolutely perfect triangle that meets all the requirements of geometry; nor can it refer, for the same reason, to all individual triangular objects. And yet it can hardly be said that geometry does not refer to anything at all. Hence our assertion must refer to 'the' triangle, pure and simple. But what is this triangle, which is to be found nowhere in nature? It has none of the physical characteristics we usually ascribe to bodies. For one thing, it is not localized in space. All its properties derive from the fact that it is a triangle and nothing else; we must

acknowledge that it exists in some way, although it is an existence not perceived by the senses, accessible only to reflection.

Nominalists reject this line of reasoning. We have the right to acknowledge the existence of a thing, they say, only when experience obliges us to do so. No experience obliges us to assume that our general knowledge about the properties of 'the' triangle corresponds to a certain entity different from individual triangular bodies and possessing a separate existence from them. It is true that our science requires the use of conceptual instruments that describe certain ideal states, which are never achieved in the empirical world. Not only the mathematical sciences but also physics make use of such constructs. More particularly, the physics initiated by Galileo must inevitably make use of descriptions of ideal situations, in which certain observable features of the real world are carried to an abstract point of refinement. Study of the properties of such ideal situations helps us understand the real situations that only approximate them more or less closely. But these ideal situations – the concept of a vacuum in mechanical theory, self-contained systems, figures in geometry – are creations of our own that serve as a superior, more concise and more general description of empirical reality. There is no reason to suppose, because we assume such situations for the convenience of our calculations, that they must actually exist anywhere in reality. The world we know is a collection of individual observable facts. Science aims at ordering these facts, and it is only thanks to this ordering work that it becomes a true science, i.e., something that can be put to practical use and that enables us to predict certain events on the basis of others. All our abstract concepts, all the schemata of the mathematical sciences, and all the idealizations drawn up in the natural sciences are contained in these ordering systems. Only thanks to them can we give experience a coherent, concise form, that is easy to remember and purified of the accidental deviations and deformations that are necessarily present in every individual fact. Though absolutely perfect circles are found neither in nature nor in the products of human technology, we can produce circular bodies that quite closely approximate to this ideal, thanks to the fact that we operate with the perfect circle in our abstract calculations. A system ordering our experiences must be such that it does not introduce into experience more entities than are contained in experience. But since it inevitably uses abstractions among its means it must also be such that we do not forget that these abstractions are no more or less than means, human creations that serve to organize experience but that are not entitled to lay claim to any separate existence.

According to nominalism, in other words, every abstract science is a method of abridging the recording of experiences and gives us no extra, independent knowledge in the sense that, via its abstractions, it opens access to empirically inaccessible domains of reality. All the general entities, the abstract creations, with which the old metaphysics filled the world, are fictions, for they illegitimately ascribed existence to things that have no existence save as names or words. In the language of the old controversies universality is merely a characteristic of linguistic constructs or – according to some interpretations – of mental acts associated with operations involving these constructs. In the world of actual experience, however, hence in the world pure and simple, there are no such things as 'universals'.

3. The phenomenalist, nominalist conception of science has another important consequence, namely, *the rule that refuses to call value judgements and normative statements knowledge.* Experience, positivism argues, contains no such qualities of men, events, or things as 'noble', 'ignoble', 'good', 'evil', 'beautiful', 'ugly', etc. Nor can any experience oblige us, through any logical operations whatever, to accept statements containing commandments or prohibitions, telling us to do something or not to do it. More accurately: it is clear that it is possible to supply logical grounds for judgements made on the basis of a declared aim on the effectiveness of the means employed; evaluations of this type have a technical character and may be qualified as true or false to the extent that they have a technical sense, i.e., to the extent that they tell us what operations are or are not effective in achieving a desired end. Examples of such technical judgements would be statements to the effect that we should administer penicillin in a case of pneumonia or that children ought not to be threatened with a beating if they won't eat. Such statements can clearly be justified, if their meaning is respectively that penicillin is an effective remedy against pneumonia, and that threatening children with punishment to make them eat harms their characters. And if we assume tacitly that as a rule it is a good thing to cure the sick and a bad thing to inflict psychological damage on children, these statements can be justified, even though they do have the form of normative judgements. But we are not to assume that any assertion of values that we accept for themselves, rather than in relation to something else, can be justified by experience. For instance, the principle that human life is an irreplaceable good cannot be so justified: we may accept it or we may reject it, but we must be conscious of the arbitrariness of our option. For on the phenomenalist rule we are obliged to reject the assumption of values as

characteristics of the world for they are not discoverable in the same way as the only kind of knowledge worthy of the name. At the same time the rule of nominalism obliges us to reject the assumption that beyond the visible world there exists a domain of values 'in themselves', with which our evaluations are correlated in some mysterious way. Consequently we are entitled to express value judgements on the human world, but we are not entitled to assume that our grounds for making them are scientific; in other words, the only grounds for making them are our own arbitrary choices.

4. Finally among the fundamental ideas of positivist philosophy there is a belief in the essential *unity of the scientific method*. To an even greater extent than the previous principles, the meaning of this one admits of various interpretations. For all that, the idea itself is invariably present in positivist discussion. In its most general form it expresses the belief that the methods for acquiring valid knowledge, and the main stages in elaborating experience through theoretical reflection, are essentially the same in all spheres of experience. Consequently we have no reason to assume that the qualitative differences between particular sciences come to anything more than characteristics of a particular historical stage in the development of science; we may expect that further progress will gradually eliminate such differences or even, as many authors have believed, will reduce all the domains of knowledge to a single science. It has often been supposed that this single science in the proper sense of the term will be physics, on the grounds that of all the empirical disciplines it has developed the most exact methods of description, and that it encompasses the most universal of the qualities and phenomena found in nature – those without which no others occur. This assumption – that all knowledge will be reduced to the physical sciences, that all scientific statements will be translated into physical terms – does not, to be sure, follow from the foregoing positivist rules without further assumptions. Moreover, belief in the unity of the scientific method can be specified in other ways as well. However, this interpretation is fairly common in the history of positivism.

Around these four briefly stated rules positivist philosophy has built up an extensive network of theory covering all the domains of human knowledge. Defined in the most general terms positivism is a collection of prohibitions concerning human knowledge, intended to confine the name 'knowledge' or 'science' to the results of those operations that are observable in the evolution of the modern sciences of nature. Throughout its history the particular concern of positivism has been to turn a polemical cutting edge to metaphysical speculation of every kind, and hence against all reflection that either cannot found its conclusions on empirical data or formulates its judgements in such a way that they can never be contradicted by empirical data. Thus, according to the positivists, both the materialist and the spiritualist interpretations of the world make use of terms to which nothing corresponds in experience: it is not known how the world of our experience would be different from what it is, were we to assume that it is not, as materialists think, a manifestation of the existence and movement of matter, or were we to assume that it is not as the adherents of religious denominations think, controlled by the spiritual forces of Providence. Since neither of these assumptions entails consequences enabling us to predict or to describe additional features of the world, there is no reason to concern ourselves with them. Thus positivism constantly directs its criticisms against both religious interpretations of the world and materialist metaphysics, and tries to work out an empirical position entirely free of metaphysical assumptions. This position is consciously confined to the rules the natural sciences observe in practice. According to the positivists, metaphysical assumptions serve no purpose in these sciences, whose aim is to formulate the interdependence of phenomena without penetrating more deeply into their hidden 'natures' and without trying to find out whether the world 'in itself' has features other than those accessible, directly or indirectly, to experience.

2

Two Traditions

G.H. von Wright

Two main traditions can be distinguished in the history of ideas, differing as to the conditions an explanation has to satisfy in order to be scientifically respectable. The one tradition is sometimes called *Aristotelian*, the other *Galilean*. The names suggest that the first has very ancient roots in the intellectual history of man, while the second is of relatively recent origin. There is some truth in this, but it should be taken with a grain of salt. What I here call the Galilean tradition has an ancestry going back beyond Aristotle to Plato. One should also beware of thinking that the Aristotelian tradition today represents merely the fading survival of obsolete elements from which science is gradually becoming 'liberated'.

As to their views of scientific explanation, the contrast between the two traditions is usually characterized as causal *versus* teleological explanation. The first type of explanation is also called mechanistic, the second finalistic. The Galilean tradition in science runs parallel with the advance of the causal-mechanistic point of view in man's efforts to explain and predict phenomena, the Aristotelian tradition with his efforts to make facts teleologically or finalistically understandable. [. . .]

The great awakening or revolution in the natural sciences during the late Renaissance and the Baroque era was to a certain extent paralleled in the nineteenth century in the systematic study of man, his history, languages, *mores* and social institutions. The work of Ranke and Mommsen in historiography, Wilhelm von Humboldt, Rasmus Rask, Jacob Grimm in linguistics and philology, Tylor in social anthropology, is comparable to the achievements, two or three centuries earlier, of Copernicus and Kepler in astronomy, Galileo and Newton in physics, or Vesalius and Harvey in anatomy and physiology.

Since natural science was already established on the intellectual stage, and the humanistic studies with a scientific claim were

From *Explanation and Understanding*, Routledge, London, 1971, pp. 1–7 and 169–73.

newcomers, it was but natural that one of the chief issues of nineteenth-century methodology and philosophy of science concerned the relationship between these two main branches of empirical inquiry. The principal stands on this issue can be linked with the two main traditions in methodological thinking we have distinguished.

One stand is the philosophy of science most typically represented by Auguste Comte and John Stuart Mill. It is usually called *positivism*. The name was coined by Comte, but used with due caution it is also appropriate for the position of Mill[1] and for an entire intellectual tradition extending from Comte and Mill not only down to the present day but also upward in the stream of time to Hume and the philosophy of the Enlightenment.

One of the tenets of positivism[2] is *methodological monism*, or the idea of the unity of scientific method amidst the diversity of subject matter of scientific investigation.[3] A second tenet is the view that the exact natural sciences, in particular mathematical physics, set a methodological ideal or standard which measures the degree of development and perfection of all the other sciences, including the humanities.[4] A third tenet, finally, is a characteristic view of scientific explanation.[5] Such explanation is, in a broad sense, 'causal'.[6] It consists, more specifically, in the subsumption of individual cases under hypothetically assumed general laws of nature, including 'human nature'.[7] The attitude towards finalistic explanations, i.e. towards attempts to account for facts in terms of intentions, goals, purposes, is either to reject them as unscientific or to try to show that they can, when duly purified of 'animist' or 'vitalist' remains, be transformed into causal explanations.[8]

Through its emphasis on unity of method, on the mathematical ideal-type of a science, and on the importance of general laws to explanation, positivism is linked with that longer and more ramified tradition in the history of ideas which I have here called Galilean.

Another stand on the question of the relationship between the sciences of nature and of man was a reaction against positivism. The antipositivist philosophy of science which became prominent towards the end of the nineteenth century is a much more diversified and heterogeneous trend than positivism. The name 'idealism' which is sometimes used to characterize it is appropriate only for some facets of this trend. A better name for it seems to me to be *hermeneutics*. Representatives of this type of thought included some eminent German philosophers, historians and social scientists. Perhaps the best known of them are Droysen, Dilthey,

Simmel and Max Weber. Windelband and Rickert of the neo-Kantian Baden School are related to them. The Italian Croce and eminent British philosopher of history and art Collingwood may be said to belong to the idealist wing of this anti-positivist trend in methodology.

All these thinkers reject the methodological monism of positivism and refuse to view the pattern set by the exact natural sciences as the sole and supreme ideal for a rational understanding of reality. Many of them emphasize a contrast between those sciences which, like physics or chemistry or physiology, aim at generalizations about reproducible and predictable phenomena, and those which, like history, want to grasp the individual and unique features of their objects. Windelband coined the label 'nomothetic' for sciences which search for laws, and 'ideographic' for the descriptive study of individuality.[9]

The antipositivists also attacked the positivist view of explanation. The German historian–philosopher Droysen appears to have been the first to introduce a methodological dichotomy which has had great influence. He coined for it the names *explanation* and *understanding*, in German *Erklären* and *Verstehen*.[10] The aim of the natural sciences, he said, is to explain; the aim of history is to understand the phenomena which fall within its domain. These methodological ideas were then worked out to systematic fullness by Wilhelm Dilthey.[11] For the entire domain of the understanding method he used the name *Geisteswissenschaften*. There is no good equivalent in English, but it should be mentioned that the word was originally coined for the purpose of translating into German the English term 'moral science'.

Ordinary usage does not make a sharp distinction between the words 'explain' and 'understand'. Practically every explanation, be it causal or teleological or of some other kind, can be said to further our understanding of things. But 'understanding' also has a psychological ring which 'explanation' has not. This psychological feature was emphasized by several of the nineteenth-century antipositivist methodologists, perhaps most forcefully by Simmel, who thought that understanding as a method characteristic of the humanities is a form of *empathy* (in German *Einfühlung*) or re-creation in the mind of the scholar of the mental atmosphere the thoughts and feelings and motivations, of the objects of his study.[12]

It is not only through this psychological twist, however, that understanding may be differentiated from explanation. Understanding is also connected with *intentionality* in a way explanation is not. One understands the aims and purposes of an agent, the meaning of a sign or symbol, and the significance of a social institution or religious rite. This intentionalistic or, as one could perhaps also call it, semantic dimension of understanding has come to play a prominent role in more recent methodological discussion.

If one accepts a fundamental methodological cleavage between the natural sciences and the historical *Geisteswissenschaften*, the question will immediately arise of where the social and behavioural sciences stand. These sciences were born largely under the influence of a cross pressure of positivist and antipositivist tendencies in the last century. It is therefore not surprising that they should have become a battleground for the two opposed trends in the philosophy of scientific method. The application of mathematical methods to political economy and other forms of social study was an inheritance of the eighteenth-century Enlightenment which found favour with nineteenth-century positivists. Comte himself coined the name 'sociology' for the scientific study of human society. Of the two great sociologists of the turn of the century, Emile Durkheim was essentially a positivist as far as his methodology is concerned,[13] while in Max Weber a positivist colouring is combined with emphasis on teleology (*zweckrationales Handeln*) and empathic understanding (*verstehende Soziologie*).[14]

Notes

1. Cf. Mill (1865) and the references to Comte and positivism in Mill (1843), especially in Bk VI.
2. There are different ways of characterizing 'positivism'. One characterization links positivism with a phenomenalist or sensualist theory of knowledge, and modern positivism with a verificationist theory of meaning. Another characterization links it with a 'scientistic' and 'technological' view of knowledge and its uses. Mill is more of a positivist in the first sense than is Comte. Comte's positivism is above all a philosophy of science. (See Comte, 1830, 'Avertissement de l'Auteur'.) His ultimate ambition was to be a champion of the 'positive', scientific spirit in the study of social phenomena. (Comte, 1830, Leçon I, sec. 6.) With this he combined a firm belief in the usefulness of scientific knowledge for social reform. [. . .]
3. Comte (1830), 'Avertissement', Leçon I, sec. 10. [. . .]
4. Comte (1830), Leçon I, sec. 6 (on the notion of a 'physique sociale') and Leçon II, sec. 11.
5. Mill (1843), Bk III, ch. xii; Comte (1830), Leçon I, secs 4 and 24. [. . .]
6. Mill (1843), Bk III, ch. xii, sec. 1: 'An individual fact is said to be explained, by pointing out its cause, that is, by stating the law or laws of causation, of which its production is an instance.' Comte repudiated the search for 'causes'. He associated it with the 'pre-positivist', metaphysical stage in the development of science. In positivist science the role of causes is taken over by general laws. Cf. Comte (1830), Leçon I, sec. 4, and Comte (1844), Pt 1, sec. 3.
7. Mill (1843), Bk VI, ch. iii, sec. 2. [. . .]

8. Cf. Comte (1844), Pt I, sec. 6. [. . .]
9. Windelband (1894).
10. Droysen (1858). [. . .]
11. Dilthey (1883, 1894, 1900, 1910). [. . .]
12. Simmel (1892), particularly ch. I, and Simmel (1918).
13. The methodological standpoint of Durkheim is best studied in Durkheim (1893) and (1894). His positivist attitude notwithstanding, some of Durkheim's chief ideas, for example those concerning the 'representations collectives' of the social consciousness, could be profitably reinterpreted, I think, in the terms of a hermeneutic methodology of understanding.
14. On Weber's position see in particular Weber (1913) and Weber (1921), Pt I, ch. i.

References

Angel, R.B. (1967) 'Explanation and prediction: a plea for reason', *Philosophy of Science*, 34.

Caws, P. (1965) *The Philosophy of Science*. Princeton, NJ: Von Nostrand.

Comte, A. (1830) *Cours de Philosophie Positive*.

Comte, A. (1844) *Discours sur L'esprit Positif*.

Dilthey, W. (1833) *Einleitung in die Geisteswissenschaften*.

Dilthey, W. (1894) *Ideen über eine beschreibende und zergliedernde Psychologie*.

Dilthey, W. (1900) *Die Entstehung der Hermeneutik*.

Dilthey, W. (1910) *Der Aufbau der geschichtlichen Welt in den Geisteswissenschaften*.

Droysen, J.G. (1858) *Grundriss der Historik*.

Durkheim, E. (1893) *De la Division du Travail Social*.

Durkheim, E. (1894) *Les Règles de la Méthode Sociologique*.

Hanson, N.R. (1959) 'On the symmetry of explanation and prediction', *Philosophical Review*, 68.

Hempel, C.G. (1942) 'The function of general laws in history', *Journal of Philosophy*, 39.

Hempel, C.G. (1965) 'Aspects of scientific explanation', in C.G. Hempel, *Aspects of Scientific Explanation and other Essays in the Philosophy of Science*. New York: Free Press.

Kuhn, T.S. (1962) *The Structure of Scientific Revolutions*. Chicago: University of Chicago Press.

Mill, J.S. (1843) *A System of Logic*. London: John W. Parker.

Mill, J.S. (1865) 'Auguste Comte and positivism', *Westminster Review*.

Popper, K. (1935) *Logik der Forschung*. Vienna: Julius Springer.

Scheffler, I. (1957) 'Explanation, prediction and abstraction', *British Journal for the Philosophy of Science*, 7.

Simmel, G. (1892) *Die Probleme der Geschichtsphilosophie*. Leipzig: Duncker & Humblot.

Simmel, G. (1918) *Von Wesen des historischen Verstehens*. Berlin: E.S. Mittler & Sohn.

Weber, M. (1913) 'Über einige Kategorien der verstchenden Soziologie', *Logos*, 4.

Weber, M. (1921) *Wirtschaft und Gesellschaft: Grundriss der verstehenden Soziologie*. 4th edn, Tübingen: J.C.B. Mohr.

Windelband, W. (1894) 'Geschichte und Naturwissenschaft', reprinted in *Präludien*, 3rd edn. Tübingen: J.C.B. Mohr.

3

Qualitative Research and Psychological Theorizing

Karen L. Henwood and Nick F. Pidgeon

This paper is concerned with the debate about qualitative and quantitative research methods, and why this debate is important to psychology. One of our key contentions is that doing qualitative research cannot be reduced merely to questions of gathering, analysing and reporting non-numeric data. Rather, a whole range of epistemological issues, as well as wider ones of research practice, are raised. Some of the epistemological issues have been aired before in well-known criticisms of the status of the experiment in psychology (Gergen, 1978a; Harré and Secord, 1972; Orne, 1962; Tajfel, 1972). These criticisms have been valuable in raising ethical questions for psychologists, and in securing the ground for an increasing interest in psychology in interview and fieldwork research. However, their more radical implications have generally been neglected. We suspect that this is because they are perceived to fall within an epistemological framework which is incommensurate with the natural science approach underpinning the experimental method. We shall argue that psychology can benefit from a closer look at the epistemological and technical dimensions of the recent quantity–quality debate as conducted in the human sciences in general (for example, Bryman, 1988; Lincoln and Guba, 1985). In particular we wish to draw attention to issues and strategies for theory generation and criteria for assessing the adequacy of research.

What is Qualitative Research?

Alan Bryman (1988) has argued that a good deal of confusion exists amongst human scientists due to lack of clarity over what constitutes qualitative and quantitative research. Part of the confusion comes from the narrow association of qualitative methodology either with particular modes of data gathering (typically interviews

From *British Journal of Psychology*, 83, 1992, pp. 97–111.

or fieldwork) or its non-numeric character (for example, verbal protocols, verbatim transcriptions of subjects' discourse, fieldnotes from participant observation studies, or archival material). However, method is more than data alone. The gathering, analysis and interpretation of data is always conducted within some broader understanding of what constitutes legitimate inquiry and warrantable knowledge. In this respect, the quantity–quality debate has been anchored within two apparently opposed epistemological positions. The two poles are known variously as 'experimental', 'hypothetico-deductive' or 'positivist' and the 'naturalistic', 'contextual' or 'interpretative' approaches respectively.

The natural science approach held to underpin the experimental method is the dominant paradigm in psychology and other forms of quantitative social research. This paradigm emphasizes universal laws of cause and effect based on an explanatory framework which assumes a realist ontology; that is, that reality consists of a world of objectively defined facts. The hypothetico-deductive method is the principal means by which causal relationships are established. Within this account of method, the scientist's ideal strategy is the experimental control of subsets of variables in the service of testing (either verification or falsification) of *prior* theory. In practical terms, much of the work of the natural scientist concerns the methodological minutiae of operationalization and measurement. Quantification – the sum of standardization, measurement and number – is crucial to the natural science approach, because it renders the concepts embedded in theoretical schemes or hypotheses observable, manipulable, and testable. It is also taken to be a necessary (if not always sufficient) condition for the findings of research to be replicable and generalizable, and for predictions upon the basis of observed regularities to be made. Not surprisingly, therefore, quantification is traditionally seen as the *sine qua non* of scientific method.

The alternative epistemological position is expressed in the naturalistic or interpretative paradigm. It is the result of a long history of critique of the positivist scientific method as the sole basis for understanding human activity (for example, Hammersley, 1989). The nineteenth-century German historian and philosopher Wilhelm Dilthey argued that a clear distinction should be drawn between the disciplines of *Naturwissenschaften* (natural science) and *Geisteswissenschaften* (the moral or human sciences). In Dilthey's view ([1894] 1977), whilst the former could be prosecuted by the external observation and explanation of regularities in physical events, the human sciences should be premised upon the search for *Verstehen* (meaning or understanding). Dilthey directed this critique at the early experimental psychology of the time, arguing, unsuccessfully, against its uncritical adherence to the natural science model and its reductionist approach to human consciousness. The naturalistic paradigm, as characterized today, draws upon these broad insights, and their echoes in the related traditions of hermeneutics and phenomenology. This paradigm is described by a number of characteristics. These include a commitment to constructivist epistemologies, an emphasis (at least in its pure ethnographic form) upon description rather than explanation, the representation of reality through the eyes of participants, the importance of viewing the meaning of experience and behaviour in context and in its full complexity, a view of the scientific process as generating working hypotheses rather than immutable empirical facts, an attitude towards theorizing which emphasizes the emergence of concepts from data rather than their imposition in terms of *a priori* theory, and the use of qualitative methodologies for research. Qualitative methods are privileged within the naturalistic approach because they are thought to meet a number of reservations about the uncritical use of quantification in social science practice: in particular, the problem of inappropriately fixing meanings where these are variable and renegotiable in relation to their context of use; the neglect of the uniqueness and particularity of human experience (cf. the nomothetic–ideographic debate in psychology); and because of concern with the overwriting of internally structured subjectivities by externally imposed 'objective' systems of meaning.

Framing the distinction between quantitative and qualitative research in terms of these two epistemological poles is important in alerting us to the fact that there are competing claims regarding what constitutes warrantable knowledge. This idea has been common currency in the literature on the philosophy of science for some years now (for example, Collins, 1985; Feyerabend, 1975; Kuhn, 1962), and is extremely useful in understanding the emergence of counter-paradigmatic movements in psychology and the human sciences. For example, in social psychology it is argued that one important consideration is to understand the way versions of social and psychological reality are constructed in discourse and social texts (Henriques *et al.*, 1984; Hollway, 1989; Parker, 1989; Potter and Wetherell, 1987). The meta-theoretical concern of discourse analysts within psychology is with a constructivist epistemology which leads them to advocate the primacy of qualitative methods. Similarly, for ethical, epistemological and emancipatory reasons, traditional quantitative methods are increasingly being rejected by feminist researchers in psychology.

Qualitative methods are being adopted by these researchers because they are viewed as being sensitive to women's experiences seen in their own terms, and as empowering women in their efforts to work for change (for example, Duelli Klein, 1983; Griffin, 1986).

In discussing choices made during the process of research it is important that we do not overemphasize the significance of the epistemological distinction. Bruno Latour's (1987) discussion of the role of number and formalism in science is instructive here. It suggests that quantification is but one manifestation of the common practice of deriving coherent, mobile and combinable inscriptions in science. By this argument qualitative and quantitative research procedures are but different forms of the analytic practice of re-representation in science, in that both seek to arrange and rearrange the complexities[1] of 'raw' data. Also, programmatic statements about how psychological and social realities ought to be studied and what constitutes proper knowledge thereof are rarely followed up by the *exclusive* use of either qualitative or quantitative methods. For example, discourse analysts have used a questionnaire-type approach (Potter and Collie, 1989) and some feminist psychologists have used Q-sort and factor analytic methods (Kitzinger, 1986).[2] And where a researcher does rely on either qualitative or quantitative methods this will tend to be justified on pragmatic rather than epistemological grounds. Alan Bryman presents one view in suggesting that 'the distinction between qualitative and quantitative research is really a technical matter whereby the choice between them is to do with their suitability in answering particular research questions' (1988: 108–9). That is to say, the researcher should always bear in mind that methods are not so much valid in and of themselves, but rather will be more or less useful for particular research purposes.

On the other hand, there is an equivalent danger in minimizing the epistemological dimension to the issue. The effect of this would be to characterize the choice between qualitative and quantitative research methods as a *purely* technical matter, and risks a reversion to the position where research is evaluated only in relation to the classical canons of reliability, validity and objectivity. Two examples of this in psychology are provided by the methods of content analysis (Krippendorff, 1980) and protocol analysis (Ericsson and Simon, 1984). The focus of both is upon the classification of data in ways that maximize the reliability and validity of the coding system, and on facilitating the testing of prior theoretical concerns. These two examples are qualitative in the narrow sense of being methods of dealing with non-numeric data but, as we illustrate below, do not offer the potential benefits that qualitative methods such as grounded theory and discourse analysis open up to psychology.

It is clear that the issue of what constitutes qualitative methodology is not a simple one. It follows from our argument so far that one could attempt to classify research methods according to some kind of typology related to the numeric/non-numeric and traditional/new-paradigm dimensions. Such a classification scheme would inevitably be both fuzzy and imperfect. Therefore, we will not dwell upon locating particular research strategies within this typology or any other. A more immediate concern is to avoid viewing qualitative and quantitative methods as deriving from incommensurable paradigms. In practical terms this would deny the possibility of strengthening research through the use of a principled mixture of methods.[3] It would also risk simply repeating the inconclusive and divisive debate of the 1970s, and carries the implication that qualitative methods are only relevant to specialist domains in psychology, such as clinical or social. This would do a disservice to psychology as a whole because it would obscure the radical and exciting implications that are explicitly raised by considering qualitative methods (in the broadest sense) in relation to the scientific process and the generation of knowledge. In particular we focus in the next section on the issue of the generation of scientific theories, and how this might enrich psychological theorizing.

The Generation of Theory

There is a simplistic view of qualitative methods as local description anchored around single case studies, eschewing theoretical concerns. This is so in some traditional ethnography, where the purpose of research is the detailed description of patterns of cultural life through the eyes of participants in that culture, and is valuable for the role that it plays in debunking ethnocentric myths that researchers and their audience may hold. However, this idea is not fully representative of core ideas in contemporary ethnography (for example, Hammersley and Atkinson, 1983) and in qualitative research generally. Here it is recognized that any intellectual analysis entails some degree of abstraction away from the purely phenomenological (Rock, 1973). In this respect both qualitative and traditional quantitative approaches share a common concern with theory as the goal of research. Nevertheless, the relationship between theory and the research process is a different one in qualitative and quantitative research. Implicit in the discussion so far has been a distinction between the use of empirical research for the testing of prior theory and the rather different goal of generating theory from data. In the hypothetico-deductive mode the emphasis is on the former: *a priori* theory is assumed to *direct* the processes of collection, analysis, and interpretation of data. In contrast to this in the naturalistic paradigm, and for a variety of reasons, researchers may be unwilling or unable to fully specify their theoretical concerns in advance of the study. The emphasis in the latter tradition is therefore to *move from data towards theory*.

In talking about the generation or discovery of theory, qualitative researchers make explicit what tends to be only implicit in much scientific practice. In the traditional philosophy of science literature, the idea that a distinction can be made between the context of discovery and the context of justification has a long pedigree (for example, Reichenbach, 1938: 7). By this account, it is apparent that the methodology of science itself has focused almost exclusively upon techniques for justification, either as verification or criticism, and neglected those of discovery. The issue of discovery is a complex one, and has typically been mystified both by scientists and philosophers. Ironically, an extreme view is that 'how it happens that a new idea occurs to a man [sic] – whether it is a musical theme, a dramatic conflict, or a scientific theory – may be of great interest to empirical psychology; but is irrelevant to the logical analysis of scientific hypotheses' (Popper, 1980: 31)! It is clear to us that, unless all scientists are engaged merely in 'normal science' (Kuhn, 1962), discovery must play a fundamental role in the scientific process, with psychology being no exception. However, we must be clear in eschewing a naïve view of the notion of discovery in science. What comes to be recognized as a 'discovery' involves more than the creativity and cognitive resources of the individual researcher. Research in the sociology of scientific knowledge has alerted us to the role of the social networks within which scientific ideas become constituted and legitimized as new and significant (Woolgar, 1988a). For this reason the notion of theory *generation* is preferable to discovery in accommodating key aspects of the social practice of science. To talk in terms of discovery assumes a model of the individual researcher dispassionately uncovering pre-existing objectively defined facts. The notion of theory generation, however, highlights the process of inserting new discourses within old systems of meaning – the active, constitutive process of representation and re-representation in science (Latour, 1987).

Clearly there are contexts where there is a need for psychologists to generate theory. Leaving aside the question of how full-scale paradigm shifts occur, there are occasions where existing theory is incomplete, inappropriate, or entirely absent (see also Gergen, 1978b). We can quote at least two examples relating to this from our own research experience. The first example concerns the field of cognitive science and intelligent knowledge-based systems research, where efforts are being made to elicit knowledge from human specialists in order to build so-called 'expert systems'. It is clear that prior theories concerning contextual aspects of an expert's knowledge in any particular domain will often be largely absent, and that under such circumstances the inquiry must take a more generative approach (Pidgeon *et al.*, 1991). A second example, from the social psychology of ageing, is of research framed originally within an intergroup relations and speech accommodation paradigm being reoriented to focus instead on strategies for the management of painful self-disclosure and age identity. Open-ended interpretative analysis of localized and context-specific verbal interactions led to the overhauling of initial assumptions about the relevance of stereotypically driven speech, and to their replacement by a concern for situated interaction routines and everyday understandings of age identification and representation. This research illustrated how detailed inspection of participants' discourse can illuminate quite different features of the processes of social ageing than would have been possible if research had continued within preset theoretical terms (for example, Coupland *et al.*, 1988; Coupland *et al.*, 1991; Henwood, 1990).

Grounded Theory

A significant contribution can be made by qualitative research to psychology in the provision of explicit skills and techniques to aid in the generation of theory. This statement conveys more than the idea of using open-ended pilot studies merely to prepare the ground for subsequent quantitative research (a useful, if restricted, role that qualitative methods have played in the past in psychology). Rather, qualitative methodology can be seen as playing a central role in the quest for psychological knowledge, and be reported on in its own right. We would agree with David Rennie *et al.* (1988) that a useful approach in this regard is that of *grounded theory*. Barney Glaser and Anselm Strauss (1967) advocate a particular approach to qualitative analysis that is now being widely used in the human sciences, although not as yet to any great extent in psychology. Their principal concern in writing the monograph *The Discovery of Grounded Theory* (1967) was to free researchers in sociology from the theoretical strait-jackets of a few 'grand' theories. They originally used the term 'grounded theory' to refer to theory that is generated in the course of the close inspection and analysis of qualitative data, an idea which is now a central tenet of naturalistic research. The term has, since, also become associated with the specific data analysis strategies formulated by Glaser and Strauss, which we go on to describe below. We cannot provide a detailed account of the techniques of generating grounded theory here: the interested reader is directed to the original source plus B.A. Turner (1981), Martin and Turner (1987), and Strauss and Corbin (1990). An excellent summary making specific reference to psychology is Rennie *et al.* (1988).

In approaching research without any strong prior theory, qualitative researchers are inevitably faced with the problem of making sense of a vast amount of unstructured data. Glaser and Strauss advocate that researchers begin by allowing an array of concepts and categories to emerge from systematic inspection of a data corpus. This necessitates the development of an open-ended indexing system, where the researcher works systematically through the basic data transcripts generating labels to describe both low-level concepts and the more abstract features deemed relevant. This may be characterized as a means of moving towards a data description language. The exercise of generating grounded theory is in this respect very different from that of, for example, traditional content analysis, where the researcher's task is to allocate instances to a set of predefined, mutually exclusive and exhaustive categories.[4] In the early phases of grounded theory, the researcher is endowed with maximum flexibility in generating new categories from the data. This is a creative process which taxes fully the interpretative powers of the researcher, who is disciplined by the requirement that low-level descriptions, in Glaser and Strauss's terms, *fit* the data well. Success in generating good grounded theory which is faithful to the data depends upon maintaining a balance between full use of the researcher's own intellect and this requirement of fit.

As analysis proceeds the researcher builds up a set of categories each of which is referenced to one or more instances in the data. Whilst there is no orthodoxy here, there are a number of more or less routine operations that help the researcher move toward a conceptually rich understanding, and systematic integration of the low-level categories into a coherent theoretical account. These include: theoretical saturation of categories (coding of instances until no new examples of variation are found); writing definitions of categories that have achieved saturation; writing memoranda recording all of the analyst's observations during the course of the analysis; linking categories together, often involving the creation of new overarching categories at higher levels of abstraction; and seeking more data where this appears necessary to elucidate aspects of the emerging theory. A key orienting idea in all of this is the method of constant comparative analysis. Here the researcher is urged to be constantly alert to the similarities and differences which exist between instances, cases, and concepts, to ensure that the full diversity and complexity of the data are explored.

Glaser and Strauss have been rightly criticized on the grounds that theoretical reflection cannot be delayed until so late in the research process (Bulmer, 1979), and more pointedly for espousing a form of 'inductivist positivism' (Stanley and Wise, 1983: 152). Glaser and Strauss themselves note this possible contradiction in their work when they state that 'the researcher does not approach reality as a tabula rasa' (1967: 3). This difficulty arises from the philosophical proposition that legitimate data are necessarily defined through theory (Feyerabend, 1975), and raises the question of what grounds grounded theory! A resolution of this is to view any 'emergent' theoretical account as the result of a constant interplay between data and conceptualization, a 'flip-flop' between ideas and research experience (Bulmer, 1979). A number of inter-related features shape this interplay and mark out the differences between grounded theory and the hypothetico-deductive method. These include the assumption that the relationship between theory and data will at first be ill-defined; acceptance of the need to be tolerant of, and indeed to seek out and explore, ambiguity and uncertainty in this relationship when constructing a category system that is both relevant to the problem and fits the data; and the exhortation to researchers to avoid premature closure or fixing of theory whenever new insights might arise. In practice, the researcher at first perceives only unstructured chaos in the data, as if looking through unfocused conceptual lenses. But as analysis proceeds, and order is generated, the lenses become more sharply focused.

Our own experience of using grounded theory in the analysis of qualitative data has convinced us of the utility of this approach for generating theory in psychology. The operations described briefly above typically generate a rich, deep and well-integrated conceptual system, organized at various levels of theoretical abstraction all of which in some way articulate with the data. As such, it engenders great confidence in the researcher in her or his theoretical account. A researcher's confidence in the account is a necessary condition, but not a sufficient one, for evaluating the adequacy of the emergent theory. The next section therefore discusses the critical issue of criteria for evaluating the 'goodness' of generative, qualitative research.

Criteria for Judging the Quality of Research in Psychology

Discussions of criteria for judging psychological research are generally limited to questions about specific aspects of methodology such as reliability and validity, and characteristics of theory including parsimony, empirical content, internal consistency, and generality. For qualitative methods to be taken seriously in psychology, however, a broader-based discussion around these issues is required. In our view, merely applying the above canons to evaluate generative qualitative research risks undermining the benefits that can be gained from their use (Marshall, 1985). Nonnumeric methods such as content analysis, which are underpinned by the hypothetico-deductive model, are routinely evaluated using conventional reliability and validity criteria (for example, Krippendorff, 1980: chs 12 and 13). And parallel criteria of 'trustworthiness' have been derived with general qualitative methods in mind (Miles and Huberman, 1984). But, we can go further than this, to argue for the need for radically different means of evaluating such research. The classical criteria rest on the norm of objectivity which assumes the independence of the knower and the known. By this account one important goal of method is to limit wherever possible the effects of researcher bias, where bias is defined to be a deviation from some empirical truth or fact. The naturalistic paradigm, on the other hand, challenges the dualistic distinction between knower and known, leading to the realization that the personal is always present in research (Polanyi, 1958; Stanley and Wise, 1983). The corollary of this is that criteria for judging the quality of research cannot be reduced to tactics for eradicating observer bias.

Once the norm of objectivity has been questioned in this way, there is no easy resolution to the problem of judging the adequacy of a particular piece of research. A powerful case can be made for methodological anarchy, to ensure the proliferation of new theoretical ideas (Feyerabend, 1975)! This points up a radical elaboration of the notion of accountability in the research process. Whereas the traditional canons, in essence, seek to eliminate idiosyncrasy and creativity, criteria for judging the quality of generative research must recognize aspects of these personal characteristics in the search for theory that is relevant and good.

There are no methodological criteria capable of guaranteeing the *absolute* accuracy of research. However, a number of good practices have been suggested by qualitative researchers which can be used to guide both the progress of the study and its ultimate evaluation by researchers and their peers. These practices illustrate the rigour of qualitative research, thus challenging the traditional dichotomy (for example, Gherardi and Turner, 1987) between 'hard' quantitative and 'soft' qualitative research. On the other hand, to use Catherine Marshall's phrase (1985), they do not overly 'sanitize' the research process, and for this reason do not stifle the researcher's theoretical imagination.

Keeping Close to the Data: the Importance of Fit
We have already alluded to the fact that a basic requirement of good qualitative research is that the categories constituting the building blocks of emergent theory should fit the data well. One way of working towards this, recommended by Barry Turner (1981), is to write comprehensive definitions summarizing why phenomena have been labelled in a certain way. This exercise produces a public product which makes explicit the initially tacit conceptual classifications perceived by the individual researcher. As such, it allows both the researcher and peers to evaluate fit.

Theory Integrated at Diverse Levels of Abstraction
Good theory should be rich, complex and dense, and integrated at diverse levels of generality. The analyst's memoranda are a key resource here, for explicating the synthesized structure of the emergent theory. Glaser and Strauss argue that 'the synthesis provides readily apparent connections between data and lower and higher level conceptual abstractions of categories and properties' (1967: 37). The goal here is to ensure that the theory at all levels of abstraction is meaningfully related to the problem domain. Glaser and Strauss describe theory that exhibits this property as theory that 'works'.

Reflexivity
Science is often distinguished from everyday understandings in terms of its self-consciousness about methodology. Much of contemporary psychology still shares with the positivist paradigm a reflection upon method that is restricted by adherence to a realist ontology. This promotes the ideal of scientific inquiry as a neutral, impartial activity. Naturalistic research, in contrast, acknowledges the ways in which research activity *inevitably* shapes and constitutes the object of inquiry; the researcher and researched are characterized as interdependent in the social process of research. This can be termed the reflexive character of research (for example, Hammersley and Atkinson, 1983). The term 'reflexivity' is, of course, a complex one and has, over the years, acquired many and

varied usages (for example, Woolgar, 1988b; Steier, 1991). However, one practical implication of accepting the inevitable role of the researcher in the research process is that this should be highlighted and revealed in the documentation of qualitative studies. For example, the feminist researcher Shulamit Reinharz contrasts the conventional approach to conducting and reporting science, where researchers' attitudes are not revealed, recognized or analyzed (in the attempt to be 'objective' and 'value free'), with the alternative or feminist view that researchers' attitudes should be fully described and discussed and their values 'acknowledged, revealed and labelled' (1983: 172). In a similar vein, Yvonna Lincoln and Egon Guba (1985) advise the keeping of a 'reflexive journal'. They suggest that such a journal should include the daily schedule and logistics of the study, a personal diary where reflections are noted on the role of one's own values and interests, and a log of methodological decisions and accompanying rationales.[5]

Documentation
The keeping of a reflexive journal is but one facet of the important process of building up documentation in qualitative research. This exercise provides an account of what is done, and why it is done, at all phases in the research process. As well as reflecting upon values and assumptions, and writing memoranda and definitions for categories, researchers should also document such things as initial concerns and how these may change, sampling decisions, hunches about the quality of the data gathered, and observations about the context of data generation. In building up such a set of documents the researcher is laying a 'paper-trail' open to external audit (Lincoln and Guba, 1985: ch. 13) by immediate colleagues and more distant peers. The exercise provides a means of tracking the progress of (and stimulating) creative thought, and acts as a useful vehicle for increasing researcher reflexivity.

Theoretical Sampling and Negative Case Analysis
Sampling is an important consideration in qualitative research. Since the goal is the elaboration of a conceptually rich, dense, and contextually grounded theory, there is no compunction to sample multiple cases where this would not extend or modify emerging theory. Sampling is therefore explicitly driven by theoretical concerns. A key consideration in theoretical sampling is so-called 'negative case analysis' (for example, Kidder, 1981). This parallels the Popperian strategy of ingeniously seeking wherever possible to falsify working hypotheses derived from the emergent model in that, as analysis of initial cases proceeds, further cases would be

selected for their disconfirming potential. However, in the Popperian account of this strategy, the end goal would be the logical corroboration of existing theory by *failure* to falsify. This contrasts sharply with the goal of negative case analysis in qualitative research, which is to aid in the generation of conceptually dense, grounded theory. Exploring cases which do not fit an emerging conceptual system is invaluable because it serves as a device for challenging initial assumptions and categories, and for modifying and elaborating theory where necessary.[6] Negative case analysis may be viewed as a particular manifestation of the method of constant comparative analysis, since this also seeks to systematically explore differences in the expanding data corpus.

Sensitivity to Negotiated Realities
One frequently cited, but hotly contested, approach to validating theory in qualitative studies is the suggestion that, as a consequence of good fit, it should be readily recognizable to participants in the study who have provided data. Whilst there is a good case for this under some circumstances, there are also many reasons to be cautious of taking respondents' accounts wholly at face value; for example, people may not always be fully aware of reasons for their actions, and accounts may be offered to perform a variety of non-obvious and context-specific functions (for example, allocating blame to others, warranting particular claims to truth) which go beyond the mere provision of information. One approach, which overcomes some of the immediate difficulties of respondent validation, is the suggestion that researchers seek to construct a negotiated joint reality with participants (Westkott, quoted in Duelli Klein, 1983; see also Regoczei and Plantinga, 1987). This facilitates the exploration of reasons why respondents' and researchers' interpretations may differ, and serves as a further source of data with which to elaborate the developing theory (see also Dingwall, 1981). Beyond this, there will be occasions where the researcher cannot accept the stricture to negotiate reality with participants on their own terms; for example, when studying the beliefs of fascist groups (Billig, 1977). More generally, it must be recognized that such negotiations cannot be characterized necessarily as part of a free and democratic process, as some accounts of the naturalistic paradigm would hold. They inevitably take place within relationships of power which exist between and around the researcher and researched (see Gubrium and Silverman, 1989).

Transferability
The question of the extent to which findings from a particular study can be said to have a more general significance is important in science. In qualitative research, where sampling decisions have not been made on statistical grounds, one suggestion is that researchers talk in terms of the transferability, rather than generalizability, of findings (Lincoln and Guba, 1985). Most narrowly, this term refers to applying the findings of a study in contexts similar to the context in which they were first derived. This observation is important in that it places a special onus on the qualitative researcher to fully report on the contextual features of a study, and is one reason why detailed reporting of case studies is important. However, it is necessary to guard against naïve empiricism here, and also not to treat context as just an adjunct to theory (Jaeger and Rosnow, 1988). In our view, rich and dense grounded theory, which is contextually sensitive at diverse levels of abstraction, will in itself suggest its own sphere of relevance and application (compare J.C. Turner, 1981).

Concluding Comments

A final issue that we wish to raise is that of communicating the outcome of any study to others. The naturalistic view is that relying upon correspondence with the empirical world as the ultimate arbiter of truth is both impractical and untenable. Rather, the more pragmatic argument can be made that the outcomes of research will be evaluated in terms of their persuasiveness and power to inspire an audience (Feyerabend, 1975; see also Latour, 1988). The argument can be made that the conventions of quantification and statistical reporting in psychology function in precisely this way (John, 1992). In a similar vein, following the guidelines for good practice set out above should help to increase the persuasiveness of findings of qualitative research. Theory that is represented at diverse levels of abstraction, but which nevertheless fits the data well, should be challenging, stimulating, and yet highly plausible in the sense of clearly reflecting substantive aspects of the problem domain. Echoing this, Rennie *et al.* make the point that the generation of grounded theory 'gets close to the bone' (1988: 145) and Marshall describes the process of conducting research in this way as 'productive, fun and appropriate' leading to 'the "aha" experience of discovery' (1985: 370). We would concur that these are some of the major benefits of qualitative research.

Qualitative research methods *are* being used in psychology.

When conducted rigorously and intelligently, they require considerable commitment and hard work on the part of the researcher. We
would maintain that qualitative methods engender a commitment
to doing research in this way because they tend to lead to the
generation of good, relevant and persuasive theory. As yet, the
strategies adopted by qualitative researchers on the ground for
developing good theory have not been reflected to any significant
extent at a general methodological level in psychology. We hope to
have contributed to this process in this paper.

Notes

We wish to thank Caroline Kelly, Stephen Frosh, Barry Turner and an anonymous
reviewer for commenting upon an earlier version of the manuscript. John Bowers
made a number of insightful comments on the text, and directed our attention to
the important work of Bruno Latour.

1. Where qualitative and quantitative research may be seen to differ here is in
    their approach to re-representing complexity. In the former, an heuristic princi-
    ple for the researcher is not to lose sight of complexity where this might have
    interpretative value. In the quantitative paradigm, however, number is the
    means by which the many become the summarized few. While such a process
    holds powerful benefits, in terms of rendering data inscriptions controllable by
    the scientist, its very strength – that of simplification – is also its Achilles' heel!
    For example, Silvio Funtowicz and Jerry Ravetz (1986, 1990) argue that many
    important aspects of number (units, spread, and the quality or 'pedigree' of the
    processes of their derivation) are easily lost in the retelling. This is evident in
    psychology, where the fashion for using inferential statistical techniques by
    default rather than principled choice, and the common reliance upon statistical
    significance as the main criterion of interpretative worth (John, 1992), may well
    obscure many relevant features of data (cf. also Tukey, 1977).
2. Sandra Harding points out that 'the use of quantitative studies . . . have been
    favoured targets of many feminist social science critics . . . [but that] there are
    probably few methods of gathering evidence or theoretical frameworks that
    cannot be made to yield gold to feminist miners' (1987: 109).
3. Powerful pragmatic arguments can be made for using a principled mixture of
    qualitative and quantitative research methods under particular circumstances
    (see Bryman, 1988, chapter 6; Silverman, 1985, chapter 7). Most commonly
    accepted in psychology would be the practice of grounding quantitative research
    by prior use of qualitative investigation, to ensure that quantitative measures
    assess issues that are relevant to the research problem in context and salient to
    participants. A second possibility is to use qualitative and quantitative research
    methods in parallel; here 'simple counting techniques can offer a means to
    survey the whole corpus of data ordinarily lost in intensive qualitative research'
    (Silverman, 1985: 140). Arguments can also be found for a quantitative phase
    preceding qualitative research. For example, Steve Reicher and Nick Emler
    (1986) used an initial quantitative survey in order to establish relevant
    comparison groups for their subsequent qualitative interviews.
4. Recently, a more open-ended form of content analysis, using fuzzy rather than

crisp categories, and which holds much potential as an exploratory generative technique, has been developed by Lea Scherl and Michael Smithson (1987).

5. For some contrasting, and critical, comments on the notion and promotion of reflexivity in research see Bruno Latour (1988). He expresses reservations about what he terms 'meta-reflexivity', the major function of which is to promote scepticism in any scientific account. Accepting the pragmatic need for one's own version of scientific knowledge to be persuasive, he identifies the practice of 'infra-reflexivity' as a preferable alternative. By this he is advising the deployment of any stylistic device in order to narrate a more compelling and plausible account.

6. Recent criticisms of Popper in the philosophy of science have pointed out that simple falsification is untenable as the logical arbiter of truth in science, since any theoretical conjecture will always be surrounded by supporting assumptions (for example, Lakatos, 1970). A falsifying instance will always be ambiguous in its implications, therefore, since it may be due to the conjecture being inappropriate, one or more of the supporting assumptions being inappropriate, or both. By this account, differences between Popperian falsification and the use of negative case analysis in qualitative research become less pronounced: both can be seen as offering opportunities for the exploration of the complexities of data and theory.

References

Billig, M. (1977) 'The new social psychology of "fascism"', *European Journal of Social Psychology*, 7 (4): 393–432.

Bryman, A. (1988) *Quantity and Quality in Social Research*. London: Unwin Hyman.

Bulmer, M. (1979) 'Concepts in the analysis of qualitative data', in M. Bulmer (ed.), *Sociological Research Methods*. London: Macmillan.

Collins, H.M. (1985) *Changing Order: Replication and Induction in Scientific Practice*. London: Sage.

Coupland, N., Coupland, J., Giles, H., Henwood, K. and Wiemann, J. (1988) 'Elderly self-disclosure: interactional and intergroup issues', *Language in Society*, 8 (2): 109–33.

Coupland, J., Coupland, N., Giles, H. and Henwood, K. (1991) 'Formulating age: dimensions of age identity in elderly talk', *Discourse Processes*, 14: 87–105.

Dilthey, W. ([1894] 1977) *Descriptive Psychology and Historical Understanding*. English trans. The Hague: Martinus Nijhoff.

Dingwall, R. (1981) 'The ethnomethodological movement', in G. Payne, R. Dingwall, J. Payne and M. Carter (eds), *Sociology and Social Research*. London: Croom Helm.

Duelli Klein R. (1983) 'How to do what we want to do: thoughts about feminist methodology', in G. Bowles and R. Duelli Klein (eds), *Theories of Women's Studies*. London: Routledge & Kegan Paul.

Ericsson, K.A. and Simon, H.A. (1984) *Protocol Analysis: Verbal Reports as Data*. Cambridge, MA: MIT Press.

Feyerabend, P.K. (1975) *Against Method*. London: Verso.

Funtowicz, S.O. and Ravetz, J.R. (1986) 'Policy-related research: a notational scheme for the expression of quantitative technical information', *Journal of the Operational Research Society*, 37 (3): 243–7.

Funtowicz, S.O. and Ravetz, J.R. (1990) *Uncertainty and Quality in Science for Policy*. Dordrecht: Kluwer.

Gergen, K.J. (1978a) 'Experimentation in social psychology', *European Journal of Social Psychology*, 8: 507–27.

Gergen, K.J. (1978b) 'Toward generative theory', *Journal of Personality and Social Psychology*, 36 (11): 1344–60.

Gherardi, S. and Turner, B.A. (1987) *Real Men Don't Collect Soft Data*. Dipartimento di Politica Sociale, Quaderno 13, Università di Trento, Italy.

Glaser, B.G. and Strauss, A.L. (1967) *The Discovery of Grounded Theory: Strategies for Qualitative Research*. New York: Aldine.

Griffin, C. (1986) 'Qualitative methods and female experience', in S. Wilkinson (ed.), *Feminist Social Psychology: Developing Theory and Practice*. Milton Keynes: Open University Press.

Gubrium, J.F. and Silverman, D. (1989) *The Politics of Field Research*. London: Sage.

Hammersley, M. (1989) *The Dilemma of Qualitative Method: Herbert Blumer and the Chicago Tradition*. London: Routledge.

Hammersley, M. and Atkinson, P. (1983) *Ethnography: Principles in Practice*. London: Routledge.

Harding, S. (ed.) (1987) *Feminism and Methodology*. Milton Keynes: Open University Press.

Harré, R. and Secord, P.F. (1972) *The Explanation of Social Behaviour*. Oxford: Blackwell.

Henriques, J., Hollway, W., Urwin, C., Venn, C. and Walkerdine, V. (1984) *Changing the Subject: Psychology, Social Regulation and Subjectivity*. London: Methuen.

Henwood, K. (1990) 'Stereotyping and self disclosure: a discourse approach to ageing', paper presented at the Future of Adult Life: Second International Conference, Leeuwenhorst, The Netherlands, July.

Hollway, W. (1989) *Subjectivity and Method in Psychology: Gender, Meaning and Science*. London: Sage.

Jaeger, M.E. and Rosnow, R.L. (1988) 'Contextualism and its implications for psychological inquiry', *British Journal of Psychology*, 79: 63–75.

John, I.D. (1992) 'Statistics as rhetoric in psychology', *Australian Psychologist* (in press).

Kidder, L.H. (1981) 'Qualitative research and quasi-experimental frameworks', in M.B. Brewer and B.E. Collins (eds), *Scientific Inquiry and the Social Sciences*. San Francisco: Jossey-Bass.

Kitzinger, C. (1986) 'Introducing and developing Q as a feminist methodology: a study of accounts of lesbianism', in S. Wilkinson (ed.), *Feminist Social Psychology: Developing Theory and Practice*. Milton Keynes: Open University Press.

Krippendorff, K. (1980) *Content Analysis: An Introduction to its Methodology*. London: Sage.

Kuhn, T.S. (1962) *The Structure of Scientific Revolutions*. Chicago: University of Chicago Press.

Lakatos, I. (1970) 'Falsification and the methodology of scientific research programmes', in I. Lakatos and A. Musgrave (eds), *Criticism and the Growth of Knowledge*. Cambridge: Cambridge University Press.

Latour, B. (1987) *Science in Action*. Milton Keynes: Open University Press.

Latour, B. (1988) 'The politics of explanation: an alternative', in S. Woolgar (ed.), *Knowledge and Reflexivity: New Frontiers in the Sociology of Knowledge*. London: Sage.

Lincoln, Y.S. and Guba, E.G. (1985) *Naturalistic Inquiry*. Beverly Hills, CA: Sage.

Marshall, C. (1985) 'Appropriate criteria of trustworthiness and goodness for qualitative research on education organizations', *Quality and Quantity*, 19: 353–73.

Martin, P.Y. and Turner, B.A. (1987) 'Grounded theory and organizational research', *Journal of Applied Behavioural Science*, 22 (2): 141–57.

Miles, M.B. and Huberman, A.M. (1984) *Qualitative Data Analysis*. Beverly Hills: Sage

Orne, M.T. (1962) 'On the social psychology of the psychological experiment: with particular reference to demand characteristics', *American Psychologist*, 17: 776–83.

Parker, I. (1989) *The Crisis in Modern Social Psychology: And How To End It*. London: Routledge.

Pidgeon, N.F., Turner, B.A. and Blockley, D.I. (1991) 'The use of grounded theory for conceptual analysis in knowledge elicitation', *International Journal of Man-Machine Studies*, 35: 151–73.

Polanyi, M. (1958) *Personal Knowledge: Towards a Post-Critical Philosophy*. Chicago: University of Chicago Press.

Popper, K.R. (1980) *The Logic of Scientific Discovery*, 4th edn. London: Hutchinson. (First edn 1959.)

Potter, J. and Collie, S. (1989) ' "Community care" as persuasive rhetoric: A study of discourse', *Disability, Handicap and Society*, 4 (1): 57–64.

Potter, J. and Wetherell, M. (1987) *Discourse and Social Psychology*. London: Sage.

Regoczei, S. and Plantinga, E.P.O. (1987) 'Creating the domain of discourse: ontology and inventory', *International Journal of Man-Machine Studies*, 27: 235–50.

Reichenbach, H. (1938) *Experience and Prediction: An Analysis of the Foundations of the Structure of Knowledge*. Chicago: University of Chicago Press.

Reicher, S. and Emler, N. (1986) 'Managing reputations in adolescence: the pursuit of delinquent and non-delinquent identities', in H. Beloff (ed.), *Getting into Life*. London: Methuen.

Reinharz, S. (1983) 'Experiential analysis: a contribution to feminist research', in G. Bowles and R. Duelli Klein (eds), *Theories of Women's Studies*. London: Routledge & Kegan Paul

Rennie, D.L., Phillips, J.R. and Quartaro, G.K. (1988) 'Grounded theory: a promising approach to conceptualization in psychology?', *Canadian Psychology*, 29 (2): 139–50.

Rock, P. (1973) 'Phenomenalism and essentialism in the sociology of deviance', *Sociology*, 7 (1): 17–29.

Scherl, L.M. and Smithson, M. (1987) 'A new dimension to content analysis: exploring relationships among thematic categories', *Quality and Quantity*, 21: 199–208.

Silverman, D. (1985) *Qualitative Methodology and Sociology*. Aldershot, Hants: Gower.

Stanley, L. and Wise, S. (1983) *Breaking Out: Feminist Consciousness and Feminist Research*. London: Routledge & Kegan Paul.

Steier, F. (ed.) (1991) *Research and Reflexivity*. London: Sage.

Strauss, A.L. and Corbin, J. (1990) *Basics of Qualitative Research: Grounded Theory Procedures and Techniques*. Newbury Park, CA: Sage.

Tajfel, H. (1972) 'Experiments in a vacuum', in J. Israel and H. Tajfel (eds), *The Context of Social Psychology: A Critical Assessment*. London: Academic Press.

Tukey, J.W. (1977) *Exploratory Data Analysis*. Reading, MA: Addison-Wesley.

Turner, B.A. (1981) 'Some practical aspects of qualitative data analysis: one way of organizing some of the cognitive processes associated with the generation of grounded theory', *Quality and Quantity*, 15: 225–47.

Turner, J.C. (1981) 'Some considerations in generalizing experimental social psychology', in G.M. Stephenson and J.M. Davis (eds), *Progress in Applied Social Psychology*, Vol. 1. London: Wiley.

Woolgar, S. (1988a) *Science: The Very Idea*. London: Tavistock.

Woolgar, S. (ed.) (1988b) *Knowledge and Reflexivity: New Frontiers in the Sociology of Knowledge*. London: Sage.

4

The Elements of Critical Social Science

Brian Fay

A critical theory wants to explain a social order in such a way that it becomes itself the catalyst which leads to the transformation of this social order. How can an explanatory theory accomplish this?

Assume for a moment that a society is marked by fundamental structural conflict and that this conflict produces deep suffering in its members. Indeed, assume further that this conflict has reached such a proportion that it threatens to lead to the breakdown of the society – that, in other words, the society is in crisis. Moreover, assume that one of the causes of this situation is the systematic ignorance that the members of this society have about themselves and their society – that, in other words, one of the causes of the crisis and its attendant suffering is what has been traditionally called the false consciousness of some or all of its members. Furthermore, assume that the sufferers themselves wish their suffering could cease. Lastly, assume that the social order is such that if the sufferers came to have a different understanding of themselves, they would be able to organize themselves into an effective group with the power to alter their basic social arrangements and thereby to alleviate their suffering. Now this situation provides the perfect ground for a critical social scientist. Such a scientist could focus on the social crisis and explain it as in part the result of the false consciousness of the members of the society in question. Such an explanation would constitute a critique of themselves and their society at least for the sufferers, and, if offered in the proper manner, could lead to a change in their consciousness and subsequently to the transformation of this society itself.

Of course, not all crises are at least in part caused by the false consciousness of those experiencing them. Not all conflicts develop to the point of crisis either. Moreover, not all instances of false consciousness are amenable to the education I described. Nor will

From *Critical Social Science: Liberation and its Limits*, Polity, Cambridge, 1987, pp. 27–31.

the elimination of false consciousness always yield the requisite changes in lifestyle and social condition that are needed to eliminate the suffering that is at issue. And even if such changes did occur, they might yield a greater amount of net suffering than the original position contained. If any or all of these were to be the case, the scenario for a critical social science that I portrayed would be undermined. Why, then, did I pick this particular scenario as the one appropriate for describing how a social scientific theory might be suitably critical? Answering this question will provide a good way of revealing the elements which comprise any critical theory.

The place to begin is with the fact that any critical theory is propagated with the idea that it will itself be the catalytic agent in the overthrow of a given social order. Now this means that a critical theory requires that liberation from a social order occur partly as the result of the absorption of itself by its audience – that liberation result from 'the enlightenment of the subjects of critical theory' (to use a phrase often found in the literature). Such a process of enlightenment is sometimes called 'raising the consciousness' of the oppressed.

What sort of enlightenment is involved here? The crucial element is providing the means whereby the members of its audience can come to see themselves in a radically different way from their current self-conception. Critical theorists do this by offering a theory which explains why these people are frustrated and unsatisfied, why they are doomed to continue in this condition, given their conception of themselves and their social order, and why it is that they have these conceptions. By doing this, critical theorists want to show them that as long as they conceive of their capacities and interests as they do, and as long as they understand their social order as they do, they will remain thwarted. Moreover, this essentially negative tack is combined with a more positive one. For critical theorists will also offer to their audience an alternative conception of who they are, providing them with a new and radically different picture of their psychic economy and their social order.

But of course enlightenment by itself is not enough. Liberation requires that a group not only come to understand itself in a new way, but that it galvanize itself into revolutionary activity in which its oppressors are overthrown. To have the practical force it requires, critical theory must become an enabling, motivating resource for its audience – it must, in short, empower them. This empowerment has emancipation as its goal. The whole point of a critical theory is to redress a situation in which a group is experiencing deep but remedial suffering as a result of the way their lives are arranged. Its aim is to overturn these arrangements and to put into place another set in which people can relate and act in fuller, more satisfying ways.

The practical intent of critical social science is thus achieved only when all three phases of the tripartite process of enlightenment, empowerment, and emancipation are completed. But for this to happen, the arrangements which are responsible for the suffering of a group addressed by a critical theory must partly depend on the ignorance of the members of this group – otherwise, how could the learning of a mere theory have the desired effect? This in turn means that what I have called a group's false consciousness must be a causal factor in sustaining these arrangements. This is why in my scenario for a critical theory I made false consciousness causally operative in maintaining the social order at hand.

But why, when describing this scenario, speak of social crises rather than, say, social conflict? The answer to this question cannot be given strictly in terms of the idea of such a science. But it can be fashioned out of this idea combined with some quite plausible assumptions about human motivation. In the first place, in order for a critical theory to fulfil its practical task it must be the case that the people whom it is supposed to liberate will at some stage be willing – indeed ready – to listen and to act on its message. But it is highly unlikely that this will be the case unless the level of discontent they are experiencing is really quite high; otherwise, what might be called the 'natural resistance' to fundamental change will act as a counterweight to the desire for change, and will induce these people to accommodate themselves to the discontent they are suffering.

But there must be more than just a high level of discontent. Anthropologists have described certain sorts of societies in which there is deep conflict built right into the very structure of these societies, but in such a way that at critical moments when it threatens to blow the society apart there are mechanisms to moderate the tension and so preserve the social order as a whole. Such societies are indeed quite stable, even though marked by high levels of discontent. Such situations are not fertile ground for a critical social science; what is needed is a situation in which some sort of choice is *forced* on people because they are no longer able to function as they have done in the past. In a crisis situation, people cannot resist change and continue with the 'old ways'. It is likely that only when this sort of situation occurs can a critical theory gain a foothold, because only in this kind of choice-demanding situation will its potential audience be primed for it.

But what about a situation in which a critical social theory would lead to a radical change in a society and which, as a result, would alleviate the suffering once characteristic of it, but would do so by producing another sort of society with a new and worse form of suffering? A critical social theory would be inappropriate in this sort of situation precisely because the idea of such a theory demands that it produce an amount of net good greater than or equal to that of the original situation it seeks to explain and alter. The reason it must do this derives from the idea of critique which is central to the notion of critical social science. Any critique worthy of the name must claim that the situation it is criticizing is a relatively evil one. It thus would make no sense for a critical social scientist to condemn a social arrangement and call for its alteration, while at the same time admitting that the alternate arrangements which would emerge will be worse than the original.

Thus, I think it ought to be clear why I chose the scenario I did to introduce the notion of critical social science. For a social theory to be critical and practical as well as scientifically explanatory, the conditions described in it must be met. Specifically, these are: first, that there be a *crisis* in a social system; second, that this crisis be at least in part caused by the *false consciousness* of those experiencing it; third, that this false consciousness be amenable to the process of *enlightenment* I described; and fourth, that such enlightenment lead to *emancipation* in which a group, empowered by its new-found self-understanding, radically alters its social arrangements and thereby alleviates its suffering. It is only when this set of conditions occurs that a social science can be truly critical.

Knowing this scenario provides the basis for ascertaining the various elements which a critical theory would have to contain in order to fulfil its aspirations. In particular, such a theory would have to offer a critique of the self-understandings of the members of its audience; an explanation of why these self-understandings, though in some sense false, continue to be employed by these members; an account of why these understandings now can be undermined and how this can specifically be done in present circumstances; an alternative interpretation of the identity – the capacities and real interests – of this audience; a demonstration of the crisis nature of the workings of the society under discussion; and an identification of those aspects of this society which need to be changed if the crisis is to be resolved in a positive way for its audience. By offering this complex set of analyses to the relevant group at the appropriate time in the appropriate setting, a social theory can legitimately hope not only to explain a social order but to do so in such a way that this order is overthrown.

5

Traditions in Documentary Analysis

Victor Jupp and Clive Norris

The Origins of Documentary Analysis

In terms of the contemporary social scientific analysis of documents, the work of Thomas and Znaniecki is always taken to have had an early and seminal influence. *The Polish Peasant in Europe and America* was first published between 1918 and 1920 and ran to five volumes. Although it is rarely read these days, except by those with a specialist interest, it was held in high esteem in its time, especially by those associated with the Chicago school of sociology; and it is still considered to be the classic example of documentary research (although it also addresses important, and wider, theoretical issues). The research focused on Polish immigration into the United States at the turn of the century, a time when Poles accounted for about one quarter of all immigrants. The greatest impact was felt in Chicago, which was at that time a key centre for American sociology, and Thomas and Znaniecki worked firmly within the Chicagoan tradition. Their analysis moves between social structure and the individual, for example examining effects on the host community and at the same time examining the subjective experiences of individual immigrants. This is typical of the eclecticism of the Chicagoans. *The Polish Peasant* is most renowned for its use of personal and other documents. These include letters which emigrés sent back home, a major life history of one Polish peasant, material from a newspaper established by Polish immigrants, official documents from agencies in Poland, and records and reports from social work agencies and courts in the United States.

The details of *The Polish Peasant* need not delay us here. It is, however, worthy of reference because it established the documentary method among the tools of social science research. What is more, it did so in a way that expressed the theoretical eclecticism of the Chicago school of sociology, especially the intertwining of positivism with a more 'appreciative' stance of what was later to become known as interactionist sociology. The tension between the positivist approach to documentary analysis and interactionist-interpretive ideas about documentary analysis is one that played an important role in the development of the use of documents in social science research. This is a theme to which we shall return later.

While documents and life histories were used subsequently by others in the Chicago tradition, these sorts of data largely fell out of use in sociology in the United States from 1940 onwards. The documentary tradition is not, however, confined to Chicagoan sociology and developments emerging from it. In fact documents have been used in a wide range of disciplines including psychology, social psychology, social anthropology, political science, sociology, criminology and history. But where they were used the interpretative approach was predominantly replaced by more positivist, quantitative content analysis, focusing on three main analytic elements. These elements were the *communication*; the *sender(s)*; and the *recipient(s)*, and the basic research designs of content analysis were organized around these three elements. This is symbolized in the classic formulation of content analysis as the study of 'who says what, to whom, how and with what effect?' (Lasswell *et al.*, 1952: 12). The three research designs typically clustered around the following research questions: What are the characteristics of the content? What inferences can be made about the causes and generation of the content? What inferences can be made about the effects of the communication?

One should not underestimate the extent to which a diversity of approaches has prevailed in documentary analysis. Nevertheless, it is not unreasonable to suggest that the positivist paradigm dominated the analysis of documents at least until the 1960s. However, the increasing popularity towards the late 1960s of micro-sociological theories such as symbolic interactionism, labelling theory and ethnomethodology provided a major challenge to the ascendancy of positivism. These micro-sociological approaches also focused on the communication or document, the sender, and the recipient – but with a different theoretical emphasis. The documents were not taken for granted as objective means by which inferences could be made about causes and effects but as 'social constructions' by particular individuals at particular times which could be the object of varying interpretations by different 'audiences', with varying effects. The notion of a direct, deterministic and unilinear link through from sender to communication to recipient was played down.

The critical paradigm – especially developments since the mid-1970s – has brought a different strand to the documentary tradition. This paradigm was influenced initially by Marxism but has branched out in different directions. Consistent with the main theoretical and political slants of this paradigm, the main focus is on the relationship between documents and social structure, class relations, social control, social order, ideology and power, and involves what has come to be called 'discourse analysis'. As with the positivist and the interactionist paradigms, there is internal diversity and within it there are several 'sub-plots'. For example, one sub-plot is founded on Marxist sociology and another, which is closely associated with the French social theorist Michel Foucault, has played an important role in giving communications – or what he calls 'text' and 'discourse' – a greater profile in the broad umbrella of critical analysis. He treats text or discourse not as a resource to explain the world but as an object of inquiry in its own right. Plummer distinguishes Foucault's approach from others we have considered, as follows:

> Foucault's use of documents is as 'a text' where the human authorship is of no interest, where the subject is denied and where the informational value of the document is of little concern. It is merely an independent discourse through which power relations are constituted, and the text hence comes simply to exemplify this wider theory. (1982: 132)

Foucault, then, is not interested in what texts tell us about the biographies of individual authors. Rather, he is interested in what the texts reveal about the mechanisms by which power is exercised. This adds a different, and more recent, strand to the documentary tradition. We shall consider Foucault's ideas and implications for methodological work later.

An examination of traditions of documentary analysis indicates that a consideration of methods of social inquiry cannot be isolated from a consideration of theory. Specific research questions are underpinned by more general theoretical paradigms – such as positivism, interactionism, Marxism – which have in-built assumptions about the nature of the social order and about how it can be 'captured' and explained. The position which we take here is that theory does not by itself provide any 'correct' answers or explanations. Rather, the theory-method interchange is best viewed in terms of theory setting 'research agendas' for inquiry. Such agendas are in terms of the basic assumptions of underlying paradigms and also include concepts derived from specific formulations. Theory defines what is problematic and also provides prescriptions as to how such problems are to be conceptualized. In turn, this generates guide-lines as to unit and level of analysis, the form of data to be generated, the questions to be asked of such data, the form of analysis and interpretations to be adopted.

The general principle that methods of social inquiry cannot be discussed in isolation from theory will be illustrated in subsequent sections by specific reference to the analysis of documents and texts. We shall focus on the interchange between documents and texts and three broad theoretical paradigms – the positivist, the interpretative and the critical; with particular reference to developments in criminology.

These three paradigms have played an important part in the development of the documentary tradition. In some, but not all, respects one can view these approaches as being in some order of progression insofar as the interpretative documentary approach developed as a challenge to the ascendancy of positivist content analysis, and critical analysis emerged in the 1970s to correct what were seen as failings in both positivist and interpretative approaches. Nevertheless, all three still form a part of social inquiry in general, and the analysis of documents and texts in particular. To a large degree this accounts for the diversity and plurality in social research.

Positivism and Documents

This is not the place to go into the detailed features of positivism nor into the different nuances which can and have been placed on the meaning of the word. Here we shall treat the basic assumptions of sociological positivism as being that social phenomena are 'objective' and exist externally to the individuals who make up society or a social group. Positivist research aims to follow the principles of natural scientific research and proceeds by the formulation and testing of hypotheses with a view to making inferences about the causal connections between two or more social phenomena or 'facts'.

In terms of the analysis of documents this approach is exemplified by *content analysis*. Holsti (1969) itemizes five features of content analysis as follows. First, the procedures should be *objective*, that is, each step in the research process (for example, categorization and coding schemes) should be carried out on the basis of explicitly formulated rules. In this way different researchers following the same procedures will get the same results. Second, procedures must by *systematic*, that is the rules must be applied with consistency. Third, content analysis should have *generality*, by which he means that findings must have theoretical relevance, for example the characteristics of the sender or of the recipient. Fourth, content analysis is typically *quantitative* and can include counting the frequency with which certain themes or words appear. 'There is clearly no reason for content analysis unless the question one wants answered is quantitative' (Lasswell *et al.*, 1952: 45, quoted by Holsti, 1969: 5).

Finally, content analysis is typically concerned with the *manifest* content and surface meaning rather than with deeper layers of meaning. This is a crucial feature which is typified in the writings and work of Berelson, a leading American content analyst:

> Content analysis is ordinarily limited to the manifest content of communications and is not normally directly in terms of the content intention which the content may express nor the latent responses which it may elicit. Strictly speaking content analysis proceeds in terms of what-is-said and not in terms of why-is-the-content-like-that (e.g. 'motives') or how-people-react (e.g. 'appeals' or 'responses'). (1952: 16)

Finally, we can note how the positivist approach to documents is very similar to the positivist approach to the use of official statistics on, say, crime. Just as the latter assumes that the level of crime in society can be objectively measured and represented by crime statistics, content analysis assumes that there are attributes, attitudes and values relating to individuals, and that these are *represented* unambiguously in the manifest contents of documents held in the criminal justice system. It is because of this that the positivist approach to content analysis as typified in Berelson's work is also referred to as the *representational model*.

As indicated earlier, content analysis typically focuses on three main elements – the communication – the sender(s) and the recipient(s). Seeking to answer one or other of three questions:

What are the Characteristics of Content?
Studies concerned with this question were very prevalent in political science in the United States during the 1940s and 1950s. In the main they were longitudinal trend studies which were concerned with changes in political values as expressed in newspaper editorials. Some of these studies were cross-cultural (see, for example, Lasswell *et al.*, 1952; Pool *et al.*, 1952). Studies of the content of communication, especially within American political science studies, were often closely allied to the gaining of political and military intelligence. Apart from the work on political values cited above, other studies focused on trends in political decision making, styles of political rhetoric and techniques of persuasion (for example, Lasswell's [1942] research on war propaganda). A distinctive feature of such work was its unquestioning stance towards the contents of the documents and towards the role of the documents and their contents in maintaining existing power relations. This is in contrast to the critical paradigm which emerged during the 1970s.

What Inferences can be Made about the Causes and Generation of the Content?

Typical examples of research concerned with this come from studies in psychology and social psychology which seek to make inferences about the personality characteristics and the attitudes or the values of the writers from the contents of the diaries and letters they write. However, such work is not restricted to psychologists. Sociologists and social anthropologists have also examined documents to make inferences about sources of social and cultural values, but their emphasis is less upon individual features such as personality traits and more upon documents as expressions of such social and cultural values. For example, social anthropologists typically have used a whole range of artefacts to make claims about the cultural values of the group, tribe or society from which they emanated.

What Inferences can be Made about the Effects of Communications?

Media analysis provides a typical example of a primary concern with the effects of the content of communication. In the main this has concentrated around debates, not just in academic circles but also in the political arena, about the effects of the contents of television programmes on young children and their subsequent development and also about the possible relationship between exposure to violent television and video programmes and the subsequent committing by some individuals of violent acts.

The Interpretative Tradition and Documents

Although 'appreciative' approaches to the study of documents developed following the publication of *The Polish Peasant*, in the 1960s they became much more strident as critiques of, and responses to, the assumptions of the *representational model*. The critiques clustered around a number of theoretical strands including humanism, labelling theory, interactionism and new deviancy, all of which pay particular attention to the situated interpretations of documents. It is for this reason that we refer to it as the interpretative tradition. There is always a danger of making too much of the positivist–interpretative divide and of drawing the dividing line too sharply. Nevertheless, there are differences. In contrast to positivism, the interpretative tradition holds the basic assumption that social phenomena are of an essentially different order from natural ones. They are not objective, external and preordained but socially constructed by individuals. Therefore, it is argued, positivist approaches to the study of such phenomena are inappropriate.

The interpretative tradition is epitomized, for example, in Cicourel's (1964) critique of Berelson's *representational model*. (It is interesting to note that Cicourel was also influential in critiques of the positivist use of official statistics, see for example, Kitsuse and Cicourel, 1963; Cicourel, 1968.) Cicourel is critical of two assumptions of the *representational model*. First, the assumption of a correspondence between intent, content and the effect on different audiences; and, second, the assumption 'that there is a common universe of discourse among the relevant parties, so that the manifest content can be taken as a valid unit of study' (Cicourel, 1964: 149). Cicourel's argument is that the *representational model* takes for granted that which is problematic, namely the way in which meanings are assigned both by authors and audiences. What is missing from Berelson-type analysis 'is any explicit reference to the normative rules governing communicator, audience and analyst interpretations of the meanings of one another's communications' (Cicourel, 1964: 151). In *The Social Organization of Juvenile Justice* (1968) Cicourel examines the everyday practices of police, probation officials and courts, including the documents produced by these, and argues that these play a crucial role in generating delinquency. Documents are vital mechanisms by which individuals are processed, labelled and subsequently confirmed as 'delinquents'. Cicourel's work was an important influence on interactionist and interpretative sociology and also on the interpretative analysis of documents and conversations.

Another approach within this tradition of analysing documents is typified by Plummer's *Documents of Life* (1983). Plummer suggests that, in their differing ways, the counter positions of positivism and realism (which is characterized by abstract theorizing about structure) have both removed the 'subject' from social inquiry. To correct this he argues for a 'corrective sociology' – which he describes as humanist – which would retain social structure in any analysis but seek to combine it with the 'subject' and with the way in which he or she both constructs and experiences the social world. The following quote describes how the interpretative perspective can be seen to contribute to a humanist corrective sociology.

> This corrective sociology may be called 'humanistic' and has at least four central criteria. It must pay tribute to *human subjectivity and creativity* – showing how individuals respond to social constraints and actively assemble social worlds; it must deal with concrete human experiences – talk, feelings, actions – through their *social, and*

especially economic, organization (and not just their inner, psychic or biological structuring); it must show a naturalistic 'intimate familiarity' with such experiences – abstractions untempered by close involvement are ruled out; and there must be a self-awareness by the sociologist of the ultimate *moral and political role* in moving towards a social structure in which there is less exploitation, oppression and injustice and more creativity, diversity and equality. A list like this is open to detailed extension and revision, but it is hard to imagine a humanistic sociology which is not at least minimally committed to these criteria. (Plummer, 1983: 5)

An example of the use of documents in line with Plummer's call for a humanistically corrective sociology is to be found in Cohen and Taylor's (1972) study *Psychological Survival*, an account of long-term prisoners in Durham Prison. In contrast to official, positivistic research sponsored by the Home Office, which used a battery of questionnaires and personality tests to formally test hypotheses about the effect of long-term imprisonment, Cohen and Taylor's aim was to focus on the way in which inmates subjectively experienced and interpreted long-term imprisonment. Cohen and Taylor's main research tool was informal interviewing or as they called it 'talk'. However, as the research progressed and became more structured, inmates were asked to produce essays, stories and poems, about their experience of long-term imprisonment and their feelings about it. These documentary sources provide the basis for further 'talk' and also were used as data to shed light on their subjective experience of long-term imprisonment.

The Critical Tradition

The early 1970s witnessed a gradual shift, especially but not exclusively in criminology, towards a more radical and critical approach. On the one hand, this approach was critical of the positivism, empiricism, conservatism and reform-orientation of conventional, mainstream or 'official' criminology, and on the other, castigated the liberal-democratic humanist approaches for playing down the importance of social structural arrangements, power, ideology and social conflict, especially class conflict.

The critical approach was symbolized by the 'new criminology' project (Taylor *et al.*, 1973), which represented an attempt to produce a comprehensive and radical criminology. It grew out of earlier humanist new deviancy approaches and incorporated many of their ideas. For example, it had a concern with everyday social interactions, say those between police officers and youths, and also with the social processes by which the law is applied in particular instances. However, it argued that such a concern was not by itself sufficient since adequate attention was not being paid to differential power relations in such interactions and processes, nor to the origins of such power relations in structural – especially class – divisions and conflicts. In doing this the new criminology project sought to create a theoretical approach that would link humanist-interactionist theories to Marxist concerns with historical processes and structural arrangements.

The new criminology project has been criticized on a number of counts. It is reductionist in the way in which it sought to reduce all explanations of crime and the operation of the criminal justice system to class conflict, thereby marginalizing explanations in other terms. It had a tendency to idealize working-class crime rather than recognize its reality for sections of the working class themselves: a criticism most closely associated with the so-called 'new left realists' (see, for example, Matthews and Young, 1986). However, the new criminology did provide a new emphasis and impetus to criminological thinking, it offered new areas for exploration and moved criminology, at least partially, away from its positivist, conservative and functionalist stronghold. Since that time the radical and critical paradigm has branched out in different directions and it is by no means characterized by internal coherence. However, as a whole, the critical paradigm has offered alternative – but not new – concepts for inclusion on the research agenda. These concepts include social structure, social conflict, regulation of social order, ideology, power and control.

The critical paradigm is heavily theoretical (and overtly political) and is not, by inclination, interested in traditional research methods. Part of the reason for this comes from the theoretical and political aversion to the highly formal, quantitative and positivist approaches of conventional criminology. However, the critical paradigm is not against empirical investigation *per se*. For example, critical analysis typically will be very interested in examining the role which the formal, quantitative positivist methods (for example, crime statistics, surveys of prisoners, experiments in prisons) and their conclusions play in the maintenance of social order by the state's crime control apparatus – investigations that may be termed reflexive critical analysis. It is also interested in carrying out its own research, but only with those methods which give access to the key concepts of the critical paradigm. Such methods tend to be qualitative, naturalistic and non-positivist and include life history and other informal interviews, observational methods especially participant observation case studies and social history research.

What role, then, is there for the use of documents and texts in the critical paradigm? We can enlist once again the notion that theory can set research agendas. The central concepts and emphases of the critical paradigm raise key questions which can be examined via documents and texts. In this way, the critical paradigm brings a distinctiveness to analysis of documents and texts as data which differentiates it from the other approaches we have discussed. Such questions can involve:

- A concern with analysis at a societal and social structural level (and therefore with the role of official, quasi-official and other public documents which operate at this level).
- An emphasis upon conflict between social groupings and on the dynamics of struggles between them (and hence upon the role of documents and texts in such conflicts and struggles).
- An emphasis on power and control in the relation between social groupings (and hence on documents and texts as mechanisms by which power can be exercised by one group over another and by which one group controls and regulates the actions of another).
- An interest in ideology as a means by which existing structures and social arrangements are legitimated and maintained (and therefore an interest in documents and texts as legitimating devices whose contents seek to achieve such legitimacy by gaining popular consent for the existing state of affairs).
- A commitment to not taking for granted what-is-said (and therefore to not rely on the manifest content of documents, and also taking a critical stance to them by examining their role in relation to ideology, power and control).
- A commitment to changing the existing state of things (and hence of not solely adopting a critical stance towards documents and texts but also putting forward alternative definitions, explanations and solutions from those which dominate and prevail in official documents and texts).

Discourse Analysis

Earlier we referred to the influence of discourse analysis within what we have termed the critical paradigm. Here we want to consider discourse analysis in a little more detail. Discourse analysis represents an important development within the critical tradition and although it is closely associated with the writings of Michel Foucault it is not restricted to him. During the 1970s there were fundamental changes in the theorizing about the way in which social meanings are constructed, and one such strand of this theorizing resulted in major developments in the analysis of all speech and writing, or what we shall describe here as 'discourse'. It is important to recognize that discourse analysis has itself followed many paths and it has stimulated the interest and imagination of those working in psychology, sociology, philosophy, history, literature, linguistics as well as criminology. These different disciplines have different emphases and bring to the surface different aspects of discourses and their analysis. We cannot possibly hope to reproduce those differences here and therefore choose to offer the slant most typically associated with sociology and criminology.

For McDonnell (1986) a fundamental feature of discourse is that it is social, that is that the words which are used and their meanings depend on where they were used, by whom and to whom. Therefore, the words and their meanings can differ according to the social relations and the institutional settings within which they are produced, reproduced and sometimes reshaped. The implication of this is that discourse analysis assumes that there is no such thing as a fundamental and universal discourse which is shared by all. In this sense discourse analysis is at odds with a structuralist position which holds that language has an underlying structure and therefore is a common code. This does not mean that there is no possibility of a universal code, simply that discourse analysis rejects the notion that such a universality is inevitable. However, the rejection of structuralist principles does not mean that discourse analysis embraces the interpretative approach, where individuals are seen as the primary sources of social meanings. In contrast, it argues that knowledge and discourses must be analysed in terms of different points or stages in history, and also in terms of social relations prevailing at these points rather than in terms of individual constructions.

The assumption that discourses can differ according to the social relations and institutional settings with which they are shaped means that at any given point there can be different discourses, each of which puts forward certain concepts, explanations and solutions, thereby rejecting others. In fact, a discourse does not exist in isolation but in relation to others. Further, discourses can be, and frequently are, in conflict with one another in the way in which they promulgate concepts, explanations and solutions and seek to marginalize others. McDonnell illustrates this feature of discourses: 'Managerial discourse spoken to workers can act against them: spoken to managers, it may still in the end act against workers; and in such ways a discourse takes effect indirectly or directly through its relation to, its address to, another discourse' (1986: 3).

One can move beyond the notion of conflicting discourses to think in terms of hierarchies of discourses within which one person's or one group's discourse – its definitions, explanations and solutions – carry little weight in relation to others and therefore have little credibility as 'knowledge' or as what is seen as 'right' and 'correct'. As Worrall has argued, discourse analysis embraces all aspects of communication: 'not only its content, but its author (who says it?), its authority (on what grounds?), its audience (to whom?), its object (about whom?), its objective (in order to achieve what?)' (1990: 9). In her study of women's experience of the criminal justice system, Worrall demonstrates how the discursive practices of criminal justice personnel, such as magistrates, include: 'the prohibition of certain topics on the grounds of "irrelevance", the disqualification of certain individuals from being authorized speakers and the rejection of certain statements as illegitimate' (1990: 9). (This is not dissimilar to Becker's [1967] notion of 'hierarchies of credibility' within which there are differing definitions of what is and is not deviant, each of which is endowed with a different level of credibility.) Social conflict and hierarchies of credibility are very closely linked to the exercise of power within society and within institutions and groups. It is not surprising, therefore, that the concept of power is vital to discourse analysis via the theoretical connection between the production of discourses and the exercise of power. The two are very closely interwoven and in some theoretical formulations are viewed as one and the same.

We can identify two broad strands of theorizing, each of which is concerned with the relation between power and discourse, but in differing ways. One of these is associated with Althusser (see, for example, 1971) and analyses of discourses and power at a macro societal level. It places particular emphasis on the production of ideologies and discourses at this level. Ideologies develop antagonistically and emerge from, but are not wholly reducible to, class conflict. The apparatus of the state plays an important part in the production of ideology in seeking to legitimate existing social divisions. In focusing on the apparatus and process of production of ideology, Althusser offers an 'external analysis' which is concerned with the politics of discourse as opposed to an 'internal analysis' which is primarily concerned with the internal logic and sequence of meaning within any discourse (see Hindess and Hirst, 1977; McDonnell, 1986). What is more, in ultimately tracing the production of ideologies and discourses back to class conflict and class struggle, this form of analysis shares common ground with other varieties of Marxist analysis (although there are also differences).

A second broad strand which can be identified is that associated with Foucault. Foucault's writings cover a vast range of topics and develop many new and influential theoretical concepts. Here we can only summarize the rudiments and even then we can only consider the way in which these relate to the analysis of documents and texts. Foucault was concerned with the question of why different forms of knowledge and discourse emerge at certain points in time (for example, why particular forms of punishment are dominant at particular points in history). Within this he theorizes about the interconnectedness between knowledge and power; for Foucault they imply each other: 'Power produces knowledge, they imply one another: a site where power is exercised is also a place at which knowledge is produced' (Smart, 1989: 65). Discourses are the very means by which people communicate and they include moral norms or imperatives for behaviour. They are mechanisms of power and control, but they are not beyond resistance from other, alternative discourses. Although Foucault was concerned with why different forms of knowledge and discourse emerge at certain points of time, he had no notion of the inevitability of history and in this respect he offers a form of analysis which differs from that of Marxism. There is one further crucial difference in that Foucault argues that there is not one focus of knowledge and power – the state – but several. His viewpoint is that strategies of power and social regulation are pervasive and that the state is only one of several points of control. This is an important divergence from Marxist analysis. For Foucault there are many semi-autonomous realms in society, where the state has little influence, but where power and control is exercised. In this way Foucault's notion of the pervasiveness of loci of regulation and control encourages research about discourses in a range of institutional settings.

Conclusion

We have treated documents and texts as forms of data which can play a vital part in social inquiry. We have also emphasized that the ways in which such data are addressed are themselves closely related to the theoretical approaches which are brought to such data. Three main theoretical approaches have been examined in relation to the analysis of documents and texts and we have highlighted three forms of analysis – positivist content analysis, interpretative analysis of documents, and critical or discourse

analysis. We have suggested that the role of theory is to offer
agendas for social inquiry, perhaps by the analysis of documents
and texts. We have examined the agendas offered by positivist and
interpretative theoretical approaches but we have put greatest
emphasis on the research agendas offered within critical research.
We have emphasized that the critical paradigm does not exhibit an
internal coherence and inevitably there are differences within it.
However, in order to point the way forward we offer the following
'agenda', organized around a series of questions to be asked of
data. In the main this is based on a distillation of ideas from
discourse analysis which, especially in its Foucauldian form, has
welded sophisticated theorizing to the prospect of social inquiry.
An agenda could be as follows:

1. What public and/or institutional discourses are important in
   terms of knowledge of what is 'right' and what is 'wrong'?
2. In what kind of documents and texts do such discourses appear?
3. Who writes or speaks these discourses and whom do they
   represent or purport to represent?
4. What is the intended audience of such discourses?
5. What does a critical reading of these documents uncover in
   terms of:
   (a) what is defined as 'right' and 'wrong' and therefore what
       is seen as problematic;
   (b) what explanation is offered for what is seen as
       problematic;
   (c) what therefore is seen as the solution?
6. What does a critical reading of these documents tell us about
   (a) what is not seen as problematic;
   (b) which explanations are rejected or omitted;
   (c) which solutions are not preferred?
7. What alternative discourses exist?
8. How do these relate to 'internal differentiation' within and
   between semi-autonomous realms of control?
9. What does a critical reading of these alternative discourses tell
   us?
10. Is there evidence of negotiation with, or resistance to, domi-
    nant discourses?
11. What is the relationship between the discourses and social
    conflict, social struggle, hierarchies of credibility, order and
    control, and most of all, the exercise of power?
12. Are discourses, knowledge and power pervasive or reducible to
    class, class conflict and struggles refracted through one source,
    the state?

Finally, we can add one further question which is one that is asked not of data but of the methodological and political role of the researcher: does a critical reading of dominant discourses inevitably lead to the construction of alternative and competing discourses by the social researcher?

References and Further Reading

Althusser, L. (1971) 'Ideology and ideological state apparatus (notes towards an investigation)', in his *Lenin and Philosophy and Other Essays*, trans. B. Brewster. London: New Left Books.

Becker, H. (1967) 'Whose side are we on?', *Social Problems*, 14 (3): 239–47.

Berelson, B. (1952) *Content Analysis in Communicative Research*. New York: Free Press.

Cicourel, A.V. (1964) *Method and Measurement in Sociology*. New York: Free Press.

Cicourel, A.V. (1968) *The Social Organization of Juvenile Justice*. New York: John Wiley.

Cohen, S. and Taylor, L. (1972) *Psychological Survival: The Experience of Long-Term Imprisonment*. Harmondsworth: Penguin.

Hindess, B. and Hirst, P. (1977) *Mode of Production and Social Formation*. London: Macmillan.

Holsti, O.R. (1969) *Content Analysis for the Social Sciences and Humanities*. Reading, MA: Addison-Wesley.

Kitsuse, J. and Cicourel, A.V. (1963) 'A note on the use of official statistics', *Social Problems*, 11 (2): 328–38.

Lasswell, H.D. (1942) 'Communications research and politics', in D. Waples (ed.), *Print, Radio and Film in a Democracy*. Chicago: University of Chicago Press.

Lasswell, H.D., Lerner, D. and Pool, I. (1952) *The Comparative Study of Symbols*. Stanford, CA: Stanford University Press.

McDonnell, D. (1986) *Theories of Discourse: An Introduction*. Oxford: Blackwell.

Matthews, R. and Young J. (eds) (1986) *Confronting Crime*. London: Sage.

Plummer, K. (1983) *Documents of Life*. London: Allen & Unwin.

Pool, I. de Sola, Lasswell, H.D. and Lerner, D. (1952) *Symbols of Democracy*. Hoover Institution Studies Series C, Symbols: no. 4. Stanford, CA: Stanford University Press.

Smart, B. (1989) 'On discipline and social regulation: a review of Foucault's genealogical analysis', in D. Garland and P. Young (eds), *The Power to Punish*. London: Gower.

Taylor, I., Walton, P. and Young, J. (1973) *The New Criminology*. London: Routledge & Kegan Paul.

Thomas, W.I. and Znaniecki, F. (1958) *The Polish Peasant in Europe and America*. New York: Dover. (Original edn published 1918–20.)

Worrall, A. (1990) *Offending Women: Female Law-Breakers and the Criminal Justice System*. London: Routledge.

PART 2

POLITICS

6

Decolonializing Applied Social Sciences

Rodolfo Stavenhagen

It lies perhaps in the destiny of the social sciences that they should not only reflect the dominant forms of social organization of their times, but also – as they have done ever since they grew out of the social and political thought of the. Enlightenment – that they should become major vehicles for the expression of the radical countercurrents and critical conscience that these very forms of organization have brought forth. This dialectical relationship between the social sciences and society finds its way into the ambiguous and frequently conflictive roles that social scientists as individuals are called upon to play in modern society.

It has lately been found necessary in some quarters to decry anthropology in general, and its applied variety in particular, for its links to colonialism and imperialism. I believe this to be a healthy development, for the historical relation between colonialism and imperialism as world-wide systems of domination and exploitation on the one hand, and the use of social science in the management of empire, on the other, has up to recently been overlooked or ignored. It can no longer be neglected, and it has become clear to many of us that the methods, the theories, the various 'schools of thought', the very objects of study and observation in anthropology and other social disciplines have been deeply colored by this historical relationship.[1]

Let me add right away that I am deeply convinced of the very important contributions that anthropology and the other social sciences have made to the advancement of knowledge, irrespective

From *Human Organization*, 30 (4), 1971, pp. 333–44.

of their various relationships with colonialism and imperialism; and particularly to knowledge of and about the so-called underdeveloped countries. I am also one of those who recognize the deep strain of humanism, progressivism, liberalism and radicalism that has been imbedded in the development of anthropology, and even in some of its colonialistic varieties.

Thus it seems to me that it is equally mistaken to deny the evident historical relationships between colonialism and anthropology (or between imperialism and the so-called sociology of development) – a question that lies in the domain of the sociology of knowledge – as it is to simply treat these disciplines as handmaidens of colonialist or imperialist domination.

For it is precisely out of the science of society that the most powerful critiques of colonial systems, imperialist domination, totalitarian political structures and bourgeois class society have sprung. New generations of radical social scientists have arisen – mainly in the Third World – who question some of the basic assumptions upon which social science in the industrial countries seems to stand. Yet it must be recognized that these social scientists themselves are a product of the way social science in general has developed.

I think we may look at the issues involved from two angles: the uses or application of social scientific knowledge in general, and the professional practice of applied social science.

Like all knowledge, social scientific knowledge forms part of humanity's cultural heritage. It is there to be used or applied by those who can and know how to make use of it. While social scientists may be held partially responsible for the uses to which the knowledge they produce is put, they can do little to actually control the process if they remain within the established rules of the scientific game (research, publish, teach). It is the rules of the game that must be changed.

I think the issue hinges on two important aspects: the nature and quality of the research, and the diffusion of the information to potential users. But these two aspects are intimately linked, and they condition each other.

Anthropological studies are commonly criticized for being concerned with small-scale, part societies and it is held that this approach does not enable them to see wider issues and relationships necessary for a meaningful understanding of reality. The radical critique demands a holistic approach in terms of global social units and total societies. It is however not sufficient to simply state that tribal or peasant peoples, or village communities, are integrated into wider wholes (a truth that has not escaped anthropologists from the beginning). The task for anthropology is to unravel the mechanisms which relate the traditional anthropological unit of study to the wider society, to discover the mutual relationships and interconnections; to analyze cleavages, conflicts and contradictions. This is a question not of ideology, as some would have it, but of research methodology and adequate theory.

In general, anthropology – by concentrating on the small-scale, the isolated, the traditional – has not handled the theoretical aspects involved in these links and relationships satisfactorily. Few anthropologists who have carried out field work among tribal or peasant peoples have had a theory – even a general theoretical orientation – to help them explain such linkages. Unlike sociologists and political scientists, anthropologists have not given much attention to the interpretation of the national societies of which the object of their study is a part. On the average, anthropologists have been rather naïve concerning national social structures or world systems. (I do not mean studies of national cultures or national character, which are quite numerous.) In fact, anthropological studies in underdeveloped countries have been much too culture bound, in the two meanings of this term. On the one hand, despite disclaimers to the contrary in the name of cultural relativism, whenever problems of social change are considered, we find linear models based on the assumption that modernization or development will lead necessarily to some kind of social structure similar to the capitalist industrial, middle-class, consumer societies we are ourselves a part of. On the other hand, by stressing, and more often than not, by reifying culture as a concept, anthropology has been unable to handle the problems involved in the analysis of total social systems.

Theories about national societies (or world-wide systems, for that matter), are of course not true or false in any absolute sense; they are simply more or less relevant in attempting to explain adequately a set of observable facts and their interrelationships. None of the existing theories, as far as I can judge, are directly verifiable or testable (in the laboratory sense that some 'scientific purists' would like to have it). They necessarily reflect the value orientations of those who use them, but in their capacity to explain particular sets of facts they will in the long run turn out to be more or less adequate. And this of course has to do with what, indeed, one wishes to explain.

We may recall, some years back, the discussion between Robert Redfield and Oscar Lewis about the interpretation of the social structure of the Mexican peasant village, Tepoztlán. We cannot, for sure, state that one of the opposing interpretations is true and the other false. We can only say that certain facts seem to be explained better by one interpretation than by the other. A similar discussion – with important implications for action programs – has arisen around the concept of 'peasant resistance to change' (see Huizer, 1970). Whether we accept theories attempting to explain 'peasant conservatism' or prefer those that emphasize 'peasant rebelliousness,' will depend on our value orientations, and our choice will, in turn, determine the importance we attribute to different kinds of empirical data.

At a certain level of generality, theories about social structure and the dynamics of social forces are simply not testable in the immediate sense; they will only stand or fall in historical perspective; they should more correctly be considered paradigms. But I would go one step further; to paraphrase a piece of good old Anglo-Saxon folk wisdom: the proof of the theory is in the *praxis*. What I mean by this is that in the long run any theory of society, and particularly of social change, will be validated by its utility as an instrument of action in the hands of organized social groups.

Karl Marx formulated it thus: 'Theory becomes a material force as soon as it has gripped the masses.' This leads to the question of ideology and value orientations in relation to theory: an empirically validated theory becomes knowledge (not 'truth' in any absolute sense); knowledge is necessarily relative, not always unambiguous and subject to constant revision; it may become ideology when used as a guide for action; and if validated by *praxis* (that is, by the organized, purposeful behaviour of social groups) it ceases to be 'mere' theory and becomes social reality. It may be countered that this argument leads into the trap of the self-fulfilling prophecy. I don't think that this should deter us, because if we accept that man is not only a blind creature of historical forces but also shapes his own history, with the necessary bounds that this same history imposes on him, then the self-fulfilling prophecy becomes one of many dynamic forces that mankind uses to forge its future.

What does this mean in concrete terms? To take an example from common anthropological subject matter, it is generally agreed that community development programs are not as successful as they should be (or they turn into outright failures), because they are unable to really mobilize community participation. And this is so because they are based on wrong assumptions, deriving from inadequate theoretical orientations, about the social structure of rural villages and their links to the wider society. Specifically, they ignore or play down the patterns of dominance, power structures and conflict potential between differentially located social groups (that is, social classes) at the local and regional levels, if they do not actually (as is often the case) perpetuate the very inequalities they pretend to overcome. When, however, the issues of social struggle become clear (because they have been adequately identified and analyzed – and not usually by the social scientist, but by the interested parties themselves), then communities (or a good part of them) do become dynamic forces for progressive social change. Witness the mobilization potential of peasants around the agrarian reform issue in most Latin American countries.

Most commonly held social theory has been unable to cope with these phenomena, and usually social scientists are belatedly called upon to explain *ex post* what should have been clear from the beginning. That is why I hold that the most fruitful social theory is the one that may be validated not by any amount of statistical verification, but by the practical day-to-day problem solving of real life issues. These practical problems are of increasing concern to social scientists throughout the world and they raise the need to address ourselves to the question of the relation between the researcher and the wider society within which he acts.

I am always touched by the prefaces to published monographs on Latin America, in which the grateful author expresses his acknowledgment to Don Simpatico, Doña Gracias and the other helpful inhabitants of San Pedro or San Miguel (or whatever the name of the barrio or the village might be), but for whose collaboration and hospitality the study might never have been written. Yet how frequently do those communities and those helpful informants whose lives are so carefully laid bare by proficient researchers actually get to know the results of the research? Is any effort made to channel the scientific conclusions and research findings to them; to translate our professional jargon into everyday concepts which the people themselves can understand and from which they can learn something? And, most importantly, to which they can contribute precisely through such a dialogue? Would it not be recommendable that efforts be made by the sponsoring institutions, with direct participation of the researchers themselves, to ensure that research findings be freed from the bonds of the specialized journals, the university libraries or the limbo of government files? Can books about peasants be brought to the attention of, discussed with and used by, peasant organizations? Can studies on urban migrants be made to help labor unions and neighborhood voluntary associations to better understand, and thus solve, their problems? Cannot studies on social movements, popular rebellions and revolutions be shorn of their scientific and scholarly paraphernalia and made available to the revolutionaries themselves?

I am assuming that the scientific value of such work is good enough to deserve being involved in such a process of de-elitization. This is not, however, always the case. I am not sure whether much anthropological production would survive the crucial confrontation with its Object – transformed for that purpose from Object into acting Subject. Not only do we face the need for a process of de-elitization, but also of demystification and the direct responsibility of the researcher must be engaged here. (Some years ago C. Wright Mills proposed this in *The Sociological Imagination* (1959) but I daresay that only a handful of social scientists have followed his lead.)

It is a sad reflection on the state of our art that on the very few occasions that members of groups studied by anthropologists have the opportunity to comment on our profession they feel it necessary to do so in most unflattering terms. Quite aside from his wit, a recent statement by a leading spokesman of American Indians to the effect that his people have been cursed above all others in history because they have anthropologists should give pause for thought to many (Deloria, Jr., 1969: 83). And it would be wrong to simply shrug this literary omelette off as a bit of harmless egghead breaking. I have often wondered what would remain of concepts such as the culture of poverty, created by the cultured and the rich, if the poor had any say in the diagnosis of their own problems (on this, see Valentine, 1968 and *Current Anthropology*, 1969). Or what the results would be when *encogido*-ridden peasants encountered *entrón*-anthropologists on an equal footing (see Erasmus, 1968).

In French-speaking Black Africa intellectuals and students tend to grade visiting foreign social scientists (particularly Frenchmen) according to their degree of mental decolonization before they begin to judge their professional capacities. In these countries the identification between colonialism and ethnology is such that the very name and nature of the discipline is in disrepute and rejected by many Africans. (See Jaulin, 1970 and Copans, 1970–1 for a critique of French neocolonial ethnology.)

Still, in most cases, scholars in academic communities (particularly when they go back to their own foreign countries) can do relatively little to control the uses or misuses (or simply the non-use) of the fruits of their labour. We often hear it said amongst radicals that social scientific produce is really only of use to repressive governments, the exploiting classes or the self-seeking imperialists. Some younger radical social scientists now refuse to publish their work, or to carry out research at all, on these grounds. While it is certainly necessary at times to delay or refuse publication of research findings because of possible harm it may cause to the groups involved, those who stand on this as a matter of principle will simply radicalize themselves out of meaningful social scientific activity. The point here, it seems to me, is to save social science and to ensure its use for humanitarian, not destructive, ends – but not to abandon the field altogether.

As I said earlier, I believe a part of the problem is the diffusion to the desired publics of the product of research. Yet it is not only a question of information transmittal *per se*; for the nature and characteristics of this transmittal (if built into the research itself, through a creative dialogue between researcher and Object–Subject of research), will turn it into a process of mutual learning and will thus change the very nature of the scientific activity. This – transposed to the problem area of research – is what Paulo Freire calls *dialogics* in his *Pedagogy of the Oppressed* (1970).

Yet precisely one of the more criticable and increasingly criticized aspects of social science – at least as far as the Third World is concerned – is that it is mainly concerned with studying the oppressed – from the outside. It should have become abundantly clear in recent years that the causes of oppression, or exploitation, or deprivation (relative or absolute), or simply backwardness and traditionalism, are to be found in the functioning of total systems, in the nature of the relationships binding the oppressed and their oppressors (or, if these words shock the sensibilities of those who think they are too value-laden, we may say the deprived and the privileged), into a total system. We must thus try to channel to the former not only scientific knowledge about themselves, but also about how the system works. And this requires giving attention to the other pole of the relationship, and perhaps the most important pole: that of the dominant groups.

The truly comprehensive understanding of social forces in a process of social change requires more than an analysis of the so-called underprivileged social groups or of social movements against established systems of domination. It requires the study of the system of domination itself, and particularly of the mechanisms whereby the social groups at the top, that is, the elites, fit into the general structure; how they react to and participate in the process of change; how they operate to maintain, adapt or modify existing systems. It is here that I see a vast new field of inquiry opening up for the radical social scientist. Compared to studies of Indians, peasants, tribal peoples, urban poor, marginal migrants and so forth, the scientific study of elites and decision-making at the upper echelons of the social edifice is still very sketchy. One would think that because of his social origins, his university education and his general place within the social structure, the social scientist should be well placed to carry out such studies; yet up to now his scientific and mental equipment does not seem to have carried him into this direction. By concentrating his attention upon the 'underdogs' in society, the social scientist has revealed precisely those tendencies which are most subject to the radical critique: the paternalistic or 'colonial' approach to the study of society. More than any of the other social disciplines, anthropology has been bound by these limitations. And perhaps for this very reason it is incumbent upon anthropology to break with its own past and set out upon new paths.

How many studies do we have of political elites and their decision-making processes; of the functioning of bureaucracies; of entrepreneurs (not only as innovators or modernizers but as political and economic interest groups); of foreign business communities in underdeveloped countries; of corruption among labor leaders; of advertising and the manipulation of ideologies, opinions, attitudes, tastes and the innermost emotions; of the role of estate owners in the maintenance of traditional agrarian society; of regional and local *cacicazgos* or *coronelismo*; of the influence of foreign diplomatic missions on national politics; of ecclesiastical hierarchies; of military cliques; of the role of the mass media; of oppressive educational systems; or simply of the varied and multiple aspects of repression (physical, cultural, psychological, economic) that dominant groups use to maintain the *status quo*? When studying Indian communities, how often have we analyzed regional political systems? When studying peasant villages, how frequently have we given attention to the operation of national market systems? When describing the urban poor, what role do we attribute to real estate speculation and economic interest in the development of cities? When addressing ourselves to the rural migrant in the process of industrialization, how conscious are we of the role and function of the multinational corporation in determining levels of investment, technology and employment opportunities? When judging the effects of community development, health or nutrition programs at the local level, how much do we actually know of the bureaucratic and political processes involved? Admittedly, these are difficult areas for the field worker to get involved in. And by tradition we have chosen the path of least resistance. It is easier to walk into a peasant hut than into an executive office; besides, the peasant is not likely to ever read our field report.

Nevertheless, if social science is to avoid becoming irrelevant to the social change process as it is occurring in the underdeveloped countries, then we must face these new challenges, make use of our sociological imagination, become observers, perhaps even participant observers of those institutions and areas of activity which are of significance. This is not easy, and such a change of focus will encounter enormous – but I hope, not insurmountable – difficulties.

Social scientific knowledge has long since ceased to be merely an academic fixture. Like all scientific knowledge, it has become (and increasingly so) an element of power (economic, social, political). Hence the rapid proliferation of 'think tanks', data banks, documentation centers, clearinghouses, etc. The academic researcher (particularly the younger one) is no longer able to select his research activity simply by following his intellectual whims. His choice is governed by available funding, university institutes specializing in this or that area, 'scientific fashion' (which is perhaps as tyrannical in its own way as are women's fashions in theirs), and other institutional considerations. Under these circumstances the accumulation of knowledge follows predetermined patterns over which the individual researcher exercises relatively little control. In the face of this situation, he can take one of three alternatives:

(a) He can simply continue producing information – like an assembly line worker produces spare parts – without regard to its ultimate use. But surely such scientific alienation stands in direct contradiction to the role of the intellectual in society as a humanist and a social critic.

(b) Or he can produce knowledge suited to prevailing and established interpretations of society, accepting and using in his work the premises upon which are predicated the continuity and stability of existing social systems. I would include under this heading the majority of studies on, say, acculturation, social class mobility, modernization, socioeconomic correlates of individual attitudes and behavior, community monographs, etc., within the framework of functionalism and behavioralism. While such research has contributed considerably to an accumulation of knowledge in general, it has had little influence on changing prevailing patterns of the uses to which such knowledge is put and on the distribution of productive knowledge among different social groups. I am here consciously drawing an analogy between the accumulation of capital and the accumulation of knowledge in a capitalist society, insofar as both processes are an expression of the prevailing mode of social and economic organization.

(c) Thirdly, he can attempt to offer alternative explanations; explore new theoretical avenues; and exercise his intellectual critique of established or accepted 'truths', and at the same time promote the redistribution of knowledge in the fashion suggested earlier. At this point, the accumulation of knowledge may become dangerous in the eyes of those who control the academic or political establishment, and our scientist will have diminishing access to research funds, his contract may not be renewed, he may be forced to leave the university; and in extreme cases he will be obliged to leave the country or may be imprisoned. In some Latin American countries (such as Brazil and Argentina) this process has been notorious in recent years – but I do not think that it is specific to the southern part of the hemisphere or to the Western hemisphere at all.

While the accumulation of knowledge is an element of power, it does not necessarily always serve to maintain existing power structures. On the contrary, it may – and must – become an instrument for change which, through the awakening and development of a creative critical conscience, enables the powerless, the oppressed, the downtrodden, the colonized, first to question, then to subvert (for emphasis on the positive aspects of subversion, see Fals Borda, 1970), and finally to modify existing systems.

This leads directly to a consideration of an emerging role of the social researcher which will go beyond the well proven technique of participant observation: the role that I would call of activist observation, that is, of the militant *cum* observer. By this I mean the true synthesis between research on, and participation in, the social change process, not – as is so often the case – from the vantage point of the administrator, the outside manipulator or the transitory participating visitor (a common breed of applied anthropologist); but rather at the level of the political organizer, the social agitator (in the noblest expression of that much maligned term), or the 'fish in the water' (to use a relevant Chinese metaphor). Thus action and research would be joined both in the interests of furthering knowledge and of contributing to change.

Not only will activist observation improve scientific understanding of social process as it is actually occurring (and not as it is reconstructed after the fact), but it may also help to transform non-research-minded activists or militants into careful observers of their own action. This is not of course a standard recipe for anthropology in general, for not every kind of social movement can hope to count a qualified social scientist among its members, committed to its goals. It is rather an idea for committed social scientists who are interested in certain kinds of social movements not only as observers but perhaps even mainly as participants. And, hopefully, it will help to improve the quality of the social action itself.

That this is not idle speculation is clearly demonstrated by the very active commitment of many a social scientist in Latin America's revolutionary movements. May I be permitted to publicly express here my humble admiration and homage to those (social scientists and all the others) who have thus become involved, and particularly to those who have met death and suffered torture, imprisonment and persecution in their pursuit of some of man's most noble ideals. But personal emotion aside, these very revolutionary movements have shown the desperate need for social scientific analysis; that is, for the constant interplay between theory, facts and practice. Would not some of the errors and tragic mistakes that many of these movements have incurred have been avoided if, instead of simply applying theories and schemas mechanistically, they had engaged in some sort of continuing analysis of the social reality that they themselves were helping to shape? Or is this too much to expect from social science as well as from revolutionary movements? I confess that I do not possess a ready-made answer to this question.

But despite the advantages of posing research problems at this level, there are large fields of study where this approach simply is not feasible. Moreover, there is the thorny question of perspective and objectivity. One of the principal contributions of social science to social knowledge has been precisely the development of research techniques and methodology that has enabled individual researchers to distinguish more or less clearly between social fact and social norm, between what is actually going on and what they would like to see happen. This contribution of social science should not be thrown overboard by radical social scientists. The vantage point of scientific, theoretically-grounded observation by trained observers, the comparative perspective so dear to anthropologists and sociologists, the ability of social scientists to free themselves from narrowly determined perspectives of social class, minority group or subculture, is a precious achievement. And this may be an important contribution to the adequate study of the social movements to which the researcher as an individual is committed.

There is, furthermore, the very important role of the social scientist as a teacher, and not only in the university. The world-wide student revolt against the university and schools in general as systems of domestication should be of particular relevance to social scientists in helping them to 'decolonialize' themselves in their own academic environments. Social scientists as teachers can become powerful forces in the decolonialization process at all levels. We have a responsibility in helping to promote educational systems for the liberation of the human being, and not his domestication and subservience to established systems of domination.

[. . .]

The social scientist [. . .] cannot remain true to the ethical principles of his science and at the same time refuse to take a stand on the wider ideological and ethical issues of the societal processes in which he is involved as a practitioner. [. . .] It is not a question of science versus politics, but of one kind of science-in-politics versus another.

Certainly no amount of applied social science, whether romantic, official, bureaucratic or radical, can alter by itself the social forces that are at work. But the committed social scientist has an obligation to raise the issues, to ask the embarrassing questions, to carry the critique through to its conclusions, to create new models in place of the ones he is obliged to discard. And if he can, to take the necessary action.

Note

1. The issues raised in this paper are neither new nor original and the author is conscious of treading on ground that has been broken before. He sees it rather as a contribution to the Great Debate that has taken place in the social sciences in recent years and in which many colleagues from various disciplines and different countries have participated. (See for example the discussion in *Current Anthropology*, 1968; and among Latin American sociologists the debate between Fals Borda and Solari in the journal *Aportes*, 1968–71.)

References

Copans, J. (1970–1) 'Quelques reflexions', *Les Temps Modernes*, 293–4.

Current Anthropology (1969) 'Review of C.A. Valentine, *Culture and Poverty*', 10: 2–3.

Deloria, V. Jr (1969) *Custer Died for Your Sins: An Indian Manifesto*. New York: Avon Books.

Erasmus, C. (1968) 'Community development and the encogido syndrome', *Human Organization*, 27: 65–73.

Fals Borda, O. (1968) 'Ciencia y compromiso', *Aportes*, 8.

Fals Borda, O. (1970) 'La crisis social y la orientación sociológica: una réplica', *Aportes*, 15.

Freire, P. (1970) *Pedagogy of the Oppressed*. New York: Herder & Herder.

Huizer, G. (1970) '"Resistance to change" and radical peasant mobilization: Foster and Erasmus reconsidered', *Human Organization*, 29: 303–12.

Jaulin, R. (1970) *La paix blanche: introduction à l'ethnocide*. Paris: Seuil.

Mills, C. Wright (1959) *The Sociological Imagination*. New York: Oxford University Press.

Valentine, C.A. (1968) *Culture and Poverty: Critique and Counter-Proposals*. Chicago: University of Chicago Press.

7

Towards a Methodology for Feminist Research

Maria Mies

'New wine must not be poured into old bottles.'

I Introduction

After more than a decade centered on mobilization, consciousness-raising and struggles on issues such as equal rights, abortion laws, rape and violence against women, the women's movement is still gaining momentum, drawing more and more women into its vortex. This quantitative expansion, particularly in the rich capitalist countries, however, has also given rise to specific problems. There seems to be an ever-rising wave of rebellion against patriarchy and sexism, accompanied by expectations of women's solidarity and emancipation. But this rebellion, these expectations, have not yet led to a clear understanding of the relationship between women's exploitation and oppression (sexism), on the one hand, and the overall class exploitation and oppression of workers and peasants. Many women who have been in the movement since its beginnings feel increasingly worried about this lack of analysis and direction. One of the outcomes of this uneasiness is the recent emphasis on feminist research and theoretical work. In many universities in Europe and the USA feminist women have been able to set up centers for Women's Studies. In a number of disciplines women have formed feminist groups or associations. In West Germany, for example, feminist social scientists formed an association for 'Feminist Theory and Practice in Social Sciences'. Similar associations were started on other disciplines as well as on an inter-disciplinary base. During the summer vacations, so-called Women's Summer Universities in Berlin are being organized which attract thousands of women. This keen interest in the study of sexism and in women's history, women's anthropology, etc., and the endeavors to establish a feminist theory of society, has led to

From Bowles, G. and Klein, R.D. (eds), *Theories for Women's Studies*, Routledge & Kegan Paul, London, 1983, pp. 117–39.

a spate of literature, books, journals, pamphlets on women's issues. Not only are there many feminist publishing houses and bookshops exclusively run by women, but the general bookshops have discovered women as a new market and invariably reserve some shelves for women's literature. This new theoretical interest, in itself an encouraging sign of the deepening of the movement, has thrown up a number of theoretical questions for which no ready-made answer is available in the existing system of academic work. The main problem that Women's Studies face on all fronts is the male bias or androcentrism that prevails in practically all disciplines, in most theoretical work done through centuries of scientific quest. This androcentrism is manifested not only in the fact that universities and research institutions are still largely male domains, but more subtly in the choice of areas of research, in research policies, theoretical concepts and particularly in research methodology. The inadequacy of predominant research methods was first painfully felt by feminist historians, who tried to reconstruct women's history. Women's contribution to history is hardly recorded in the history books. Within a framework of science that is based on written records only, this means that their contribution does not exist for as far as historical science goes. It is this experience which has given rise to the expression: the 'hidden women'. The virtual exclusion of women, of their lives, work and struggles from the bulk of research can be adequately epitomized in Bertolt Brecht's phrase: 'One does not see those who are in the dark'. When women now try to bring light into this darkness, they encounter specific methodological problems, because the prominent social science research methodology, mainly the quantitative survey method, is itself not free from androcentric bias. The present paper, therefore, tries to address itself to the methodological problems of feminist social scientists who want to study women's issues. Its aim is to lay down some methodological guidelines, which may be further discussed and developed into a new methodological approach consistent with the political aims of the women's movement. It is the outcome of my experience as a social scientist and a participant in the women's movement.

Criticism of the dominant quantitative social science research methodology started earlier than the women's movement. My first doubts about the scientific relevance and ethical justification of this methodology were raised when I was working as a teacher and researcher in a Third World country. Here I realized that the research situation as such, due to colonialism and neo-colonialism, was a situation of clear dominance between research subject and research object, which tended to lead to distorted data.[1] In the

USA, however, criticism of the established social science research methodology came up in connection with the protest movement against American involvement in Latin America and Southeast Asia. Scholars like Horowitz (1976), Wolf and Jorgenson (1970), and Huizer (1973) raised their voices against this kind of research as a tactical tool in the 'Counter-insurgency-and-containment-of-Communism' strategy of the USA. The emphasis of their criticism was on political and ethical questions.

In West Germany, at about the same time (1967–72), the positivist and functionalist theory of society, propagated throughout the Anglo-Saxon world, and the quantitative analytical research methodology were being attacked by the theoreticians of the Frankfurt school: Horkheimer, Adorno, Fromm, Habermas, *et al.*, who evolved the critical theory of society from a dialectical and historical point of view. The focus of their criticism was the claim of value neutrality and the structural separation between theory and practice of positivism. They attacked the scientific irrelevance, the elitism and inherent class bias of this approach and tried to revive the emancipatory potential which social theory had had in the eighteenth century, the beginning of the bourgeois epoch. The criticism of 'Critical Theory', however, remained confined to the magic circle of academic institutions. It did not reach the working masses and thus reproduced the structural separation between theory and practice, characteristic of the capitalist mode of production. In the mid-1970s an effort was made to bridge this gap by the proponents of action research, first evolved by Lewin (1948).

The thoughts which follow on a methodology for feminist research grew out of the debates on these three waves of criticism against positivism as the dominant social science theory and its accompanying methodology. Therefore, they will repeat many points which are already known. However, they are the outcome of my involvement in the women's movement and of my experience in action research projects. They are not to be understood as prescriptions to be followed dogmatically, but as an invitation for methodological experiment and innovation. The assumption underlying these guidelines is the following: *there is a contradiction between the prevalent theories of social science and methodology and the political aims of the women's movement.* If Women's Studies is to be made into an instrument of women's liberation, we cannot uncritically use the positivist, quantitative research methodology. If Women's Studies uses these old methodologies, they will again be turned into an instrument of repression. New wine should not be poured into old bottles.

Thesis: When women begin to change their situation of exploitation and oppression, then this change will have consequences for the research areas, theories, concepts and methodology of studies that focus on women's issues.

'Women's Studies' means more than the fact that women have now been discovered as a 'target group' for research, or that an increasing number of women scholars and students are taking up women's issues. If Women's Studies is to contribute to the cause of women's emancipation, then women in the academic field have to use their scholarship and knowledge towards this end. If they consciously do so they will realize that their own existence as *women* and *scholars* is a contradictory one. As women, they are affected by sexist oppression together with other women, and as scholars they share the privileges of the (male) academic elite.

Out of this split existence grows a double consciousness which must be taken into account when we think about a new methodology. Women scholars have been told to look at their contradictory existence, that is, at their subjective being as women as an obstacle and a handicap to 'pure' and 'objective' research. Even while studying women's questions they were advised to suppress their emotions, their subjective feelings of involvement and identification with other women in order to produce 'objective' data.

The methodological principle of a value-free, neutral, uninvolved approach, of an hierarchical, non-reciprocal relationship between research subject and research object – certainly the decisive methodological postulate of positivist social science research – drives women scholars into a schizophrenic situation. If they try to follow this postulate, they have constantly to repress, negate or ignore their own experience of sexist oppression and have to strive to live up to the so-called 'rational' standards of a highly competitive, male-dominated academic world.

Moreover, this methodological principle does not help us to explore those areas which, due to this androcentric bias, have so far remained 'invisible'. These include: women's social history, women's perception of their own situation, their own subordination and their own resistance. Women in the universities have also shown a tendency to ignore these areas out of motives of self-preservation.

The contradictory existential and ideological condition of women scholars must become the starting point for a new methodological approach. The postulate of truth itself makes it necessary that those areas of the female existence which so far were repressed and socially 'invisible' be brought into the full daylight of scientific analysis. In order to make this possible, feminist women must deliberately and courageously integrate their repressed, unconscious female subjectivity, that is, their own experience of oppression and discrimination into the research process. This means that committed women social scientists must learn to understand their own 'double consciousness' as a methodological and political opportunity and not as an obstacle.

[. . .]

In the following I shall try to lay down some methodological guidelines for feminist research. These will be followed by an account of an attempt to put these guidelines into practice in an action research project.

II   Methodological Guidelines for Feminist Research

1. The postulate of *value free research*, of neutrality and indifference towards the research objects, has to be replaced by *conscious partiality*, which is achieved through partial identification with the research objects. For women who deliberately and actively integrate their double-consciousness into the research process, this partial identification will not be difficult. It is the opposite of the so-called 'Spectator-Knowledge' (Maslow, 1966: 50) which is achieved by showing an indifferent, disinterested, alienated attitude towards the 'research objects'. Conscious partiality, however, not only conceives of the research objects as parts of a bigger social whole but also of the research subjects, i.e. the researchers themselves. Conscious partiality is different from mere subjectivism or simple empathy. On the basis of a limited identification it creates a critical and dialectical distance between the researcher and his 'objects'. It enables the correction of distortions of perception on both sides and widens the consciousness of both, the researcher and the 'researched'.

2. The vertical relationship between researcher and 'research objects', the *view from above*, must be replaced by the *view from below*. This is the necessary consequence of the demands of conscious partiality and reciprocity. Research, which so far has been largely an instrument of dominance and legitimation of power elites, must be brought to serve the interests of dominated, exploited and oppressed groups, particularly women. Women scholars, committed to the cause of women's liberation, cannot have an objective interest in a 'view from above'. This would mean that they would consent to their own oppression as women, because the man–woman relationship represents one of the oldest

examples of the view from above and may be the paradigm of all vertical hierarchical relationships.

The demand for a systematic 'view from below' has both a scientific and an ethical-political dimension. The scientific significance is related to the fact that despite the sophistication of the quantitative research tools, many data gathered by these methods are irrelevant or even invalid because the hierarchical research situation as such defeats the very purpose of research: it creates an acute distrust in the 'research objects' who feel that they are being interrogated. This distrust can be found when women and other underprivileged groups are being interviewed by members of a socially higher stratum. It has been observed that the data thus gathered often reflect 'expected behavior' rather than real behavior (Berger, 1974).

Women, who are committed to the cause of women's liberation, cannot stop at this result. They cannot be satisfied with giving the social sciences better, more authentic and more relevant data. The ethical-political significance of the view from below cannot be separated from the scientific one: this separation would again transform all methodological innovations in Women's Studies into instruments of dominance. Only if Women's Studies is deliberately made part of the struggle against women's oppression and exploitation, can women prevent the misuse of their theoretical and methodological innovations for the stabilization of the *status quo* and for crisis management. This implies that committed women scholars must fight, not only for the integration of women's issues into the academic establishment and research policies but also for a new orientation regarding areas and objectives of research. The needs and interests of the majority of women must become the yardstick for the research policy of Women's Studies. This presupposes that women in the academic world know these needs and interests. The 'view from below', therefore, leads to another postulate.

3. The contemplative, uninvolved 'spectator knowledge' must be replaced by *active participation in actions, movements and struggles* for women's emancipation. Research must become an integral part of such struggles. Because Women's Studies grew out of the women's movement, it would be a betrayal of the aims of the movement if academic women, who were never involved in any struggle or were never concerned about women's oppression and exploitation, should try to reduce Women's Studies to a purely academic concern, restricted to the ivory tower of research institutes and universities, thus blunting the edge of all this

discontent.[2] To avert this danger, Women's studies must remain closely linked to the struggles and actions of the movement.

The concept of integrating praxis and research was concretely formulated by Mao Tse-Tung in his essays on contradiction and praxis. It must be emphasized that this concept goes beyond the prevalent understanding of action research. Action research has not been able so far to solve the dilemma of trying to establish a materialist praxis and theory which integrate the understanding of science and knowledge within a paradigm in which the separation from praxis is one of the most important structural prerequisites. But the demand to link praxis and research consistently follows an historical, dialectical and materialist theory of knowledge. According to this concept, the 'truth' of a theory is not dependent on the application of certain methodological principles and rules, but on its potential to orient the processes of praxis towards progressive emancipation and humanization. This potential, however, is not acquired in the sheltered world of academic institutions but in participation in social processes and in reflection about them.

Max Weber's famous principle of separating science and politics (praxis) is not in the interests of women's liberation. Women scholars who want to do more than a mere paternalistic 'something for their poorer sisters' (because they feel that, as a privileged group, they are already liberated) but who struggle against patriarchy as a system, must take their studies into the streets and take part in the social actions and struggles of the movement.

If they do so, their contribution will not be to give abstract analyses and prescriptions but to help those involved in these struggles to discover and develop their own theoretical and methodological potentials. The elitist attitude of women social scientists will be overcome if they are able to look at all those who participate in a social action or struggle as 'sister-or-brother-sociologists' (adapting Gouldner). The integration of research into social and political action for the emancipation of women, the dialectics of doing and knowing, will lead not only to better and more realistic theories. According to this approach, the object of research is not something static and homogeneous but an historical, dynamic and contradictory entity. Research, therefore, will have to follow closely the dynamics of this process.

4. Participation in social actions and struggles, and the integration of research into these processes, further implies that the *change of the status quo* becomes the starting point for a scientific quest. The motto for this approach could be: 'If you want to know a thing, you must change it.' ('If you want to know the taste of a pear, you

must change it, i.e. you must chew it in your mouth', Mao Tse-Tung, 1968). If we apply this principle to the study of women, it means that we have to start fighting against women's exploitation and oppression in order to be able to understand the extent, the dimensions, the forms and causes of this patriarchal system. Most empirical research on women has concentrated so far on the study of superficial or surface phenomena such as women's attitudes towards housework, career, part-time work, etc. Such attitudes or opinion surveys give very little information about women's true consciousness. Only when there is a rupture in the 'normal' life of a woman – a crisis such as divorce, the end of a relationship, etc. – is there a chance for her to become conscious of her true condition. In the 'experience of crises' (Kramert, 1977) and rupture with normalcy, women are confronted with the real social relationships in which they had unconsciously been submerged as objects without being able to distance themselves from them. As long as normalcy is not disrupted they are not able to admit even to themselves that these relationships are oppressive or exploitive.

This is the reason why in attitude surveys women so often are found to subscribe to the dominant sexist ideology of the submissive, self-sacrificing woman. When a rupture with this normalcy occurs, however, the mystification surrounding the natural and harmonious character of these patriarchal relations cannot be maintained.

The motto of changing a situation in order to be able to understand it applies not only to the individual woman and her life crises, but also to collective processes. The very fact that today we are talking about a methodology for doing research in Women's Studies is the result of a change in the *status quo* that was brought about by the women's movement and not by intellectual endeavors in universities.

If women scholars begin to understand their studies as an integral part of an emancipatory struggle and if they focus their research on the process of individual and social change, then they cannot but change themselves also in the process, both as human beings and as scholars. They will have to give up the elitist narrow-mindedness, abstract thinking, political and ethical impotence and arrogance of the established academician. They must learn that scientific work and a scientific outlook is not the privilege of professional scientists, but that the creativity of science depends on its being rooted in living social processes. Methodologically, this implies the search for techniques with which to document and analyze historical processes of change.

5. *The research process must become a process of 'conscientiza-tion'*, both for the so-called 'research subjects' (social scientists) and for the 'research objects' (women as target groups). The methodology of *conscientização* was first developed and applied by Paulo Freire in his problem-formulating method.[3] The decisive characteristic of the approach is that the study of an oppressive reality is not carried out by experts but by the objects of the oppression. People who before were objects of research become subjects of their own research and action. This implies that scientists who participate in this study of the conditions of oppression must give their research tools to the people. They must inspire them to formulate the problems with which they struggle in order that they may plan their action. The women's movement so far has understood the process of conscientization largely as that of becoming conscious of one's individual suffering as a woman. The emphasis in consciousness-raising groups was on group dynamics, role-specific behavior and relationship problems rather than on the social relations that govern the capitalist patriarchal societies.

The problem-formulating method, however, sees individual problems as an expression and manifestation of oppressive social relations. Whereas consciousness-raising groups often tend to psychologize all relations of dominance, the problem-formulating method considers conscientization as the subjective precondition for liberating action. If processes of conscientization do not lead subsequently to processes of change and action, they may lead to dangerous illusions and even to regression.

6. I would like to go a step further than Paulo Freire, however. The collective conscientization of women through a problem-formulating methodology *must be accompanied by the study of women's individual and social history*. Women have so far not been able to appropriate, that is, make their own, the social changes to which they have been subjected passively in the course of history. Women do make history, but in the past they have not *appropriated* (made it their own) their history as subjects. Such a subjective appropriation of their history, their past struggles, sufferings and dreams would lead to something like a collective women's consciousness (in analogy to class consciousness) without which no struggle for emancipation can be successful.

The appropriation of women's history can be promoted by feminist scholars who can inspire and help other women to document their campaigns and struggles. They can help them to analyze these struggles, so that they can learn from past mistakes and successes and, in the long run, may become able to move from mere spontaneous activism to long-term strategies. This presupposes, however, that women engaged in Women's Studies remain in close contact with the movement and maintain a continuous dialogue with other women. This in turn implies that they can no longer treat their research results as their private property, but that they must learn to collectivize and share them. This leads to the next postulate.

7. Women cannot appropriate their own history unless they *begin to collectivize their own experiences*. Women's Studies, therefore, must strive to overcome the individualism, the competitiveness, the careerism, prevalent among male scholars. This has relevance both for the individual woman scholar engaged in research and for her methodology. If she is committed to the cause of women's liberation, she cannot choose her area of research purely from a career point of view but must try to use her relative power to take up issues that are central to the movement. Therefore, she needs dialogues on methodology with other feminists. The emphasis on interviews of individuals at a given time must be shifted towards group discussions, if possible at repeated intervals. This collectivization of women's experiences is not only a means of getting more and more diversified information, but it also helps women to overcome their structural isolation in their families and to understand that their individual sufferings have social causes.

III An Attempt to Apply these Postulates by the Action Group: 'Women Help Women', Cologne 1976–7

These methodological guidelines were not evolved merely through the study of social science literature but also through my participation in several field projects and the discussion of these experiences with women students and other colleagues. I had a first chance to try out some of these guidelines in an action research project which grew out of an initiative responding to violence against women in the family. This initiative was started by the women students of Social Pedagogy in Cologne in Spring 1976. They founded an association called 'Women Help Women' and started a campaign to get a house where women who had been beaten by their husbands or friends could find shelter.

Although this initiative did not start with an explicit interest in research, the need for documentation and analysis became urgently felt in the course of its development. The following description of our attempt to link social research to the requirements of this field project will give an idea of how some of the guidelines mentioned above can be put into practice. It should be kept in mind that it was not a systematic attempt to apply a certain methodology of social research, but that the main motive was to further the objectives of the action group. The following should, therefore, be understood as a sharing of our experience rather than as a systematic study. The aim is to invite others to experiment along similar lines.

1. A Problem must be 'Created' (Postulate 4: in Order to Understand a Thing, One has to Change it)

After an action group of fifteen women had been constituted, a position paper was drafted on its objectives, methods and organizational principles. The group then approached the Social Welfare Department of the Municipal Administration and asked for a house for battered women. There had been reports in the press about increasing wife-beating in German families and about houses for battered women in England and Holland. The reply of the Social Welfare authorities, however, was that there was no need for such a house in Cologne; there were various homes for destitute and poor women to which battered women could go. The fact that there were hardly any battered women in these homes was sufficient proof for the authorities that the problem did not exist on any large scale. The group was advised first to make a survey and to give the authorities exact figures about the extent of wife-beating in Cologne in order to prove the need for a special house for this target group.

Such surveys are usually made by commercial research institutes with the help of professional social scientists, using the techniques of questionnaires and interviews. They not only cost a lot of money (which the group did not have) but they also have the political effect that no action is taken before the results of the studies are available. In this way, a problem is often swept under the rug.

The action group therefore chose another method of proving the need for a house for battered women. It organized a street action with posters, photos of battered wives, newspaper-clippings and signatures collected from passers-by, about the need for a Women's House for battered women. At the same time, people who came to their stand were interviewed about their experiences with and their views on wife-beating. These interviews were recorded and provided first-hand data about the existence of this problem in Cologne.

These interviews also gave the group initial feedback about people's reactions to private violence in the family, about the class position of men who beat women, about people's opinion as to the causes of this private violence and about police indifference towards the problem.

This information helped the group to plan their next steps, but it was also a bit of social research which could immediately be used to further the action. The whole action was reported in the press, including some of the statements made by the people. This publication of a problem which so far had been considered a purely private affair mobilized many people to discuss the question of a Women's House.

The municipal authorities found it difficult to maintain their indifference and finally had to mobilize their own research cell to investigate the problem of wife-beating. This was the first time that any attempt had been made to obtain statistics about cases of wife-beating in the city. Neither the police nor the various social welfare homes had kept statistics about women who approached them for help. The Social Welfare Department carried out this inquiry only in the homes under their control, not in private homes. The results of the study showed that an average 100 women per month approached these homes because they had been beaten by their husbands. The homes have no means by which to help such women quickly and unbureaucratically, however, and therefore sent them back to their husbands.

With the aid of systematic publicity work in the press, on the radio and TV, the organization grew and became known in the city. Many women who had been mistreated by their husbands rang the number given in the press. Three months after the start of the project, women began to ask the group for help. At that time the group did not yet have a house and its members thus began to give shelter in their own homes to the women who asked for help.

This made the need for a Women's House all the more urgent. When the Social Welfare Department published the results of its own investigation, the action group stated that they had given shelter to about 30 women between June and September 1976. It could no longer be said that the problem of private violence against women did not exist in Cologne. Eventually the members raised enough money to pay the rent of a suitable house, and later the municipality provided a subsidy.

2. Partiality and Egalitarian Involvement in a Social Action (Postulates 1 and 3)

Members of the action group clearly stated in their position paper that they did not want to allow new hierarchies to grow or experts to dominate the organization. Therefore, they made it a precondition for membership that women who wanted to join 'Women Help Women' had to do any type of work that came up. In the long run this proved to be a correct decision. The women social scientists who joined the organization had to give up their status of uninvolved, neutral, scientific observers or experts; they not only had to take sides with and for the mistreated women, but also to participate actively and on an equal footing with non-academic women in all the work. Some pressure was exercised by the public to elect some eminent women as members of the Board of the Association. Officers of the Social Welfare Department would have felt more at ease negotiating with academics than with unknown and inexperienced young women. The action group did not yield to such pressure, however, and stuck to its egalitarian principle of organization. This had the effect that all members had to feel actively responsible for the progress of the movement. There was no bureaucratic center of authority to which responsibility could be delegated.

The result for the academic women was that their horizon in day-to-day struggles was immensely broadened. In their discussions with women who sought shelter in the Women's House they learned more about the true social conditions of German families than from any number of quantitative surveys. For the women who had started the action group, the decision that there should be no hierarchy or bureaucracy meant that they had to learn many things that women usually do not know: from dealing with officials, lawyers, policemen, to speaking at press conferences, studying Social Welfare Laws, to white-washing and painting, driving alone at night to unknown places to meet women who sought their help, etc. The principle of action and egalitarian participation was also applied to the women who sought the help of 'Women Help Women'. After a time of rest and recovery in the Women's House, they were encouraged to participate in all the activities of the organization. This was not always easy because the women who sought shelter had run away from an acute crisis situation. They expected help and looked upon the organization as an ordinary social welfare institution. It was difficult to get them to understand gradually that women's liberation rather than social welfare and charity was the aim of the action group. This understanding was furthered by the principle of active and egalitarian participation of all, including the academic women.

The difficulties that arose from this struggle towards inner democracy and integration of praxis and theory were caused by the contacts with the outer world, mainly the municipal authorities, with their highly hierarchized and bureaucratized organizations. Constant friction was caused by the fact that these bureaucracies have no latitude for egalitarian initiative.

3. Discussion and 'Socialization' of Life-Histories as Therapy, as a Basis for Collective Women's Consciousness and as a Starting Point for Emancipatory Action (Postulates 5, 6 and 7)

In the first phase of the action, intensive individual and group discussions took place with women who had run away from their homes because their husbands or fiancés had beaten them black and blue. These intensive talks were institutionalized after the group had rented a house in November 1976 and many more women rang up. (Only the telephone number was known, not the address, in case the men should follow their wives and harass them and the children.)

At first these informal yet intensive talks were mainly about the forms, duration, extent and repercussions of male violence in the family. They necessarily emphasized the psychological dimension of a woman's individual history. Since no amount of psychological counselling could solve the practical and material problems that these women faced after leaving their husbands (no job, no flat, insecurity of income, no training), it became evident that psychological introspection alone could not lead to a deeper understanding of the social forces which had put women into such a state of dependency.

It became necessary to help women understand that their own experience of male violence was not just their individual bad luck or even their fault, but that there is an objective social basis for this private violence by men against women and children. This meant that they had to understand the sociological and historical dimensions of male violence if they were to get out of the masochistic tendency to attribute the failure of their marriage to their own failure as women.

The best method by which to make women in this crisis situation aware of the sociological and historical roots of their suffering appears to be the documentation and analysis of their life histories; by making their stories public, women acknowledge that their experiences have social origins. This method, evolved as a technique of action research (Osterland, 1973), is not only an effective way by which to integrate the time dimension into social research; it is also an excellent method of conscientization. The methodology of a small-action research project which grew out of these informal talks in the Women's House is described below.

It was our objective to document, analyze and discuss the life histories of a number of women who came to the Women's House. We wanted to publish these life histories because it was our aim to conscientize and mobilize the public at large about the problem. To achieve this, much more information was needed on this hidden side of our society, which professes to be democratic and peaceful. It is the task of social researchers to provide this information.

Methodologically, the small group of women who started this project (myself and six students) tried to follow the postulates laid down above.

[. . .]

When we planned this small action research project, we had the following objectives in mind, which cover not only our research interests but are closely linked to the individual interests of the women concerned, as well as to the broader aims and perspectives of the women's movement:

(a) For the women concerned, the systematic documentation of their life histories has the effect that their own subjective biography assumes an objective character. It becomes something at which they can look from a certain distance. They are not only prisoners of their own past and present sufferings and mistakes, but they can, if they want to, draw lessons for the future from their own past history.

(b) Writing down their biographies also serves a very practical purpose. These women need documentation and hard data in order to re-organize their lives. They need such documents for their lawyers, for example, if they want to have a divorce. On the other hand, the action group also needs documentation of women's histories if it is to avoid endless Sisyphian charity work.

(c) From the point of view of research, these biographies contain data not only on the individual destinies of the women but also on objective social relations such as class, and the women's reactions towards these. The biographical method also links the individual history to the overall social history of an epoch. The individual's life manifests the contradictions and stresses of an epoch. Many of the women have experienced the war and post-war years; some are refugees from East Germany. Many of the men are workers; many are unemployed and have started drinking. The question of when the man started to beat his wife often gives insight into the interplay between crises: increased phenomena of alienation (work stress, alcoholism, job insecurity, competition) and private violence and aggression. Reflection and appropriation of individual women's histories, therefore, cannot be separated from the reflection and appropriation for feminist use of the overall social history of an epoch.

(d) Apart from the individual, practical and theoretical dimensions, the writing-down and discussion of life histories also has political and action-oriented dimensions, aiming at creating a new collective consciousness among women and mobilizing them for further social action. For this it was necessary to generalize the individual life histories, which we tried by staging the play and by the ensuing discussion of the video film.

In the collectivization and discussion of their individual experiences, the women transcend their narrow isolated horizon and begin to understand that women in general have a common social destiny. In fact, most of the women, when they listened to the stories of others, were struck by the similarity of their experiences, i.e. the commonness and monotony of the everyday violence. There was hardly anything individual or extraordinary in their narrations.

(e) Mere scientific documentation and analysis, and even a group discussion on the common destiny of women, does not lead by itself to an active collective consciousness 'for themselves'.

Only when women can use their own documented, analyzed, understood and *published* history as a weapon in the struggle for themselves and for all women will they become subjects of their own history. This implies that the documentation of their life histories – the video film, the book, the discussions – have to be integrated into the overall strategy of the women's movement. This mobilization of all women who so far had been passive victims of patriarchal structural and direct violence may transcend the scope of a small action-research project. But the fact that the women who took part in the research showed keen interest in starting a public campaign against private violence is an indicator that they are moving away from their status as mere objects of charity and social welfare and are on the way to becoming subjects of their own history.[4]

Postscript

I have often been asked whether the guidelines or postulates spelled out above could also be applied to research on women in Third World countries. In 1978–9 I carried out an ILO-sponsored research project on rural women in India, where I tried to implement some of these methodological principles. A full account of my experience is given in my reports on this subject.[5] Here I wish only to highlight a few necessary points in order to counter certain illusions which may arise regarding the scope of this approach to further social change.

We (the Indian women who assisted me and I) applied this approach in three rural areas, where we carried out fieldwork among women in the subsistence sector. In one area a social movement for the organization of landless laborers and their social betterment had been in progress for several years. The landless female laborers had already formed their own autonomous organizations, which had carried out a number of successful actions for better wages, work contracts and nightschools for women. It was not difficult to use the methodological principles spelled out above and the women participated enthusiastically in our research. They first started doing research *on us*, however, asking all sorts of personal questions regarding our husbands, children, our bodies, clothes; what we did during menstruation, whether we used cotton or cloth; and above all, why we were interested in them. In other words, they did not uncritically accept the hierarchical research situation but turned it into a dialogue. This was facilitated because we lived among them and needed to be helped in many ways. In their songs, dances, dramas, role plays, group discussions, the recording of their life histories, in mass meetings, it became evident that not only were they quite capable of analyzing and understanding their own situation, but also of drawing practical conclusions from this analysis. The project provided a forum for discussions and meetings and, as such, not only helped to conscientize these women, but created a wider network of communications for women from different villages, thus giving them a new sense of power.[6]

It would have been impossible for us, however, to mobilize and organize the scattered women through the research project *alone*. Even if it is action-oriented. Women's Studies cannot *on its own* do such work. Perhaps this should not even be attempted: the researchers usually will leave the area after a certain period of time and the women who are left behind will have to face the political consequences of their mobilization. If a research project is carefully linked to an ongoing movement, however, the separation between research and action, theory and practice can be overcome – at least we can move in that direction. The degree to which the resources and services of a research project can be used to further the aims of the movement will depend on the movement itself.

Similar autonomous organizations did not exist in the other two areas, and we thus found ourselves in the typical research situation of outsiders who had come to snoop around. In one area the situation was complicated further by the fact that for approximately the last hundred years the local women had become accustomed to being the objects of charity for the Christian church and Western business interests. It was difficult to explain to them that we had no such charity to offer, and at first they did not see any point in talking to us. They were completely atomized as workers and housewives, and although we were able to organize group discussions in which they talked about their problems, the initiative was clearly in our hands. These women belonged to a better class and caste than the women in the first area, but their consciousness and self-confidence were much lower.

We realized that a research project that does not link up with some local group which will constitute a permanent base for conscientization, mobilization and action, will remain at best a pleasant episode in the lives of the women, and will be unable to develop its emancipatory potential. In any case, women's research projects as such should not be expected to *start* a conscientization movement. This would presuppose greater commitment and involvement of the research team in a particular area than is possible for most urban-based women in Third World countries.

Even in areas where no movement was yet in progress, however, we realized that it was impossible *not* to become involved. Given the general sex-segregation and oppression of women in India, the women very soon came to tell us about their private problems with their husbands, their mothers-in-law, the quarrels in the village, etc. This 'women's gossip' was obviously encouraged by the fact that we were women, belonging to the same social category, *and* were also outsiders and researchers who were ready to listen to their stories. This general feeling of 'being on the same side' helped to overcome the usual barrier between people from different classes and cultures. The establishment of an open and friendly rapport between us and the women was mainly due to the commitment and enthusiasm of the Indian women on the research team, who were not only capable of partial identification with the problems of the rural women, but who also enjoyed being with them and temporarily sharing their lives.

Notes

This paper was first read at an interdisciplinary feminist seminar in Holland and it is published in German in *Heksenkollege: de feeks viool* (Nijmegen, Holland, 1978, out of print); and in *Beiträge zur feministischen Theorie und Praxis*, 1978.

1. Mahmood Mamdani (1973) describes the functioning of this kind of research.
2. The present world-wide interest in Women's Studies may also be attributed to certain efforts to neutralize the protest potential of the movement. In many countries there is already a gap between Women's Studies and the women's movement.
3. By *conscientização*, Freire means 'learning to perceive social, political and economic contradictions and to take action against the oppressive elements of reality'. In the following we will use the English version, 'conscientization' (Freire, 1970).
4. The results of this project were published under the title: *Nachrichten ous dem Ghetto Liebe* (1980).
5. The research report on my work in India is entitled 'Housewives produce for the worldmarket: the lace makers of Narsapur' (1982).
6. An account of this experience is given in my paper 'Peasant women get organized' (1981).

References

Berger, H. (1974) *Untersuchungsmethode und soziale Wirklichkeit* [*Research Methods and Social Reality*]. Frankfurt.

Freire, P. (1970) *Pedagogy of the Oppressed*. New York: Seabury Press.

Horowitz, I.L. (1976) *The Rise and Fall of the Project Camelot: Studies in the Relationship between Science and Practical Politics*. Harvard: MIT Press.

Huizer, G. (1973) 'The a-social role of social scientists in underdeveloped countries: some ethical considerations', *Sociologus*, 23 (2): 165–77.

Kramert, H. (1977) 'Wann wird die Selbstverständlichkeit der geschlechtlichen Abeitstellung in Frage gestellt?' ['When will the assumed sexual division of labor be questioned?']. Paper delivered in Frankfurt.

Lewin, K. (1948) *Resolving Social Conflicts*. New York: Harper & Row.

Mao Tse-Tung (1968) *Über die Praxis, Über den Widerspruch* [*On Practice, on Contradiction*]. Calcutta: National Book Agency.

Maslow, A.H. (1966) *The Psychology of Science: A Renaissance*. New York: Harper & Row.

Osterland, M. (1973) 'Lebensgeschichtliche Erfahrung und gesellschaftliches Bewusstsein: Anmerkungen zur soziobiographischen Methode' ['Life history experience and social consciousness: notes on a social-biographical method'], *Soziale Welt*, 24 (4): 409–17.

Wolf, E. and Jorgenson, J.G. (1970), 'Anthropology on the warpath in Thailand', *New York Review of Books*, 15 (9): 26–34.

8

Interventions in New Social Movements

Elim Papadakis

The central theme of this chapter is the intervention in contemporary social movements by social researchers. Many of them are intellectuals who are sympathetic to the aims and goals of a social movement and who play a part in reinterpreting the meaning of its actions and in redirecting its path. This leads us into a discussion of the implications for the aims of participants in social movements of interventions by intellectuals and social researchers, particularly those who are used by (established) organizations to secure their own legitimacy. The critique by post-modernists or Foucauldians of the Enlightenment model of field research is central to this discussion, particularly since new social movements[1] have served as a source of inspiration for both sides of the debate.

Although some writers have sought to identify common goals within such diverse social protests, others have delighted in their heterogeneity and subversive quality. Habermas (1971, 1981a, 1981b), for instance, has identified, both in the student movements of the 1960s and in the new social movements of the 1980s, a potential vehicle for the completion of the modernist project, for an ethics based on communication, rational argument and intention. Movements that do not share his vision for the completion of the project of the Enlightenment are characterized as regressive. By contrast, Foucault and the post-modernists have not only celebrated the resistance by such movements to processes of rationalization but highlighted the manner in which they represent 'local revolts . . . along the disciplinary continuum' (Walzer, 1986: 65). The study of micro-power is linked to the micro-politics of new social movements.

Despite fundamental differences in their approaches, both post-modernists and Habermas have distanced themselves from Marxist theories of social change, from the working class as the main carriers of conflicts of the future and from the sphere of production. Both

From J. Gubrium and D. Silverman (eds), *The Politics of Field Research*, Sage, London, 1989, pp. 236–57.

Habermas (who projects rational models for social change based on meta-theoretical and universalist perspectives) and Foucault (who attacks any such attempts to create overarching and totalizing schemes for social relations) (see Lash, 1985) share a concern about social actors and subjectivity being rendered instrumental. It will be argued in this chapter that the attempt to combine meta-theoretical accounts with critiques of intellectual élitism (through a focus on the construction of subjects in discourses) is the most salient aspect of discussions over the empowerment of subjects other than as objects of the professional gaze in sociological research. The opposition between modernist and post-modernist approaches may not be as pronounced if one shifts from abstract generalization to the everyday practice of new social movements. Although both Habermas and Foucault draw inspiration from new social movements, neither makes explicit how such forces will act to bring about social change (Lash, 1985).

The same cannot be said of individual researchers or organizations that, in response to the challenge from new social movements, have incorporated field research in their attempts to provide new policy directions. Going much further than the Enlightenment model of field research, the sociological interventions by Alain Touraine among social movement activists are intended to help people at the grass roots to launch a more successful and effective struggle for social change. In West Germany social researchers have been used both by the state and by new social movements to rearticulate the shift in mass attitudes over nuclear power, environmentalism, peace and alternative lifestyles.[2]

Analysis of these interventions will be used to assess the pertinence of the fears expressed by Foucauldian critics of emancipatory discourses and the normalizing role of the human sciences.

Sociological Intervention in the French Anti-Nuclear Protest

The work of Touraine has provided a point of contact, albeit in a highly ambiguous manner, between meta-theoretical accounts and diverse social movements and qualitative social research. Like Touraine (1971), some post-modernists place their work at the intersection of industrial and post-industrial society (see Lash, 1985). A close connection is hypothesized between the politics of new social movements and the development of new forms of power centred not so much around the forces of production but rather the control of knowledge and information. There is, however, a crucial difference. Touraine, in a similar vein to Habermas, is concerned with the clash between two social orders, with the discovery of a central conflict dimension (to replace that of the working class versus the bourgeoisie in capitalist industrial society). Post-modernists, on the other hand, would welcome the diversity of social conflicts and struggles, whilst eschewing attempts to impose alternative models of society.

Touraine (1981) has argued that his method of sociological intervention is the application of theories of social movements. It aims to distinguish between different *meanings* of social struggle in order to reveal the presence (or not) of a social movement. The role of the researcher is to encourage the reflexivity of social actors, to assist them with self-analysis, with interpreting the significance of their own action.[3] This novel method of research only strives for objectivity within a prescribed framework: it assumes that a social struggle can only be defined as a social move-ment if it entails a struggle against 'the holders of technocratic power', those who are at the forefront of developing new ways of managing the economy not only through control of processes of capital accumulation but also through control of knowledge and information. For instance, protesters against nuclear power are only engaged in a social movement if they can clearly define (1) an adversary ('technocratic power created by capitalism'), (2) the stake of the struggle (conflict over common cultural orientations, for instance, over ways of solving economic crises) and (3) the actors themselves (in whose name they are fighting) (Touraine, 1983: 176–7).

Whenever these struggles focus on community rather than modernization, opposition against specific nuclear power installa-tions rather than on new ways of managing the economy, the nuclear industry rather than technocracy, fear rather than level-headed analysis of social action, defensive rather than offensive struggles, grass-roots fundamentalism rather than definition of adversaries, an ethic of conviction rather than of responsibility and crusades rather than strategies, they are distancing themselves from the goals of a modern social movement.

Sociological intervention goes much further than participant observation. The methodological/theoretical rationale for interven-tion is to achieve an 'adequate understanding of motives and mean-ing' of social conflicts which would otherwise remain 'deeply hidden from the mere spectator' (Bouchier, 1982: 297). The knowledge of the sociologist becomes inextricably linked with the politics of new social movements. The researcher plays an active role by promoting discussion among activists over the meaning of their struggle. The sociologist aims to assist the activists in 'elevating' the level of their struggle to that of a true social movement. Later, an assessment is made of whether a particular struggle contains the seeds of a social movement capable of challenging technocratic power. In the study of the anti-nuclear protest (Touraine, 1983), two groups were formed and invited to discuss their struggle with interlocutors of their own choice (including sympathizers and opponents, many of whom belonged to major political and industrial organizations). The researchers actively intervened to analyse the conditions and meaning of the struggle. Hypotheses were then presented to the activists. Acceptance of these signified the likely success of the social movement, rejection signalled the inability of the activists to elevate their struggle to that of a modernizing social movement.

Touraine strives to unite the work of the researcher and the object of study (1971: 233). He distances himself from the short-term goals of a particular campaign, whilst seeking (on the basis of sociological analysis and intervention) to influence its general direction as a social movement against technocratic power. The intervention in the anti-nuclear protest, he argues, led some militants to commit their struggle 'to a new direction', to 'a much clearer perception of the conditions that would allow that struggle to exist and develop'. He concludes that for the researcher 'this recognition both of their independence and of their usefulness corresponded so completely to their intention that they found in it the justification of their work' (1983: 171).[4]

Whatever the shortcomings of his methodology, Touraine has provided valuable insights into the attitudes of militants and the chances for success of their struggle. Does this also entail a positive contribution by researchers to the direction of a grass-roots campaign? The 'success' in persuading some activists to adopt a more analytical approach and to reflect on their action is only qualified. The method of intervention was challenged by many activists and some withdrew from the exercise altogether. This draws attention to the dangers of imposing a model for emancipation by 'enlightened' social researchers. It should be stressed that this discussion would not be possible if the researchers had not made public the sources and nature of the conflicts.

The researchers wanted to test their model of a social movement against the reality of the anti-nuclear protest. It is stressed for instance that the sociologist was not a 'benevolent ally' but an analyst 'urging each individual to explain his or her position' (Touraine, 1983: 58).[5] However, this detachment (in order to further the analysis), the reluctance by Touraine to turn himself into the leader of the group is undermined by the aggressive attempt to convert through 'self-analysis' 'those tendencies which seemed at variance with the research team's image of the movement' (1983: 131). The researchers perceived themselves as prophets of an incipient social movement (1983: 194) and sought to raise the consciousness of the activists (1983: 139).

One is reminded of the warning by Foucault against a shallow and dangerous approach to emancipation and rationality. Although they were in favour of self-analysis, the researchers were reluctant to evaluate or separate the groups' influence on the researchers and vice-versa. It would, they argued, be contrary to the spirit of the intervention 'since the work of the groups consisted simultaneously in self-analysis and intervention' (1983: 113). Touraine retained this ambiguity because of his over-riding preoccupation with the discovery of *the* social movement of post-industrial society.

Even participants who shared this goal accused the researchers of 'manipulation of language'. Others reproached them for pressuring the groups into adopting a 'particular image' of their struggle, of devising abstract objectives and programmes to the detriment of the 'lived experience of the movement and, above all of the group itself' (1983: 88). The researchers might have considered how much any social movement can afford to preoccupy itself at length with discourse, with self-analysis and interpretation. In addition, the temporary withdrawal by some women resulted from their perception of yet another attempt (by sociologists) to impose a 'male logic' (1983: 89). At one stage an entire group became so aware of the attempts to create divisions between them that they created an elaborate hoax to demonstrate their unity against the researchers.[6]

These negative reactions by the participants unsettled the researchers. The latter interpreted the behaviour of the dissenters in terms of their own paradigm of modernization, whilst acknowledging perceptions of manipulation. A contrast was evoked between 'cultural withdrawal' and the commitment to a 'political counter-project' (1983: 98), between rejection of industrial–technological society 'in the name of lived experience, balance and community' and the definition of 'a new society' (1983: 120), between anti-statism linked to communitarian values and 'the makers of programmes who seemed to be reformist political manipulators or disembodied theorists' (1983: 137).

Both Touraine and Habermas argue that modernizing tendencies can only be further developed through 'rational' discourse. However, this is not an end in itself. Rather it needs to be steered by an awareness of the social uses of knowledge. In this respect, Touraine identifies social movements as the central potential carriers of social change. Whereas in the past, social action was limited by 'metasocial guarantees of social order' (such as the 'order of things, divine law, or natural, historical evolution'), the capacity of modern societies to create, destroy and transform their environment has enabled social movements to play a much more active role in 'all aspects of cultural life' (Touraine, 1985: 778). Whereas in the past, social protest was confined to established institutions, 'in modern societies social movements are located precisely where change takes place' (Eder, 1982: 10).

This perspective was adopted by many of the anti-nuclear activists. However, in order to counter the criticism that the analysis merely reflected the situation of one particular group, comment was invited from other activists who had not been involved in the intervention. The activists on the whole regarded the analysis as a 'useful way of conceiving the problems of the movement' and of bridging the gap between theory and practice (Touraine, 1983: 148). There is, however, a certain Foucauldian irony in the adoption by a major umbrella organization, the Network of the Friends of the Earth, of the terminology of the sociologists. At their 1979 annual congress, they outlined their commitment to conflicts of the future over the control of information and the technocracy (1983: 167). A major grass-roots organization was adopting an interpretation which, according to the paradigm of modernization constructed by Touraine, ran counter to the orientation of many grass-roots activists.

The researchers reported that one group of activists had taken new initiatives and committed their struggle to 'new directions' because of the intervention. Both researchers and participants 'affirmed that the knowledge it had brought, had given the militants, who had never ceased to act according to the aims of their struggle, a much clearer perception of the conditions that would allow that struggle to exist and develop' (Touraine, 1983: 171). However, a second group of activists rejected this Enlightenment model and accused the researchers of producing a biased report which had failed to analyse their 'real experiences', their attempts 'to get a real democracy working and set up certain structures, certain kinds of representation, new forms of information' (1983: 151).

The researchers could hardly refute the charge. In a model drawn up by them to plot the positions of the participants in relation to the 'highest level' of social conflict, those who had rejected the 'social management' of social movements were placed furthest away. The views of these participants on the nature of power, on the locus of social struggles, bore a strong resemblance to post-modernist concerns. To them 'the search for a social adversary can only conceal an inability to challenge oneself' (Touraine, 1983: 44). They felt that power was located 'not in the capitalist system but in individual psychology' (1983: 133), and called for each individual to 'challenge his or her own way of living or thinking' (1983: 73). These views on the nature of power and the locus of social conflict are post-modern to the extent that they show an understanding of how power is a strategy for constituting subjects. However, the focus on self-actualization also corresponds to the message of the new professionals of the psyche – counsellors, psychotherapists and other enforcers of disciplinary practices.

Touraine is aware that to focus on the modernism of the anti-nuclear protest 'might favour the action of a new managing élite' unless it is linked to a broader 'struggle against the holders of technocratic power' (1983: 121). The shared cultural orientations of the anti-nuclear protest and the technocrats provides the basis for conflict rather than 'a modernizing reformism favouring the interests of a new ruling class' (1983: 177). The critique of the anti-nuclear protest has to be 'more modernizing than the policy of the ruling class and the State, but in the opposite direction' (1983: 177). The notion of the self-management of new social movements is contrasted to the manner in which older social movements (particularly the labour movement) have been turned into 'instruments of management or co-management'. None the less Touraine has not provided a convincing model for preventing the emergence of new structures of power and domination via an élite that seeks to impose its perception of the highest level of social struggle on the remainder of the community.

The Greens in West Germany[7]

I now draw out in more detail the implications of interventions by social researchers in contemporary social movements. The focus is on the Greens in West Germany who are perceived both by many of their sympathizers and by established organizations as potentially a profound threat to prevailing structures of power and authority.

The complex intermeshing of theoretical assumptions and research interventions can be linked to responses both by sympathizers to some of the aims of contemporary social movements and by modernizing élites and professionals in state employment to problems arising in areas such as the environment and the provision of welfare services.

Four levels of intervention (which are often linked with field research) can be identified. First, the close ties between intellectual inspirers or theorists and participants in the new social movements, represented above by Touraine, are an important characteristic of the development of the Greens. Indeed, the distinction between theorists and participants is often difficult to uphold. Secondly, the attempt by the Greens to challenge prevailing structures of domination, to counter technologies of monitoring and surveillance and to broaden their social bases of support has led to a complex series of 'dialogues' between new social movements and established organizations. This has highlighted both the advantages and the pitfalls of 'communicative rationality' insofar as this concept can be operationalized. Thirdly, and related to these dialogues, supporters of the Greens in the alternative self-help movement have been at the forefront of experiments in the provision of welfare which in some respects embrace the critique and implicit rejection by Foucault of the modern social state. In other respects, these experiments have led not so much to a rejection of, but to the installation of a different form of, state intervention in people's daily lives. In other words, some of these challenges have been successfully accommodated by a modernizing welfare state. Lastly, both the state and new social movements have made use of interventions by researchers and, despite resistance among some groups, the majority of supporters of new social movements appear to accept them.

The Suspicion of Interventions by the Intelligentsia
Modernizing counter-élites, defined by knowledge and a certain level of education (see Touraine, 1971) have, with limited success, influenced the direction of new social movements. None the less, many Green activists would reject the style of the intervention carried out by Touraine in France. 'Prominent personalities' are seen to have a destructive effect on the attempt by the movements to create credible alternatives to prevailing political structures. The usefulness of intellectual inspirers is questioned by activists who draw the distinction between the capacity of such people to generate publicity for the movement and the practical skills required by militants engaged in a locally based social struggle.

There are innumerable problems facing theorists who seek to assist new social movements.[8] The gap between attempts to identify universal elements in diverse and complex social struggles (see Brand, 1986) and actual practice has led to a questioning of the role of intellectualist interventions. Boggs (1986), who regards the Greens as a prototype of post-Marxist radicalism, stresses their anti-Jacobinist orientation. None the less, the Marxist inheritance still exerts some influence.

In their most mature expression, these movements constitute counter-hegemonic struggles in the Gramscian sense to the degree they can lead to an alternative ideological framework that subverts the dominant patterns of thought and action, that challenges myths surrounding the vulnerability of the *status quo*. (Boggs, 1986: 5)

This is an accurate account of a predominant tendency within the Greens. However, it ignores the powerful anti-intellectualism that has prevailed among some sections and the purposeful opportunism involved in accepting some but not other aspects of emancipatory discourses.

This was particularly evident among the so-called Spontis who emerged in the wake of anti-nuclear and environmentalist protests in the mid-1970s and exerted a powerful influence on a burgeoning counter-cultural movement. The Spontis expressed most acutely the reaction against the Marxist orientation of the New Left, against the 'repression of instincts', 'abstract theorizing' and the emphasis on analytical approaches to social problems. The neo-Nietzschean critique of knowledge and rationality posits a mythological basis for social life, the formation of 'anti-authoritarian collectivities' in which recognition is given to the 'differences of others' (see Papadakis, 1984: 36–8). State power is conceived of in highly subjectivist terms rather than in formal abstract categories.

Their position (see Röttgen and Rabe, 1978) is close to that of Foucault and the post-modernists. Rather than consensus they would focus on dissensus (Lash, 1985: 17). For Foucault plans for reform are of little use unless they emerge from the activists engaged in a social struggle (see Silverman, 1987: 203). He is deeply suspicious of the 'emancipatory discourse' (D'Amico, 1986). Attempts to devise or imagine alternative social systems are regarded as an extension of 'participation in the present system' (Foucault, 1977: 230, quoted in Minson, 1986: 140).

Such an approach is anathema to Habermas who has argued that by equating rationality with the preservation of economic and administrative systems of action, in other words state power, new social movements may often reject reason itself (Habermas, 1981c: 140). Whereas Habermas identifies the 'emancipatory potential' of, for instance, the feminist movement and its role as a carrier of universal values (1981a: 34), a Foucauldian approach to issues such as the socialization of child care and domestic tasks would highlight 'how a certain socialization and various measures of "women's liberation" provided some of the conditions of the emergence of the involuted private modern family' (Minson, 1986: 143; see Donzelot, 1979: 221). More specifically, the extension of state child-care facilities in the German Democratic Republic has not weakened 'commitment to the nuclear family as . . . a relay of "social" disciplinary norms' (Minson, 1986: 142). Yet a simplistic adaptation of emancipatory models can often lead to a superficial assessment of such progressive measures (see, for example, Bassnett, 1986).

By juxtaposing modern and anti-modern tendencies and by hypothesizing an essential difference between a (progressive) modernizing and (regressive) cultural orientation, both Habermas and Touraine side-step the issues of how power is exercised at the micro level.[9] The underlying rationales for much of the action of social movements that do not conform to their models for emancipation tend to be discounted.

Sections of the Greens have attempted to turn away from élitist, prescriptive approaches to social emancipation. The search by Touraine for a new central conflict in society and for a new carrier for this conflict would be anathema to many. Whether this is a sign of their inability to create such a central class, or of their reluctance to act as an authoritarian vanguard, sections of the Greens, in a manner similar to Foucault, have suggested that the working class will have to formulate its own response 'from below' (see Papadakis, 1984: 216–17). Post-Marxist analyses also point to the 'pluralization of social life-worlds: the separation of public and private spheres, the growth of local autonomy, and the dispersion of various centres of life activity such as work, family, community and culture' (Boggs, 1986: 30). The attempt to transcend Marxism also implies a rejection of revolutionary intellectual élites, of social manipulation through claims of 'absolute knowledge of social totality' (Boggs, 1986: 59–60).

What requires further explanation is how these new orientations will shape field research. From a Foucauldian perspective, post-Marxist analyses need to incorporate a more thorough critique of emancipatory discourses and the normalizing role of the social sciences.

The Suspicion of Interventions through Dialogue
The involvement by the Greens in local politics and their close links to a vast network of self-help community projects was perceived by the dominant parties as a major threat to their legitimacy. Strategies were developed to accommodate 'new politics' issues and to gain some advantage from the innovations of the self-help movements. Politicians and professionals in the state apparatus who could understand these changes were in demand and, if necessary, academics were recruited to advise on these initiatives (see below on the implications of interventions through dialogue).

The architect of the Social Democratic strategy for 'dialogue' with the new social movements was Peter Glotz, who rose from the position of Senator in West Berlin to General Secretary of the party. Glotz saw himself as the mediator between two cultures which were drifting apart. He was concerned about the impact of these developments on his own party and wanted to find a basis for consensus and greater communication between established cultures and left-wing subcultures (see Glotz, 1979, 1982).

Glotz correctly anticipated the growing dilemma for his party in trying to unite a productivist ethos with an ecological orientation, in trying to articulate the concerns of its more traditionalist working-class bases of support and those of the upwardly mobile white-collar and professional middle classes. In discussions with participants in new social movements, he admitted that social democracy had neglected new political issues (such as the environment, peace and alternative lifestyles) and spiritual and ethical questions.

Among the initiatives supported by Glotz was the funding by the government of self-help projects. According to one senior public servant advising the West Berlin government on health-care projects, the alternative movement, though not necessarily offering solutions to social problems, was able to draw attention to them (interview, May 1982). These initiatives support the observation by Arney and Bergen that 'the field of medical power has changed to become incorporative and rapidly responsive to developments around it' (Arney and Bergen, 1984: 167). They can also be linked to the attempt by the state (especially under pressure from conservative parties and business interests) to reduce its own financial contribution to the public provision of welfare (see Grunow, 1986).

The Greens became deeply suspicious of the strategy of dialogue. In the words of one activist, discussions with the state

> make sense to find out what the other side wants, what tricks it is using . . . and then to expose all this . . . Among us dialogue is instantly associated with the danger of being bought off and corrupted. You assume a great deal of self-confidence if you believe that you cannot be instrumentalized by this . . . If they, the Social Democrats and the Christian Democrats, offer dialogue, they want to integrate us. (interview, May 1982; my translation)

The fear expressed by participants in the self-help movement of instrumentalization and manipulation by skilled tacticians, by the intellectuals operating from within the state bureaucracy, was shared by strategists in the Green party:

> Glotz is a problem. The strategy of dialogue by Glotz [pause] . . . I and

many others feel very cautious about it . . . [it] is a purely tactical matter, it is really a matter of the SPD attempting to recover lost support, support which had historically enabled the SPD to get into government . . . The real political questions or political goals or criteria for politics are considered by Glotz purely from a tactical viewpoint, so that one does not have the feeling that one is engaged in discussions with someone who is genuinely curious and wants to change, but rather someone who is only peering in, in the last resort, and attempting to cream off something for himself. (interview, January 1982; my translation)

According to the alternative daily newspaper, *Die Tageszeitung*, the dialogue of Glotz had 'all the charm of a trap-door'.

This fear of becoming engaged in a discourse articulated by a more powerful opponent is also justified to the extent that government advisers and politicians were very skilled and fluent in expressing themselves, in stressing the need for tolerance, for communication between the state and protest groups and for self-reflexivity. Here are two examples.

Basically both sides need to change, they must move towards each other. I don't mean that they should therefore give up their own position, but one must find ways whereby both sides can agree with each other to some extent. One shouldn't always say when a compromise has been reached that this is a victory over the other group. That draws people apart. Clearly this path towards compromise is very difficult because for years one has made compromises but always at the expense of the weaker group . . . There must be compromises which do not rob people of their identity. That is decisive. (interview, May 1982; my translation)

I live in a bourgeois marriage . . . and am not disturbed by the fact that there exist other forms of togetherness elsewhere. I welcome it. But this does not place me under pressure to change my own form of living together . . . I know various strengths and weaknesses of my way of living together and theoretically I know that of others. (interview, May 1982; my translation)[10]

Dilemmas for Radical Reformists

None the less, new social movements have attracted sympathizers who are also highly skilled communicators and who have an intimate knowledge of the workings of the bureaucracy. New social movements and the Green party have employed social scientists in a manner not dissimilar to established organizations, to provide advice on all major policy issues and on strategies for achieving programmatic goals. The focus here is on the impact of Professor Peter Grottian, a sympathizer of the self-help movement in West Berlin.

An unsuccessful attempt had been made by the Ministry of

Education to enter negotiations with some self-help groups, to discuss the possibility of funding them in a bid to gain a better insight into their operation. The groups, reflecting the attitude of suspicion towards politicians such as Glotz, initially rejected these overtures, fearing the loss of autonomy and the creation of divisions within the self-help movement. The collapse of this initiative prompted Grottian to form an organization for the funding of alternative self-help projects. There were two interrelated aims: to seek assistance from the state whilst retaining the autonomy of the groups, and to work towards a united stance among them before making such an approach.

The intervention by Grottian was decisive in persuading a large number of alternative groups to apply for funds from the state and, to some degree, in allowing even a Christian Democratic government to 'infiltrate' alternative self-help projects. Grottian was able to draw on his skill in communicating with both sides and his expert knowledge of the bureaucracy.[11] He argued that the pooling together of their demands and a carefully orchestrated public campaign particularly via the mass media would enhance the political relevance of self-help groups.

This initiative was aided by the fact that the state, even if only for purposes of short-term legitimation, *is* concerned over the lack of 'transparency' of its complex rules, regulations and structures. In West Berlin the Christian Democrats launched a campaign in favour of smaller, more transparent units of organization for the administration of welfare in which the highest levels of state authority would no longer have exclusive control and which, as far as possible, would enjoy a degree of autonomy. Other major parties also supported such measures. Although the state has drawn up criteria to identify 'worthwhile' projects (for instance, their contribution to certain aspects of health care, their capacity to encourage young people to shape their own lives and the rejection of violence as a political tactic) (see CDU Fraktion, 1982), there remains the issue of how to avoid state interference.

The initiative by Grottian was crucial in persuading a large number of groups that state interference could be reduced to a minimum. Grottian proposed that the intermediary organization he had helped to establish within the alternative movement would undertake the task of negotiating the conditions for the distribution of financial help and of submitting applications for funds: this would allow projects to deal with an organization, which though accountable to the state in the last instance, would also be much more sensitive to their needs and *modus operandi* than the established bureaucracy. He persuaded many that this would 'be better than being pushed around from one bureaucrat to another' (May 1982) but also insisted that they would have to be accountable to the organization for how they used the funds.

Attitudes within the self-help movement towards state intervention have been highly ambivalent – on some occasions they have led to discussions (over possible funding for social welfare projects) with the highest levels of the state apparatus (often via intellectuals who are sympathetic to their aims), on others they have reflected fear of manipulation and incorporation. Foucault's warning against a shallow approach to emancipation and rationality has not gone unheeded. His attempt to undermine notions of the 'whole of society' can be seen as an attack on the 'mindless identification of socialism with interventionism', on the emergence of strategies which would only 'represent a perpetuation of the present' (Minson, 1986: 143, 145).

Eräsaari has drawn on the critique by Foucault and the postmodernists to paint a bleak picture of the 'new social state' which 'institutionalizes selected community help, reshapes citizen expectations and tries to improve civic spirit and community-focused civil society' (1986: 231). He is at least correct in pointing out that the self-help movement has strengthened rather than weakened the power of the social bureaucracy, particularly in the more vulnerable areas such as youth culture and unemployment. Although conservative forces have reinforced the critique by the self-help movement of the inflexibility, inefficiency and inhuman aspects of the modern welfare state (see CDU Fraktion, 1982), it has been demonstrated that self-help groups and their supporters are predominantly middle class and do not want a reduction in the levels of state welfare (Grunow, 1986: 200).

The outcome of these developments is uncertain since they provide both a basis for the expansion of professional power (Eräsaari, 1986) and greater opportunities for challenges to it (Grunow, 1986). It could be argued that

> For many reasons – to be able to follow the discussions of the alternative movements, work with patchwork projects, identify new sociocultural strategies, etc. – critique of the social bureaucracy has already become a major resource of the new social state. Especially when the socialization or connecting work of the social bureaucracies seems in many ways to be an endless process, critical ideas are valuable because the registering of everyday phenomenologies may produce false or illusory results. (Eräsaari, 1986: 239)

Yet there is nothing new in this. The discussion by Bulmer of the Enlightenment approach highlights the willingness by policy-makers, mainly in the United States, to encourage research that forces them to question earlier assumptions (1982: 48).

Eräsaari does, however, go one step further in stressing that the final decisions on the basis of data obtained through discussions between self-help groups and professional power are made by the latter (1986: 238) (see also next section). The senior public servant (see above) who was critical of the 'dialogue behind closed doors' was making the same point. It is therefore hardly surprising that most citizens, although they have a fair understanding of notions of choice and consultation, find it difficult to conceptualize control over decision-makers (see Papadakis and Taylor-Gooby, 1987).

Eräsaari posits a general trend towards increasingly sophisticated techniques for manipulation, particularly in therapeutic forms of power which encourage people to 'become instruments of power over themselves through themselves' (1986: 239). Self-help is simply a smokescreen for self-manipulation in the interests of the state, for a reduction in state expenditure on welfare programmes. However, he can only suggest an alternative in the most general terms: through a search for 'inviolate' areas of life and through autonomy and decentralization (1986: 239)

The practicality of doing this has not been demonstrated by the self-help movement in West Germany. It has been buffeted between the search for autonomy and the need to secure financial support. Emphasis on the former has led to self-exploitation by participants who work very long hours for low pay; emphasis on the latter has forced projects to turn to the state for support, 'to negotiate with the "devil"' (see Papadakis, 1984: 202).

A major problem facing radical reformists is the general suspicion and fear of the bureaucracy. Any change in this area would require a change in attitudes based on a better understanding by the projects of the complexity of the bureaucratic process, and on greater transparency of these processes. However, initiatives for change will have to come from outside the bureaucracy. Progress in debureaucratization has been limited probably because of the 'absurdity of asking bureaucrats themselves to develop plans for debureaucratization' (Grunow, 1986: 203).

The Implications of Interventions through Dialogue

In an attempt to overcome the rigidities of the civil service, governments have come increasingly to rely on the advice of experts employed on short-term contracts to offer 'neutral' advice to the government and, through qualitative research, to explain the motives of participants in new social movements. These and other initiatives mentioned earlier highlight the ways in which both the state and new social movements attempt to articulate popular perceptions, to develop new strategies and counter-strategies. In the end we find a mixture of successful manipulation and partial implementation of popular aspirations.

Some social scientists have been employed as policy advisers by government departments because they might offer 'neutral' advice. Unlike civil servants who are more likely to offer advice on the basis of individual strategies for career advancement, academics, employed as short-term consultants, are expected to say what they think.

However, until recently such advice has usually relied on quantitative data. The state has successfully used this to secure legitimacy, to provide the necessary 'evidence' to justify particular policies and new initiatives. The rise of the Greens has led to a more rapid introduction of new techniques. The traditional use of quantitative data has proved, on its own, inadequate for these purposes. Quantitative studies commissioned, for instance, by the Office of the Federal Chancellor, had identified the shift in values across all age groups and linked it with declining support for the Social Democrats and increasing support for the Greens. However, the politicians and their professional advisers were at a loss to explain the motivational forces behind these changes. The way was open for the planning division of the Chancellor's Office to commission, for the first time, a full-scale study using qualitative field research.

The research team, in designing a frame for the survey, were influenced by Habermas's concern with the 'life-world', the social milieu of different groups in the population:

> We only took this as a theoretical consideration. Habermas stops when it comes to empirical questions. He says that there is some kind of 'new life-world'. I agree. But how do you measure it? (interview with a member of research team)

The team therefore drew up a range of milieus populated, for instance, by followers of alternative life-styles, traditional working-class families, upwardly mobile workers, hedonists, conservatives and so on. Because they were investigating new issues, they abandoned the traditional approach of classification according to socio-demographic variables. For instance, with respect to supporters of the Greens, they argued that the milieu in which they find themselves, rather than their belonging to a particular age cohort, defines their allegiance to a new social movement, their support for new values. In this the researchers were implicitly accepting some of the major assumptions of post-Marxist analyses of social change.

Although most of the data from field research have not filtered through into short-term policy implementation because of the reluctance of the bureaucracy to take it seriously, Federal Chancellors have begun to incorporate and rearticulate some of the findings in their attempts to stem the Green tide. They have found that extracts from qualitative interviews are a very useful additional source of information and have cited them in their political speeches. The extracts have been used to add an 'authentic tone' to otherwise dour political statements. Popular language and perceptions which may present a challenge to established structures are skilfully filtered into the political process.[12] Data from qualitative interviews were similarly rearticulated and incorporated into their speeches in attempts to capture the popular mood.

It should be stressed that supporters and sympathizers of new social movements and the Green Party have been very willing to discuss their views and attitudes with researchers working on behalf of the state.

The personal statements from qualitative interviews have provided a vital link for Chancellors with the voter. They are, in certain respects, a far more reliable source of information than that obtained through established channels of politicians and professional bureaucrats who are more likely to say what is 'expected' of them to the head of government. In analysing the rearticulation and incorporation of these data, the way in which they are filtered, one has to distinguish between the requirement of the government and those of party general secretaries. For instance the General Secretary of the CDU, Heiner Geissler, in a similar manner to Peter Glotz when he was General Secretary of the SPD, has made extensive use of qualitative surveys in formulating party programmes.

The government uses the qualitative material in a similar way to quantitative data, to secure legitimacy on a day-to-day basis, to sustain a particular policy or initiative. The rearticulation of popular discourse is very apparent. The parties, by contrast, have used qualitative research for long-term planning. The SPD, for instance, organized a qualitative study into the decline of active supporters and members. This led to the implementation of a new organizational structure and of new forms of intraparty communication, including the creation of a personal computer network which provided local branches with rapid access to information from the party headquarters in Bonn. The Irsee Programme of the SPD, particularly the sections on peace, ecology and economic activity, was heavily influenced by qualitative studies. Researchers from the institute that carried out the survey were involved in the formulation of the programme which refers to social movements as 'major partners in Social Democratic policy' (SPD, 1986: 34). There is an echo here of the 'recursive method' suggested by Giddens which stresses that structure should not be identified solely with constraint on human action. Rather, structure 'is both the medium and outcome of the human activities which it recursively organizes' (Giddens, 1986: 533).

The co-operation of respondents in these qualitative studies, including those from new social movements and the Greens, was achieved with very little difficulty. Some were pleased at being consulted on their opinions and that some attempt might be made to implement them. There was no concern that what they divulged might be rearticulated in order to secure greater legitimacy for either the government or a particular political party. By contrast to the efforts of Touraine in the French anti-nuclear movement, by not overtly seeking to convert respondents the researchers achieved a high measure of success simply by inciting them to express their motives and goals.

There appears to be an absence of resistance to technologies of monitoring and surveillance which incite discourse. In many respects it is hardly surprising, since contemporary social movements themselves rearticulate, filter and incorporate the language of others. The success of the Greens, the impact by their supporters in the alternative self-help movement, can be explained in terms of their more pragmatic and flexible strategies, in terms of their self-limiting radicalism (see Papadakis, 1988).

The difference between the modernist orientation of the Greens and new social movements with a premodern orientation is most evident in responses to a pilot study of right- and left-wing radicalism in West Germany carried out by the SINUS research institute. At first the left-wing radicals, who included strong sympathizers of left-wing terrorist groups, refused to participate in a study commissioned by the government. However, they reasoned that they were already well known to the state security services, that they could tell the interviewer a load of nonsense and falsify the interview and that the inducement of DM 500 would make it worth their while.

A completely different approach was required for supporters of the extreme right. Interviewers often did not reveal who had commissioned the survey and stated, for instance, that they were preparing a paper for a university seminar on German national identity. In addition, female respondents refused to be interviewed by men. Their attitude, according to one interviewer, was essentially feudal. Among them, notions of authority and dominance were much more prevalent. The only way to incite discourse was through disguising the aims of the project. As Arney and Bergen have argued, 'Technologies of domination and control impel silence; technologies of monitoring and surveillance incite discourse' (1984: 170). In this instance, the state was perceived in feudal rather than modernist terms.

There are, of course, severe limits to the influence of social researchers in all these examples. On the one hand they are indispensable intermediaries between the population and large and powerful organizations. They can, to some degree, provide or withhold information. On the other hand, they can easily be hired and fired. The content of their research, the design of their questions, often has to conform to the assumptions and goals of the agency commissioning the study or seeking their advice. Their data, however objective, scientific or authentic, can easily be interpreted to suit purposes of self-legitimation (see Müller-Rommel, 1984).

The problem for Enlightenment Reformism and for Romantic notions of authenticity lies in how to overcome the incipient élitism of their prescriptions for social change. As Silverman (1989), drawing on Foucault, has suggested, intervention in and rearticulation of discourses by subjects may provide an escape route.

This implies a complementarity of approaches, of emancipatory models and of anti-élitism, so long as they are linked to resistance to the instrumentalization of subjectivity (and support for autonomy) and to careful consideration of the operation of power at the micro level (including an understanding of prevailing institutional structures). The examples in this chapter suggest an uneasy mixture of successful manipulation and partial implementation of popular aspirations through the use of qualitative field research.

In the case of the West German Greens it is the rearticulation, for instance of the theme of nationalism by the peace movement, of widespread discontent with the inflexibility, lack of communication and accountability of the welfare state, of popular concerns with damage to the environment, and of dissatisfaction with the organizational rigidities of modern political parties and other established organizations, that has added to their popular appeal.

The incorporation and rearticulation of these issues in the programmes of major political parties should not be seen as a successful attempt to defuse the impetus of a new political power. New laws for the protection of the environment, greater funding for self-help projects and initiatives for peace and detente, however much they represent an attempt to perpetuate established political structures, may also signal significant improvements or at least a slowing down in the deterioration of the quality of life for most of the population. This success cannot, however, be attributed solely to the progressive emergence of post-industrial, modern, emancipatory discourses. Even if their interventions correlate with the aims of participants in new social movements, social researchers inevitably become part of a technology of normalization. It is for social actors themselves to rearticulate discourses. The capacity of social actors to intervene in, rearticulate and politicize the process of social change is unmistakable.

Notes

1. The term 'new social movements' is subject to diverse interpretations. The development of modern social movements has been linked with the advent of industrialization – with the need for societies to innovate in all spheres of life (see Banks, 1972) and with the dissolution of metasocial guarantees of the social order (including notions of divine law, natural historical evolution and the order of things [Touraine, 1985]). Although these interpretations underlie the meaning of the term 'new social movements' as used in this chapter, we are mainly concerned with those movements that lay strong emphasis on the democratization of society and on a reflexive approach to the creation of identity and meaning (see Cohen, 1985). This includes movements concerned with civil and social rights, alternative life-styles, sexual liberation, ecology, nuclear energy and nuclear weapons, ethnic minorities and so on.

2. The clash, for instance, between a productivist and an ecological model of development is addressed by both groups. However, the former seek to resolve the issue through a change in the political agenda (to a primary focus on measures for environmental protection), whereas the latter, whilst highly conscious of the need to incorporate environmental concerns, retain the primacy of economic growth (see Eder, 1982: 16).

3. Touraine has done this in a very self-conscious manner, drawing upon his experiences to create models for sociological intervention. Others, for instance Peter Grottian who has offered his expert knowledge to the alternative self-help movement in West Germany, have not attempted to 'theorize' their experiences even though they too have, in essence, intervened in a similar manner (see below).

4. It should be stressed that sympathy for a particular social struggle did not lead the researchers to give up their hypotheses about what constituted the highest level of social conflict. The advantage of this approach lay in creating 'criteria' which could be applied in a range of settings. A further advantage is that it does away with the 'illusion' that the researcher can be detached from material under investigation. There is a parallel here to Foucault's 'methodology' and to the argument that 'the practitioner of interpretive analytics . . . can never stand outside' the phenomena being studied (Dreyfus and Rabinow, 1986: 115).

5. 'It is not in the name of personal preferences or ideologies that we announce the visible presence of a new social movement, nor is it as the devoted interpreters of the actors and their ideology, but after an intervention in which we questioned the anti-nuclear struggle at length, placing ourselves far from its

practices and its representations, on the summit of a distant social movement' (Touraine, 1983: 180).

6. The group had staged a polemical debate between ecologists and trade unionists which was recorded on video and later played back to the researchers. Touraine, however, interpreted this psychologically, arguing that the group had attempted to purge itself of excessive tensions (Touraine, 1983: 96).

7. The term 'Greens' will be used whenever I refer to both the Green Party and new social movements. However, references will also be made to specific social movements such as those oriented towards self-help projects and alternative lifestyles, the peace movement, the ecology movement and so on. Some of the data presented in this section come from an earlier study of the Greens (Papadakis, 1984). I am particularly grateful to several supporters of and activists in the new social movements as well as to several policy advisers working for either state or federal governments for their time and effort towards discussions on the Greens. However, I remain solely responsible for any errors of interpretation or translation.

8. Cohen, in a review of literature on social movements, posits the need for greater synthesis between theories developed by social movements and social theory, between competing social theories, and between macro social theory and theories of social movements (1985: 715–16).

9. Cohen (1985) formulates the problem more in terms of addressing the prevailing institutional structures.

10. However, it would be incorrect to impute purely cynical motives to these statements or to assume collusion between the strategy of dialogue of Glotz and the views of these advisers. Several of them have criticized the failure of Glotz to take practical steps: 'The term dialogue has been misused. It has taken place behind closed doors, but with no practical consequences. I only want such discussions if they lead to something and are not simply programmatic statements. They must have consequences' (interview May 1982; my translation).

11. Grottian had previously carried out several research projects on the bureaucracy in West Germany.

12. There is a parallel to the manner in which medicine, through its discursive practices, filters 'the language of medical paraprofessionals, members of nonmedical professions, and others who present a potential challenge to orthodox medicine' (Arney and Bergen, 1984: 168).

References

Arney, W. and Bergen, B. (1984) *Medicine and the Management of Living*. Chicago: Chicago University Press.

Banks, J. (1972) *The Sociology of Social Movements*. London: Macmillan.

Bassnett, S. (1986) *Feminist Experiences*. London: Allen & Unwin.

Boggs, C. (1986) *Social Movements and Political Power*. Philadelphia, PA: Temple University Press.

Bouchier, D. (1982) 'Review of "The Voice and the Eye" by Alain Touraine', *British Journal of Sociology*, 33: 296–7.

Brand, K.W. (1986) 'New social movements as a metapolitical challenge', *Thesis Eleven*, 15: 60–8.

Bulmer, M. (1982) *The Uses of Social Research*. London: Allen & Unwin.

CDU Fraktion (1982) *Grosse Anfrage über alternatives Leben*. Drucksache 9/349. Berlin: Abgeordnetenhaus.

Cohen, J. (1985) 'Strategy or identity: new theoretical paradigms and contemporary social movements', *Social Research*, 52: 663–716.

D'Amico, R. (1986) 'Going relativist', *Telos*, 67: 135–45.

Donzelot, J. (1979) *The Policing of Families*. New York: Pantheon.

Dreyfus, H. and Rabinow, P. (1986) 'What is maturity? Habermas and Foucault on "What is enlightenment?"', in David Hoy (ed.), *Foucault: A Critical Reader*. Oxford: Basil Blackwell.

Eder, K. (1982) 'A New Social Movement?', *Telos*, 52: 5–20.

Eräsaari, R. (1986) 'The New Social State?', *Acta Sociologica*, 29: 225–41.

Foucault, M. (1977) *Language, Counter-memory and Practice*. Oxford: Basil Blackwell.

Giddens, A. (1986) 'Action, subjectivity and the constitution of meaning', *Social Research*, 53: 529–45.

Glotz, P. (1979) 'Staat und alternative Bewegungen', in J. Habermas (ed.), *Stichworte zur Geistigen Situation der Zeit*, Vol. 2. Frankfurt: Suhrkamp.

Glotz, P. (1982) *Die Beweglichkeit des Tankers*. Munich: Bertelsmann.

Grunow, D. (1986) 'Debureaucratization and the self-help movement', in E. Oyer (ed.), *Comparing Welfare States and their Futures*. London: Gower.

Habermas, J. (1971) *Towards a Rational Society*. London: Heinemann.

Habermas, J. (1981a) 'New social movements', *Telos*, 49: 33–7.

Habermas, J. (1981b) *Theorie des kommunikativen Handelns*, Vol. 2. Frankfurt: Suhrkamp.

Habermas, J. (1981c) 'Dialektik der Rationalisierung', *Aesthetik und Kommunikation*, 45/46: 129–61.

Lash, S. (1985) 'Postmodernity and desire', *Theory and Society*, 14: 1–34.

Minson, J. (1986) 'Strategies for socialists? Foucault's conception of power', in M. Gane (ed.), *Towards a Critique of Foucault*. London: Routledge & Kegan Paul.

Müller-Rommel, F. (1984) 'Sozialwissenschaftliche Politik-Beratung: Probleme und Perspektiven', *Aus Politik und Zeitgeschichte*, B 25/84: 26–39.

Papadakis, E. (1984) *The Green Movement in West Germany*. London: Croom Helm.

Papadakis, E. (1988) 'Social movements, self-limiting radicalism and the Green Party in West Germany', *Sociology*, 22: 171–92.

Papadakis, E. and Taylor-Gooby, Peter (1987) 'Consumer attitudes and participation in state welfare', *Political Studies*, 35: 467–81.

Röttgen, H. and Rabe, F. (1978) *Vulkantänze – Linke und alternative Ausgänge*. Munich: Trikont.

Silverman, D. (1987) *Communication and Medical Practice*. London: Sage.

Silverman, D. (1989) 'The impossible dreams of reformism and romanticism', in J.F. Gubrium and D. Silverman (eds), *The Politics of Field Research*. London: Sage.

SPD (1986) *Irsee Draft of a new SPD Manifesto*. Bonn: SPD.

Thompson, J. (1983) 'Rationality and social rationalization: an assessment of Habermas's theory of communicative action', *Sociology*, 17: 278–94.

Touraine, A. (1971) *The Post-industrial Society*. London: Wildwood House.

Touraine, A. (1981) *The Voice and the Eye*. New York: Cambridge University Press.

Touraine, A. (1983) *Anti-nuclear Protest*. Cambridge: Cambridge University Press.

Touraine, A. (1985) 'An introduction to the study of social movements', *Social Research*, 52: 749–87.

Walzer, M. (1986) 'The politics of Michel Foucault', in D. Hoy (ed.), *Foucault: A Critical Reader*. Oxford: Basil Blackwell.

9

A Political Classification of Evaluation Studies in Education

Barry MacDonald

After stating that the basic and utilitarian purpose of evaluation studies is to provide information for choice among alternatives, and that the choice is a subsequent activity not engaged in by the evaluators, Hemphill says: 'This fact might lead to the conclusion that an evaluation study could avoid questions of value and utility leaving them to the decision-maker, and thus not need to be distinguished from research, either basic or applied. The crux of the issue, however, is not *who* makes a decision about what alternatives or *what information* serves as the basis for a decision; rather, it is the *degree to which concern with value questions is part and parcel of the study.*'

A matter of 'degree' may not suggest a major distinction. It is necessary to be more explicit. Of course, values enter into research, in a number of ways. There are many people in this country who have resisted the conclusions of a great deal of educational research since the war, on the grounds of value bias inherent in problem selection and definition. This was notable in the response to research into educational opportunity, and seems likely to characterize the reception of current research in the field of multi-ethnic education. Other value judgements of the researcher are less perceptible and lie buried in his technology. The more esoteric the technology, the less likely are these values to be detected. Test and survey instruments are wrongly assumed to be value-free because of the depersonalized procedures of administration and analysis that govern their application. The position of the evaluator is quite distinct, and much more complex. The enterprise he is called upon to study is neither of his choosing nor under his control. He soon discovers, if he failed to assume it, that the issues of educational action and consequence he is required to elucidate are enacted in

From D. Hamilton, C. Jenkins, C. King, B. MacDonald and M. Parlett (eds), *Beyond the Numbers Game: A Reader in Educational Evaluation*, Macmillan, London, 1977, pp. 224-7.

a socio-political theatre which infiltrates the enterprise at every stage. He finds he can make few assumptions about what has happened, what is happening or what is going to happen. He is faced with competing interest groups with divergent definitions of the situation and conflicting informational needs. If he has accepted narrowly stipulative terms of reference, he may find that his options have been pre-empted by contractual restraints that are subsequently difficult to justify. If, on the other hand, he has freedom of action, he faces acute problems. He has to decide which decision-makers he will serve, what information will be of most use, when it is needed and how it can be obtained. I am suggesting that the resolution of these issues commits the evaluator to a political stance, an attitude to the government of education. No such commitment is required of the researcher. He stands outside the political process, and values his detachment from it. The researcher is free to select his questions, and to seek answers to them. He will naturally select questions which are susceptible to the problem-solving techniques of his craft.

The relevance of this issue to my present thesis is easy to demonstrate. The political stance of the evaluator has consequences for his choice of techniques of information gathering and analysis.

A great deal of new knowledge is produced by researchers and evaluators by means of techniques and procedures which are difficult to understand. Conclusions are reached and judgements made by the few who are qualified to make them. Others accept or reject these conclusions according to the degree of respect they feel towards those who make them, or the degree to which the conclusions coincide with their beliefs and self-interests.

For many years now those concerned with the failure of the educational system to make full use of the results of educational research have pleaded the case for all teachers to be trained in the techniques of research. Perhaps some of that effort should have been expended in exploring techniques that more closely resemble the ways in which teachers normally make judgements, techniques that are more accessible to non-specialist decision-makers. The evaluator who sees his task as feeding the judgement of a range of non-specialist audiences faces the problem of devising such techniques, the problem of trying to respond to the ways of knowing that his audiences use. Such an effort is presently hampered by subjecting evaluators to a research critique which is divorced from considerations of socio-political consequence. Evaluators influence changing power relationships. Their work produces information which functions as a resource for the promotion of particular interests and values. Evaluators are committed to a political stance because they must choose between competing claims for this resource. The selection of roles, goals, audiences, issues and techniques by evaluators, provides clues to their political allegiances. I will describe three distinct types of evaluation study – bureaucratic, autocratic and democratic. The last of these will be the least familiar to students of evaluation. The field has been characterized by evaluation studies which fall into one or other of the first two types. The democratic evaluation study is an emerging model, not yet substantially realized, but one which embodies some recent theoretical and practical trends. It is, in part, a reaction to the dominance of the bureaucratic types of study currently associated with American programmes.

Bureaucratic Evaluation

Bureaucratic evaluation is an unconditional service to those government agencies which have major control over the allocation of educational resources. The evaluator accepts the values of those who hold office, and offers information which will help them to accomplish their policy objectives. He acts as a management consultant, and his criterion of success is client satisfaction. His techniques of study must be credible to the policy-makers and not lay them open to public criticism. He has no independence, no control over the use that is made of his information and no court of appeal. The report is owned by the bureaucracy and lodged in its files. The key concepts of bureaucratic evaluation are 'service', 'utility' and 'efficiency'. Its key justificatory concept is 'the reality of power'.

Autocratic Evaluation

Autocratic evaluation is a conditional service to those government agencies which have major control over the allocation of educational resources. It offers external validation of policy in exchange for compliance with its recommendations. Its values are derived from the evaluator's perception of the constitutional and moral obligations of the bureaucracy. He focuses upon issues of educational merit, and acts as expert adviser. His techniques of study must yield scientific proofs, because his power base is the academic research community. His contractual arrangements guarantee non-interference by the client, and he retains ownership of the study. His report is lodged in the files of the bureaucracy, but is also published in academic journals. If his recommendations are rejected, policy is not validated. His court of appeal is the research community, and higher levels in the bureaucracy. The key concepts of the autocratic evaluator are 'principle' and 'objectivity'. Its key justificatory concept is 'the responsibility of office'.

Democratic Evaluation

Democratic evaluation is an information service to the community about the characteristics of an educational programme. It recognizes value-pluralism and seeks to represent a range of interests in its issue-formulation. The basic value is an informed citizenry, and the evaluator acts as broker in exchanges of information between differing groups. His techniques of data-gathering and presentation must be accessible to non-specialist audiences. His main activity is the collection of definitions of, and reactions to, the programme. He offers confidentiality to informants and gives them control over his use of the information. The report is non-recommendatory, and the evaluator has no concept of information misuse. The evaluator engages in periodic negotiation of his relationships with sponsors and programme participants. The criterion of success is the range of audiences served. The report aspires to 'bestseller' status. The key concepts of democratic evaluation are 'confidentiality', 'negotiation' and 'accessibility'. The key justificatory concept is 'the right to know'.

10

The Value of Quantitative Methodology
for Feminist Research

Toby Epstein Jayaratne

In the past several years the feminist community has increasingly debated the merits of traditional research in the social sciences and specifically the quantitative methodologies used in that research. Many feminists, both those in the social sciences and in other disciplines as well, argue that traditional research in the social sciences is used as a tool for promoting sexist ideology and ignores issues of concern to women and feminists (Stasz Stoll, 1974; Frieze *et al.*, 1978; Fox Keller, 1980). As a result of this and other criticisms of traditional research and quantitative methods, some feminists have suggested the increased use of qualitative research in order better to reflect the nature of human experience (Reinharz, 1979; Fox Keller, 1980; Depner, 1981). Furthermore, there has been some discussion of the need to reduce or eliminate the use of quantitative research as a valid methodology for social scientists (Reinharz, 1979). This debate between quantitative and qualitative researchers is not new. In fact, Glaser and Strauss (1967) indicate that this dialogue has been ongoing for several decades.

The primary purposes of this paper are (1) to explore briefly some of the issues surrounding this controversy from a feminist perspective and (2) to suggest some changes in the traditional quantitative research process and in traditional research environments which would make quantitative research useful for testing feminist theory.

I also advocate the use of qualitative data, in conjunction with quantitative data, to develop, support and explicate theory. My approach to this issue is political; that is, I believe the appropriate use of *both* quantitative methods and qualitative methods in the social sciences can help the feminist community in achieving its goals more effectively than the use of either qualitative or quantitative methods alone. Both quantitative and qualitative research

From G. Bowles and R.D. Klein (eds), *Theories for Women's Studies*, Routledge & Kegan Paul, London, 1983, pp. 140–61.

can be and have been effectively used by feminist researchers to promote feminist theory and goals and to document individual and institutional sexism (for example, see Weisstein, 1970; Chesler, 1972; Levitin *et al.*, 1973; Reinharz, 1979).

[. . .]

Feminist Criticism of the Quantitative Research Process and Quantitative Analysis

Feminist criticism of research in the social sciences is directed toward both the general quantitative research process and quantitative data and data analysis in particular. The primary criticisms arise because so much of traditional quantitative research seems inconsistent with feminist values. First, much social research has been used to support sexist and elitist values. Little effort has been made to explore issues of importance to women. Second, the socially relevant research which has been generated often is not utilized 'appropriately', that is, it has no real impact on social problems. Too many final reports or journal articles get dusty on the bookshelves of academicians or government bureaucrats. Third, there exist exploitative relationships among the research staff and between the staff and the respondents in the study. Too many needs or concerns of the research staff are secondary to the more immediate needs of meeting deadlines, seeking scarce funding or getting out a final report. And respondents are often seen as 'objects' of study, deceived and manipulated for the benefits of the research product. Fourth, the high standards of methodological rigor are often simply overlooked when expedient. To learn and then employ all the quality controls of a research project is not a simple task and too often the standards for appropriate use of quantitative methodology are set aside when it is convenient. Fifth, quantitative data cannot convey an in-depth understanding of or feeling for the persons under study. This final criticism of the quantitative research process concerns the objective *appearance* of the quantitative research. There is an 'objective' aura about traditional research which makes it convincing and influential. Thus, findings which are often products of poor methodology and sexist bias are interpreted by the public as fact.

While most of these claims do have merit, the conclusion by some feminists that we must reject traditional research outright is debatable. A closer examination of each of the criticisms and a discussion of possible alternative procedures will clarify other options which are available to us.

Exploration of Sexist and Elitist Issues

Anyone who glances through the indices of social science journals for the past thirty or forty years cannot deny that the great majority of research addresses issues of importance to white male academicians (Stasz Stoll, 1974; Cox, 1976; Frieze *et al.*, 1978). It has only been in the last ten years or so that some journals have consistently included research about women's issues. However slowly this change is taking place, it is now possible to find articles of relevance to women in most major social science journals. Although many established journalists in the US publish 'token' articles on women's research, some regularly include such research (see *Child Development, Journal of Personality and Social Psychology*, and *Journal of Educational Psychology*). Furthermore, there are several journals which publish research exclusively about women and much of this research is carried out using quantitative methodology (see *Psychology of Women Quarterly* and *Sex Roles*). The issues addressed in much of this recent research are of prime interest to feminists, and include a broad range of topics such as sex discrimination, child care, pregnancy, sex-role development, sexual harassment, educational equity, and spouse abuse. In addition, much of this research is carried out from a feminist perspective, and contributes to feminist theory.

Although funding for research on women's issues may be more difficult to secure in the near future, the past several years have seen an increase in research exploring issues of relevance to women. This change probably reflects not only the increased attention which women's issues have received in the popular media, but also the increased numbers of women entering graduate school and the academic job market in the social sciences. While traditional academic 'ethics' dictate the need to be relatively value-free in choosing a research area (Kerlinger, 1979), it is likely that many of these women are choosing research areas which are related to personal interests and values. According to Cox, 'women seem to be more sensitive to the issue of values in social sciences, and without abandoning scientific goals, are more candid about having values that guide them in their work' (1976: 13).

Under-Utilization of Relevant Social Findings

From a political perspective, all quality social research ought to be used in policy decisions. Obviously, this is not what happens. Many social scientists feel that their obligation to research ends with a published document; whether results from their studies have any impact on policy seems to be of little concern. This attitude is reflected in the traditional research process: most educational programs in the social sciences do not include training in the utilization and dissemination of research. In fact, it is a controversial issue as to whether researchers ought to be involved in the decision-making process at all. While there is debate as to the exact role of the researcher in policy-making, few would suggest that all researchers need to become experts in policy formulation.

Tangri and Strasburg (1979) note the importance of both traditional research conducted by researchers and the use of research in policy-making conducted by activists. They believe that while many investigators hope to see their findings utilized in policy decision-making, it is difficult for many already overburdened researchers to take on an additional role as activist. Tangri and Strasburg suggest that there can be an interaction between researchers and activists and that social researchers need not become activists in order to contribute to the political relevance of their work. While the role of the activist is to influence decision-makers, the equally important

> role of the researchers is to contribute knowledge of completed and ongoing studies relevant to the targeted problem; to help the activists frame their questions in research terms; and to develop research designs which incorporate mechanisms for ongoing evaluation. (Tangri and Strasburg, 1979: 329)

As rare as actual utilization might be, Weiss and Bucuvalas (1977) point out that decision-makers are responsive to recommendations of social scientists when those recommendations support their own views of social issues. The fact that there are a minority of policy-makers who hold values which are consistent with a feminist perspective is not promising for the implementation of policy based on the utilization of social science research which supports feminist goals. Although we need to elect and support policy-makers who are sympathetic to our views and use relevant research data to support their recommendations, as researchers we need more direct strategies.

Tangri and Strasburg (1979) have analyzed the problems of utilization of women's research on policy formulation and offer some recommendations for generating politically useful research. The authors specifically mention that the researcher should be perceived by the policy-maker as 'objective', and present findings which are statistically significant. This indicates that the use of quantitative research can be an effective tool in influencing policy-makers. These authors also point to the need to (1) make researchers more aware and employ those methods which make their data more useful to activists, and (2) change academic structures so that there is support for the use of these methods. Of course, the latter particularly will not be easy to achieve.

In another analysis of which factors affect the usefulness of research, Weiss and Bucuvalas (1977) identified one factor which consisted of items establishing 'trust' in the research. These items, which concern the methodological quality of the research, were 'statistical sophistication, objectivity, quantitative data, generalizability, validity, and additions to descriptive, causal, or theoretical knowledge' (1977: 218).

One important court decision which indicates the potential influence of quantitative data is *Griggs* v. *Duke Power Company* (1971), which was argued under Title VII of the Civil Rights Act of 1964. Prior to this case, sex discrimination could be substantiated only if one could prove intent on the part of the defendant. The decision resulting from this case, however, was that discrimination could be indicated by presenting statistics which show a different and unfair impact on a racial, sex or other group covered by Title VII. This decision set a new course for discrimination suits.

Aside from the issue of the *direct* influence of social science research on policy decisions, it is important to consider the indirect effect, that is, the influence on public opinion. Some of the results from social research, particularly those concerning current or controversial issues, find their way into the popular media, such as *Psychology Today*, women's magazines or newspapers. Often these articles, depending on the extent of coverage, influence public opinion to such an extent that, ultimately, policy decisions are also affected. While this type of 'utilization' of social research has less of an apparent effect than a more direct approach, the political efficacy of the research may be more far-reaching, since it can directly affect people's lives. For example, research which indicated the pervasiveness of wife abuse may not have resulted in immediate policy change to combat the practice. However, popular media attention was so widespread that many victims who otherwise would have felt isolated and been self-blaming, instead sought support in centers and community support programs.

Exploitive Relationships between Project Staff and
between Staff and Subjects of Study
Many of us who have been research assistants on research projects are aware of the problems of authoritarian researchers who treat their staff and/or respondents as commodities. This problem is not unique to the social sciences and often occurs in other research settings where human (and animal) subjects are used. Reinharz describes the extreme case where research is

conducted on a rape model: the researchers take, hit, and run. They intrude into their subjects' privacy, disrupt their perceptions, utilize false pretenses, manipulate the relationship, and give little or nothing in return. When the needs of the researchers are satisfied, they break off contact with the subject. (1979: 95)

In contrast, there are many researchers who are sensitive to these issues and relate well to their staff and respondents. One survey research project, whose director and staff were particularly respectful of the needs of respondents and interviewers, obtained a response rate of 98 per cent, indicating that these values were manifested in the attitudes of the research team. One interviewer, commenting on the project's success, noted the following:

I do believe one of the reasons for the high response rate of the study is the fact that interviewers do so enjoy working on the study. That is so important in getting people to do a good job. During training the interviewers were so enthused about the questionnaire and the interviewing situation that I feel this enthusiasm was transmitted to the respondents, and they in turn were eager to do their parts. (Freedman and Camburn, 1981: 24)

Both personality and personal value differences can account for some of this difference in style. However, the authoritative structure of research projects and institutions is contrary to feminist values and one might expect that feminist researchers would be sensitive to these issues. According to Cox, 'Academic feminists question the value of the individualistic, striving, competitive, aggressive style of achievement for either sex. The style of achievement in which feminists would like to work is based on cooperation, mutual respect, interdependence' (1976: 13). The fact that many feminist researchers who do traditional research are not exploitative of their staff and respondents suggests that the problem of exploitation is not inherent in the traditional research process. The occurrence of exploitation can be reduced by explicitly promoting more humanistic values in research training programs and by setting examples for others through self-evaluation when doing our own research. Furthermore, decisions which affect the funding of researchers should take into account a researcher's treatment of staff and subjects.

Abundance of 'Quick and Dirty Research'
Much of the research in the social sciences is conducted to produce quickly some publishable product. Often this research is not only poorly done but also not comprehensive or thorough enough to test theory adequately. Standards of appropriate research methodology are too often set aside due to high costs or time constraints. In

addition, poor-quality research is often a result of the researcher not having adequate research skills or training.

The structure of many academic and research institutions perpetuates this practice in several ways. The most obvious are the 'publish or perish' policies of many universities and colleges. The impact of this policy is enhanced by the policy of journals to publish 'significant' findings from 'successful' research projects. These policies often function to reward 'quick and dirty' research. For example, the untenured assistant professor who needs a long list of publications (and these are sometimes not evaluated for quality) may be more likely to use research methodology which produces significant results instead of appropriate methodology and cut corners in using other appropriate research methods since they take more time. There are further pressures from funding agencies, superiors and colleagues. These pressures can act to make good quality research less rewarding than a more expedient, but 'adequate' product.

Another complicating factor is that, as students, we learn in the classroom to view the research process in idealistic terms. We assume that most research projects are carried out 'successfully', according to the quality standards we have learned in texts or in the classroom. When we begin to engage in our own research or work with other researchers in training positions, we can become disillusioned and either change our research orientation or discontinue doing research altogether (for example, see Reinharz, 1979).

While we may not want to compromise our ideal standards, the pressures of competition are real and may in fact become more pervasive given the academic job market and the increasing scarcity of funding for social science research. There is no easy solution to this conflict. Although for some feminists the solution may lie in abandoning the research profession, it is important to have women researchers, and especially feminists, in the social sciences. Not only must we insist on high standards of research but we must direct some energy to changing the existing academic and professional structures which often reward the quantity of research and not the quality. This then becomes a political as well as a personal concern.

Tackling the traumas of research can be made easier if one comes prepared. Exposure to *both* the positive and the negative aspects of the research and a realistic appraisal of the difficulties are important in graduate school. For example, researchers who have extensive training and experience will be more likely to estimate correctly the time and cost factors in their research, allowing for the generation of good quality research within these parameters.

Finally, this discussion points up the need for feminists to differentiate between poor and quality research and to educate others to do so as well. Since the purpose of this paper is not to explicate the numerous methods for producing quality research, the reader is referred to social science research texts which cover quantitative research methods, such as Babbie (1979).

The Simplistic and Superficial Nature of Quantitative Research

Related to the problem of 'quick and dirty' research is the problem of research which takes a simplistic and superficial view of human behavior and attitudes.

The dangers of simplistic quantitative research are well known to feminists. The most obvious examples are studies which ignore sex differences or look only at sex differences as causal factors without exploring other mediating causal variables. Too often the conclusions from these studies suggest some 'inherent' difference between the sexes (see Benbow and Stanley, 1980). For example, a study which looks at *only* sex differences in maths achievement might find correctly that boys do better than girls on certain maths achievement tests. By not exploring explanatory factors, researchers leave open possible reasons for the differences. While the numbers may be accurate, the simplistic nature of the design can be misleading to the public. Although it is impossible to examine all factors related to a behavior or attitude, it is important to collect enough information so that conclusions drawn from the findings are meaningful and advance theory.[1]

Simplistic research is not inherent to quantitative research but often results from sloppy methodology. In fact, quantitative methods make the analysis of complex research designs possible. Sophisticated quantitative methods and computer techniques have been developed in recent years and are being continually brought up to date in order to handle the analysis of complex data – for example, longitudinal designs.

Although qualitative data often seem more complex than quantitative data, it sometimes depends on which questions are asked by researchers. One could imagine qualitative data which, while thoroughly descriptive in regard to an attitude (for example, boys are more active than girls), offers no insight as to the reasons for these beliefs. Good qualitative and quantitative researchers need to explore issues by asking appropriately complex questions.

While there is a practical limit to the complexity of quantitative data (and thus analysis), the limit for qualitative data seems higher since, at least theoretically, it can be as detailed as possible. For example, the quantification or coding of an open-ended response puts certain limits on the number of different responses. Cost and time factors allow a practical limit on the number of codes used and the kind of dimensions coded. Qualitative data do not necessarily need such reinterpretation before analysis. On the one hand, the more complex qualitative data are, the more difficult and less likely it is for there to be consensus in analysis. On the other hand, the more complex the qualitative data are, the less superficial and potentially more meaningful they are.

No matter how thorough the questions in quantitative research, quantitative data will yield findings which are superficial in nature, *compared to* most qualitative data. Even the most complex and sophisticated quantitative research report cannot impart the same 'in-depth' understanding of respondents as, for example, a thorough case history. This is most likely due to detailed description which is lacking in quantitative research.

It seems apparent therefore that quantitative research could benefit from the addition of qualitative data. Certainly qualitative data can support and explicate the meaning of quantitative research. Every quantitative research project should include some qualitative data, not only for use by researchers to understand their respondents better, but also to include in presentations and publications so that others may gain a deeper understanding of the quantified results.

Objective Appearance of Quantitative Data

Feminists have argued that 'quick and dirty' quantitative social science research often gets interpreted by the public as the 'truth'; the public does not distinguish between good and bad social science. Most researchers would agree that quantitative data appear to be more objective than qualitative data. However, no social researcher can claim that quantitative data are either truly objective or that they measure 'reality'. What they can claim is that 'good' quantitative data (meeting accepted standards of validity) can be used *more* objectively to evaluate theory than qualitative data. This claim is based on the fact that the principles and guidelines for quantitative data analysis have been specifically developed to produce an objective evaluation. This is true to a greater extent than in qualitative research.

To understand this dialogue more clearly it is important to distinguish between objectivity in the research process and objectivity as a part of the analysis of data. First, there can be no such thing as truly 'objective' research in the sense that the product of research is *not* subject to our own value judgements (Babbie, 1979). Personal biases impinge on the research process in many ways, particularly in theory formulation and interpretation, but also in development of design, data collection, and analysis. However, by using accepted standards of research, the final product can be less subject to those biases. Or at least one can more readily identify the biases that may have been operative. Thus while there is no absolute objectivity possible, the research product can be more or less objective and the nature of the bias can be more or less easily evaluated. For example, a research project in which interviewers openly make personal comments on a respondent's answers may produce less objective data than one in which interviewers comment little.

Second, quantitative analysis is, as much as possible, an objective evaluation of data because it is conducted according to generally accepted procedural methods based on mathematical principles.[2] These principles applied to the analysis of data result in a product which is relatively unaffected by personal bias. This is because mathematics is based on logical assumptions that are usually not open for debate. For example, suppose that a researcher is interested in why some women find it difficult to return to work after being full-time homemakers. A quantitative researcher might ask respondents to indicate the importance of various reasons. (A skilled researcher would include a comprehensive list of reasons and allow for unanticipated reasons.) Quantitative analyses could produce statistical evidence that most women feel that lack of good jobs is the most important reason. Further, the analysis could indicate either that no other reasons were important or that several other reasons were marginally or similarly important. The relative degree of importance of various factors could be specifically determined. This interpretation of the data could not reasonably be refuted because the analysis is a logical (mathematical) interpretation of data. Babbie terms this phenomenon 'intersubjectivity' and defines it as 'two scientists with different subjective orientations arriv[ing] at the same conclusion if each conducted the same experiment' (1979: 52).

A qualitative researcher exploring the same issue might ask women why it was difficult to return to work. Many reasons might be given and analysis without quantification might indicate that poor job possibilities was a major one. However, this analysis would be more subject to debate and thus personal judgment because the evaluation was not based on standards as objective as mathematical principles. Another researcher might say that job possibilities was not such an important reason and a third researcher might arrive at an altogether different opinion.

The appearance of objectivity is a powerful tool for changing public opinion. As feminists, we need to monitor closely and publicize the problems with research which appears objective – but in fact may be a product of poor methodology and/or subjective bias. (See Parsons (1981) and Parlee (1976) for examples of responses to such research.) Furthermore, we can use this power of quantitative research to our advantage to change public or political opinion in support of feminist goals. For example, we can *document* the enormous number of unwanted teenage pregnancies in support of free access to birth control. We can *document* the sex discrimination which occurs in school systems and use it to advocate change. This documentation is possible because of the use of quantitative research methods. (See, for example, Chapter 3 in Stasz Stoll (1974) for a statistical overview of sexism in our society.)

More important than using the *appearance* of objectivity for our benefit is the *actual* objectivity which quantitative methods allow in theory evaluation (that is, data analysis). As noted earlier, it is imperative for feminist theory to be assessed accurately so it can be used to direct political and research work. For example, there may be differing opinions as to why sexual harassment occurs in the workplace. Our personal values and experiences will influence our opinions as to why it occurs. If we want to combat the practice, we need to understand and assess its causes accurately. High-quality quantitative research can best do this, and the findings which result will not likely be debated on the basis of personal view. This is extremely important if we want to create effective programs and policies to reduce the incidence of sexual harassment. Directing our energies toward the correct target problem areas we define as important will help us to achieve our goals. An inaccurate evaluation of the target or problem area will result in wasted energies.

Even if one accepts the argument that quantitative data analysis is more objective than qualitative analysis, and may be important for feminist theory evaluation and for political and public opinion change, one may not accept the idea that objectivity is a valuable goal if the researcher has to be detached from her work. This emphasis on detachment in quantitative research is expressed by Kerlinger:

> The mixture of strong commitment and advocacy of political and social programs, on the one hand, and scientific research into the problems of such programs, on the other hand, seem to induce bias and what has been called selective perception. This means that we see what we want or need to see rather what is actually there. So strong is this tendency

that I have almost gotten to the point of thinking that behavioral scientists should not do research on the things they passionately advocate. Or better, when they do it, they should conceive and use exceptionally elaborate safeguards against their own biases. (1979: 17)

Too many social researchers assume that they are 'appropriately' detached if they do not have strong feelings about the issues they study. Often what they do not realize is that their views really indicate a strong commitment to the *status quo* – which is as potentially biased as any other orientation.

Feminists have argued, and correctly so, that researchers need to become more involved with and concerned about the people they study. It is critically important here to realize that to conduct 'objective' quantitative research, one does *not* have to be detached and unconcerned about the topic. Having a strong opinion about the subject of research does not necessarily mean that research decisions will be any more biased than if those opinions were not held. The use of good research methodology helps to assure against this accusation. None of us can possibly be completely objective toward our research. Therefore our methods must be as objective as possible. This is why there are clear guidelines, codes of ethics, and standards for doing quantitative research. Whatever our position, we should always make clear in our reports and publications our opinions about the subject of our research so that others will know with what initial orientation we began and carried our research.

As a feminist and a social science researcher, I have clear and strong political and personal goals for my research. The topics I choose to study and the theory I use to direct my research are strongly affected by these goals. To evaluate my theories as accurately as possible, I use some traditional research procedures and quantitative methods. Using these methods does not lessen in any way my strong commitments to feminism, or my appreciation of the value of qualitative research. And my commitment to feminism does not necessarily mean that my research is of poor quality due to bias.

Generalizing with Quantitative Research
One important part of the quantitative research process is generalizing. When researchers study a large group of people, they usually cannot gain information on all the persons in the group due to time and cost factors. They often select a smaller sample of persons from the larger group to furnish the needed information. If the sample is selected so that it is representative of the larger population, then the researcher can correctly (while accounting for

small errors) infer that the information found in the sample applies to the larger population. The validity of this inference is obviously important *if* one wishes to make generalized statements. This issue is especially critical in reviewing certain methods of qualitative research since some methods (particularly case history) do not permit generalization. Many aspects of Freudian psychology are good examples of generalization from a non-representative sample.

Generalized statements are important both for advising policy-makers of public opinion and deciding on strategies for bringing about change in public opinion itself. This can be useful to feminists, who, for example, need to know the strength of public support for the right to life amendment or the ERA, in order to develop appropriate political strategies for action.

Conclusions

As indicated above, most of the feminist criticisms of the traditional quantitative research process have merit, although an exploration of the issues surrounding these criticisms indicates the need for caution in condemning quantitative research altogether. The discussion of the criticisms also suggests methods for resolving those problems which do arise. These suggested changes in the traditional research process, which increase consistency with feminist values, will obviously not be fully implemented for some time. In the meantime, as feminists we have two plausible options for dealing with existing inconsistencies. We can either reject quantitative research altogether or value it for its benefits and work to change those elements which are antithetical to feminist ideas. (I do not consider ignoring the inconsistencies a plausible option.)

My preference is for the second option, since I believe it is the most effective method for changing the sexist structure of society to a more egalitarian one. There must be appropriate quantitative evidence to counter the pervasive and influential quantitative sexist research which has and continues to be generated in the social sciences. Feminist researchers can best accomplish this. If some of the traditional procedures used to produce that needed evidence are contrary to our feminist values, then we must change those procedures accordingly. In the process of change we not only must remember to view our research in a political context as outlined above in this paper, but we must support one another against the academic and professional pressures to compromise our standards. The better quality research that we do, the more likely that that research will influence others and ultimately help in achieving their goals.

Notes

An early version of this paper was presented at the National Women's Studies Association Conference, Bloomington, Indiana, May 1980. I would like to thank Jacquie Eccles Parsons, Marti Bombyk and Shula Reinharz for their valuable comments on the manuscript. I would also like to acknowledge the ideas and suggestions from women in the Feminist Methodology Seminar at the University of Michigan: Nicki Beisel, Marti Bombyk, Sue Contratto, Linda Kaboolian, Eleanor McLaughlin, Cindy Palmer, Paula Rabinowitz, Shula Reinharz and Betsey Taylor.

1. The criticisms of simplistic research apply mostly to areas of research in which theory is well-developed, since researchers should know and examine the major relevant factors in a study. When research is exploratory, it is more acceptable to produce 'isolated' findings needed to develop theory.
2. Although there is not absolute agreement on which mathematical or statistical method to use, there is consensus as to which methods are appropriate for which kind of data and for the kind of questions being asked of the data.

References

Babbie, E.R. (1979) *The Practice of Social Research*. Belmont, CA: Wadsworth.

Bailey, K.D. (1978) *Methods of Social Research*. New York: Free Press.

Benbow, C.P. and Stanley, J.C. (1980) 'Sex differences in mathematical ability: fact or artifact?', *Science*, 210 (12).

Bogdan, R. and Taylor, S. (1975) *Introduction to Qualitative Research Methods*. New York: Wiley.

Chesler, P. (1972) *Women and Madness*. New York: Doubleday.

Cox, S. (1976) *Female Psychology: The Emerging Self*. Chicago: Science Research Associates.

Depner, C. (1981) 'Toward the further development of feminist psychology', paper presented at the mid-winter conference of the Association for Women in Psychology, Boston.

Fox Keller, E. (1978) 'Gender and science', *Psychoanalysis and Contemporary Thought*, 1.

Fox Keller, E. (1980) 'Feminist critique of science: a forward or backward move?', *Fundamenta Scientiae*, 1.

Freedman, D. and Camburn, D. (1981) 'Some techniques for maintaining respondent participation in longitudinal studies', paper presented at the Population Association of America, Washington, DC, March.

Frieze, I.H., Parsons, J.E., Johnson, P.B., Ruble, D.N. and Zellman, G.L. (1978) *Women and Sex Roles: A Social Psychological Perspective*. New York: W.W. Norton.

Glaser, B. and Strauss, A. (1967) *The Discovery of Grounded Theory: Strategies for Qualitative Research*. Chicago: Aldine.

Griggs v. *Duke Power Co.* (1971) 401 US 424.

Jaggar, A.M. and Struhl, P.R. (1978) *Feminist Frameworks: Alternative Theoretical Accounts of the Relations between Women and Men*. New York: McGraw-Hill.

Kerlinger, F.N. (1979) *Behavioral Research: A Conceptual Approach*. New York: Holt, Rinehart & Winston.

Kroeber, T. (1969) *Ishi in Two Worlds*. Berkeley, CA: University of California Press.

Levitin, T.E., Quinn, R.P. and Staines, G.L. (1973) 'A woman is 58% of a man', *Psychology Today*, March.

Lewis, O. (1961) *The Children of Sanchez*. New York: Random House.

Liebow, E. (1967) *Tally's Corner*. Boston: Little, Brown.

McCall, G. and Simmons, J.L. (eds) (1969) *Issues in Participant Observation*. Reading, MA: Addison-Wesley.

Millett, K. (1969) *Sexual Politics*. New York: Avon.

Parlee, M.B. (1976) 'The premenstrual syndrome', in S. Cox (ed.), *Female Psychology: The Emerging Self*. Chicago: Science Research Associates.

Parsons, J.E. (1981) 'Social forces shape attitudes and performance', unpublished manuscript.

Reinharz, S. (1979) *On Becoming a Social Scientist*. San Francisco Jossey-Bass.

Schatzman, L. and Strauss, A. (1973) *Field Research*. Englewood Cliffs, NJ: Prentice-Hall.

Stasz Stoll, C. (1974) *Female and Male: Socialization, Social Roles and Social Structure*. Iowa: Wm C. Brown.

Tangri, S.S. and Strasburg, G.L. (1979) 'Can research on women be more effective in shaping policy?', *Psychology of Women Quarterly*, 3 (4).

Weiss, C. and Bucuvalas, M. (1977) 'The challenge of social research to decision-making', in C. Weiss (ed.), *Using Social Research in Public Policy-Making*. Lexington, MA: Lexington Books.

Weisstein, N. (1970) '"Kinder, Küche, Kirche" as scientific law: psychology constructs the female', in R. Morgan (ed.), *Sisterhood Is Powerful*. New York: Vintage.

11

'Race' and Statistics

Waqar I.U. Ahmad and Trevor A. Sheldon

Since World War II there has been an increase in Britain in the collection of statistics which are categorized along the lines of 'race' or ethnicity. This has not been a neutral exercise in pursuit of knowledge but has evolved hand in hand with concerns about the 'race problem' (Booth, 1988). These statistics became part of the 'numbers game' used to justify racist immigration laws and helped fuel anti-black feeling in Britain. The process of racialization of statistics reflected and reinforced racist state policies (Ohri, 1988). More recently arguments about the use of statistics in favour of black populations, in highlighting discrimination, targeting and monitoring services and so on have been put forward (Anwar, 1990). 'Ethnic data' have thus become the major tool for gaining 'race' equality in the new formalized, bureaucratized form of anti-racism.

The debate ranges from the usefulness of 'race' statistics as a potential weapon to fight 'race' discrimination to questioning the political will of the central and local state, and other organizations to fight racial discrimination. We look at the 'race' statistics debate over the last few years with particular reference to the arguments for and against collecting 'race' data, problems in defining meaningful categories for such data collection, and assessing the potential social policy relevance of 'ethnic' data, including the question in the 1991 Census. First, we look at some of the criticisms.

Arguments against Collecting 'Race' Data

Leech (1989) has summarized the many areas of criticism. Proponents of collecting 'ethnic' data often proceed as if no useful information on 'ethnicity' were available and, by implication, that the only barrier to the eradication of racial discrimination is the lack of accurate ethnic data. It is doubtful if social policy would be hampered by the exclusion of the 'ethnic question' in the Census.

From *Radical Statistics*, 48 (Spring), 1991, pp. 27–33.

One particular problem here is the difficulty in operationalizing concepts such as 'race' (only useful in relation to racism and racial discrimination) and 'ethnicity' (which effectively becomes a culturalist notion of 'race' if externally imposed and rigidly defined). There are also problems in accurate recording of ethnicity: in 1979 trials only 84 per cent of white, 41 per cent of black and 68 per cent Asian respondents recorded ethnicity correctly; in 1989 it was still low at 90 per cent, 86 per cent and 89 per cent respectively. Bhrolchain (1990) suggests that the improvement may have resulted from people now being used to answering the 'ethnic question' in their contact with local and health authorities, and employers.

Parts of the black population campaigned against the 'ethnic question' before the 1981 Census and during various subsequent field trials. This is neither paranoia, nor is opposition to the Census peculiar to the UK: for example, in 1981 The Netherlands and in 1983 the Federal German Republic cancelled their censuses because of public fears of abuse of statistics. The experience of the black population in relation to the 'numbers game' in immigration policies and more specifically the abuse of 'race' monitoring statistics by the Metropolitan Police force made such fears much more real (Bhat et al., 1988). In 1989, for example, 5 per cent of white and Asian, and 20 per cent of the 'black' respondents objected to the ethnicity question in the Census (Bhrolchain, 1990). Bhrolchain, however, remains reassured that this objection need not be taken seriously, as:

> People of black-Caribbean origin are sometimes reputed not to be enthusiastic form-fillers and some elements of their objections to the ethnicity question is likely to be due to a reluctance to answer questions in general, especially in an official context. (1990: 561)

Such cavalier victim blaming is unacceptable.

Others have questioned the political will of both the central and the local state to fight racial discrimination (Sivanandan, 1991). Moore, in his evidence to the Home Affairs Committee on the 'ethnic question' in the Census, said:

> As a social scientist currently writing on questions of race and racism in the UK, I find it extremely irritating not to have certain Census data available: given the record of government since 1961, I would nonetheless advise the black population not to collaborate in the provision of such data in the present circumstances. (quoted in Leech, 1989)

The question of ownership of such data (by minority groups) has also been raised (Booth, 1988). Summarizing her opposition to the 'ethnic question', Booth states: 'The real need is . . . not for better definitive data but a new framework of political will aimed at reducing and eradicating racial disadvantage and discrimination.'

Arguments for Collecting 'Race' Data

Often it is argued that the case for 'ethnic'/'race' data in the Census or elsewhere is no different in principle from any other type of question in as far as it is simply an example of the wider requirements of providing information relevant to policy formulation and implementation. The supporters of an ethnic question in the Census cite the following benefits: (1) some sources of central government funding such as Section 11, the Urban Programme, etc. are available for services to ethnic minorities – local authorities need accurate figures for ethnic minorities to apply for this; (2) with detailed ethnic statistics authorities can tailor their services to the clients' needs; (3) ethnic data can help in siting services in appropriate localities; (4) these data can provide evidence of discrimination at different levels within an organization which can then be tackled; (5) provide baseline data for policy formulations; (6) and can be used by ethnic minorities themselves for campaigning purposes (Bhrolchain, 1990). The supporters argue that:

> Campaigning through statistical descriptions has been an effective strategy for resource-poor social interests and one that has been successfully deployed in the United States by the Civil Rights Movement, the poverty lobby, consumer interests and by environmentalists. (Bhrolchain, 1990: 550)

Over the years the Commission for Racial Equality has campaigned vigorously for routine ethnic data collection, though it has not always been clear what exactly it means by 'ethnic data'. Supporters of the CRE, both individuals (Cross, 1980, quoted in Leech, 1989; Anwar, 1990; Bhrolchain, 1990) and institutions (such as Runnymede Trust) have variously rehearsed the above arguments. The following is illustrative of this:

> It was Census data that revealed unemployment rates among black teenagers to be twice the national average. It was Census data that was used to show how racial minorities had been concentrated in the most derelict, overcrowded and least secure sectors of inner-city housing, and how some local authorities had apparently overlooked these areas in planning development. It was Census data that helped demonstrate that, far from racial minorities making disproportionate demands on social services, the opposite was in fact the case. (Cross, quoted in Leech, 1989)

In taking this debate further we, briefly, look at issues around 'ethnic' categorization.

Conflated Concepts and Confused Categories

Both 'race' and 'ethnicity' are problematic categories. We use 'race' as a social construct with links to racisms, old and new. As 'race' as an analytical category has lost favour 'ethnicity' has been popularized. The conceptual and technical problems in opera-tionalization of these concepts for data collection are considerable; some of these are referred to in the above sections. However, we feel that the Census, and most other forms of surveys using 'ethnic questions', have failed to come to grips with these complexities. Our first concern is that the 'ethnic' question in the Census is both rigid and externally imposed: it uses a culturalist, geographical and 'nationalist' notion of 'race' dressed up as 'ethnicity'. The confu-sion is evident in the mixture of categories in the Census, based on colour (black, white), notions of 'nationality' (Pakistani, Indian), and geographical origin (Africa, the Caribbean). This appeal to cultural distinctions, national allegiances, 'natural' boundaries of inclusion and exclusion has much in common with the discourse of the 'new racism' (Husband, 1991; Sivanandan, 1991). Some (for example, Sivanandan, 1991) would claim that such categorization plays into the hands of the racists by creating and consolidating 'ethnic' differences, fragmenting the 'oppressed', separating not just 'us' from 'them' but also different sorts of 'them'. Gilroy (1990) has recently written about this conceptual inconsistency within certain areas of the anti-racist position. On the other hand are the arguments of Modood (1988), and others, strongly opposed to the use of the blanket term 'black', which he claims is equally reductionist and patronizing, rendering cherished cultural and historical values invisible in the mass of 'blackness'. We do not wish to dwell on this here; for useful introductions to some of the debates the reader may refer to, for example, Miles (1988), Modood (1988), Gilroy (1990) and Sivanandan (1991).

Even if we had no doubts about the conceptual and analytic status of 'race' or 'ethnicity' and there were no such major problems in their operationalization, there is still the question of the utility of 'ethnic' data, especially of the type employed in the Census, for research, planning and progressive political purposes.

'Ethnic' Data, Research and Social Policy

The use of 'ethnicity' as an analytical category implies the accep-tance of some notion of homogeneity of condition, culture, attitudes, expectations, and in some cases language and religion within the groups defined on an 'ethnic' basis. All these may have implications for the way forms of racism affect communities and individuals in terms of, for example, definition of their needs, provision and adequacy of services, discrimination in employment and career progression. In theory a researcher may, using appropriate 'ethnic' categories, be able to make a useful assessment of service needs, an employer may be able to monitor the employment practices as these affect different 'ethnic' groups, a health authority may offer appropriate diet and communication aids on the basis of information on the 'ethnic' mix of its population. However, what is far from clear is the utility of categories such as 'Indian' or 'Black African' for these purposes.

Let us take the example of a health authority that wishes to improve its employment practices and its service delivery with regard to minority ethnic groups. For employment monitoring the type of data used in the Census may have some validity, though we suspect that some of the categories are too broad in order to be of particular use. To offer appropriate diet these categories become meaningless. 'Indian', 'Black Caribbean', 'Black African', for example, tell nothing about diet habits. An 'Indian' may be a Punjabi, Bengali or Gujarati; Muslim, Hindu, Sikh or Christian; vegetarian or meat eater, and amongst meat eaters requiring (or wanting) halal meat or non-halal meat; rice eater or chapati eater. If the same authority wishes to improve its interpreting services then the category 'Indian' tells it nothing about the mix of languages spoken (for example, Punjabi, Urdu, Gujarati, Hindi, Bengali). Similarly, the use of this category for need assessment or as an independent variable in epidemiological studies would be far too broad to be meaningful (for example, perinatal mortality rates, and other indices of health, differ on religious and geographical basis as do lifestyles and health-related behaviours such as smoking and drinking).

We acknowledge that carefully collected information as part of a specific policy goal to improve (say) provision and location of services can be useful. We also accept that 'ethnic' data can be used by minority groups and local authorities to obtain central funds (not withstanding the criticisms of this approach, for example, Sivanandan, 1991). In addition, there are the problems for the researcher and the policy maker created by the use of non-standard 'ethnicity' categories, 'defined' on the basis of interviewer observation and country of birth, and leading to such absurd categories as 'Urdu children'. But we fear that the use of 'off-the-shelf' ethnic categories, in their 'new OPCS and Commission for Racial Equality approved' format will create a new set of problems.

We made the point earlier about 'race' and 'ethnicity' being social and political constructs; the standardization of such categories will give them a spurious air of validity, as 'natural', 'objective' and 'universal' entities. We consider such potential reification of these categories to be of more than academic significance. One of us has written on the increased racialization of research, with particular reference to health, which has done little to improve service delivery, or to advance aetiological understanding (Sheldon and Parker, 1992). We fear that the availability of routine 'ethnic' data from the Census and its adoption in the NHS 'minimum data set' will give increased impetus to this mindless empiricism. Such categories will have limited social policy relevance, yet create the illusion of high- and quality-based research activity.

The basic question to ask is 'What information do I need and why?' This fundamental question has often been ignored in research on minority ethnic groups (see, for example, Bhopal (1990) for a discussion of research on health); the reification of 'ethnic' categories will further undermine the need for a critical approach. Lastly, such categories may lead to the perpetuation of racial stereotypes of the needs, behaviours and expectations of 'Pakistanis', 'Indians', 'Black Africans', and so on, as homogeneous wholes.

Conclusion

The debate on the collection and the use of 'ethnic data' is not new and some of the issues covered in this paper have already been addressed (Anwar, 1990; Bhrolchain, 1990; Leech, 1989). Our own position is that 'ethnic' data can have a useful policy purpose, but for this the nature of the information and the level at which the independent variable of 'ethnicity' is defined must be specifically related to the policy needs. Thus, for example, to improve the acceptability of hospital food, the hospital should enquire about food habits; religion and regional background may be useful proxy variables for this – being an 'Indian' clearly is not. We are concerned that the trend towards standardization will lead to reification of 'ethnic' categories of rather dubious validity, and to a lack of critical consideration of the need for and potential use of such data. Data collection thus may become an end in itself and the rising mountains of research give the illusion of progress. Whilst we do not argue for wholesale rejection of 'ethnic' data collection, the need for and policy relevance of such data requires careful consideration. Uncritical collection and use of 'ethnic' data will aid racialization and stereotyping and thus reinforce oppression of the very minorities which the data were ostensibly meant to support.

References

Anwar, M. (1990) 'Ethnic classifications, ethnic monitoring and the 1991 Census', *New Community*, 16 (4): 606–15.

Bhat, A. *et al.* (eds) (1988) *Britain's Black Population*, 2nd edn. Aldershot: Gower.

Bhopal, R. (1990) 'Future research on the health of ethnic minorities: back to the basics – a personal view', *Ethnic Minorities Health*, 1 (3): 1–3.

Bhrolchain, M.N. (1990) 'The ethnic question for the 1991 Census: background and issues', *Ethnic and Racial Studies*, 13 (4): 543–67.

Booth, H. (1988) 'Identifying ethnic origin: the past, present and future of official data production' in A. Bhat, *et al.* (eds), *Britain's Black Population*, 2nd edn. Aldershot: Gower.

Gilroy, P. (1990) 'The end of anti-racism', *New Community*, 17 (1): 71–83.

Husband, C. (1991) 'Race, conflictual politics and anti-racist social work: lessons from the past for action in the '90s', in Curriculum Development Project Steering Group (eds), *Setting the Context*. London: CCETSW.

Leech, K. (1989) *A Question in Dispute: The Debate about an 'Ethnic' Question in the Census*. London: Runnymede Trust.

Miles, R. (1988) *Racism*. London: Routledge.

Modood, T. (1988) 'Black, racial equality and Asian identity', *New Community*, 14 (3): 397–404.

Ohri, S. (1988) 'The politics of racism, statistics and equal opportunity: towards a new perspective', in A. Bhat *et al.* (eds), *Britain's Black Population*, 2nd edn. Aldershot: Gower.

Sheldon, T. and Parker, H. (1992) 'The uses of "ethnicity" and "race" in health research: a cautionary note', in W.I.U. Ahmad (ed.), *The Politics of 'Race' and Health*. Bradford: Race Relations Research Unit, Bradford University/BICC.

Sivanandan, A. (1991) 'Black struggles against racism', in Curriculum Development Project Steering Group (eds), *Setting the Context*, London: CCETSW.

PART 3

PRACTICE

12

Research Analysis of Administrative Records

Catherine Hakim

Vast quantities of information are collated and recorded by organizations and individuals for their own purposes, well beyond the data collected by social scientists purely for research purposes. Information from records and documents enters into virtually all types of study in some degree, though usually providing only a minor part of the data. The focus here is primarily on studies which use administrative records and documents as the main source of data, and hence on the larger or more prominent collections of such information in organizations.

Administrative records are collections of documents containing mainly factual information compiled in a variety of ways (directly from those concerned, or indirectly from employers, schools, doctors and others acting as informants) and used by organizations to record the development and implementation of decisions and activities that are central to their functions. They are typically large in number; are usually high in content rigidity and narrow in content scope; and are often available for considerable stretches of time. Examples are health service records; school records; membership records of trade unions and other voluntary associations; company accounts and personnel records; marriage, birth and death registers; electoral registers; tax and social security records; police, court and prison records.

In the past statistical surveys were often based on data extracted from administrative records rather than on interview surveys. The importance of administrative records as a source of data for

From *Research Design*, Unwin Hyman, London, 1987, pp. 36–46.

research analysis has been declining, at least in industrialized countries, as specially designed research studies are carried out to replace, or to complement, records-based data. Unemployment statistics are now more commonly obtained from regular sample surveys using personal interviews, such as the CPS and the LFS, than from government unemployment registers or unemployment benefit records. Regular interview surveys such as the British Crime Survey provide an important complement to data obtained from police records.

At the same time the potential for research analysis of administrative records is expanding as more organizations are transferring such records from manual systems of files, forms and cards to computerized systems, and in the process redesigning them as management information systems which can be analysed quickly and routinely to produce summaries of particular aspects of the data. This also makes it easier to provide suitably anonymized extract tapes for social research purposes. Prior to this, the relevant information had to be extracted manually from cards, forms, or files, with all the potential for copying errors and other mistakes to occur during the extraction process, quite apart from the long time it took and any confidentiality problems raised by allowing researchers to have access to what are often confidential or private records. This new facility for producing computer tapes with selective information from administrative records for research analysis means that more data of this type is finding its way into data archives. So research based on administrative records can all too easily become conflated with secondary analysis of research data. There is a similarity, in that any research use of information from administrative records constitutes secondary analysis, given that the primary use of the records was for administrative purposes. But the similarity ends there, as there are significant differences between data collected specifically for research purposes and information which is recorded as a by-product of an organization's, or an individual's day-to-day activities. The point needs to be emphasized because economists, for example, who routinely use data collected by others, often display little concern for the source of the information they use, its quality and limitations, and frequently fail to distinguish between data from records and research data, treating both as if they were interchangeably valid and appropriate for any research analysis (Blaug, 1980: 261-2; Sayer, 1984: 161; Griliches, 1985).

Precisely because they are created and maintained by many different organizations for varied and changing purposes, it is more difficult to generalize about the characteristics, strengths and limitations of such data, and research based on them, than it is with other types of study. Collections of records and documents must be found rather than created to the researcher's specification, and their value will depend on the degree of match between the research questions addressed and the data that happen to be available. But the potential is considerable.

Varieties of Records-based Studies

The design of records-based studies has to be back to front. Instead of designing the study, and then collecting the necessary data, one obtains details of the contents and characteristics of a set of records and then identifies the corresponding research model. The builder, and the materials he has available, take a stronger leading role in the design than in the usual architect-designed study. None the less administrative records can provide the basis for longitudinal studies, quasi-experimental designs, historical research, area-based studies, international comparisons, studies of organizations and the policy process, as well as being specially useful for research on minorities and rare events.

Administrative records can provide information on topics or minority groups which is not available by any other means, or only at disproportionate cost. An obvious example is the documentary evidence and records used in historical research, to which are now being added the original records from early data collections such as the nineteenth-century population censuses and other surveys deposited in public records office or data archives. For example, Harbury and Hitchens (1979) and Rubinstein (1981) used probate records to study patterns of wealth and inheritance. A study by Furet and Ozouf (1982) used samples of marriage records to study the spread of literacy from the seventeenth century to the present day in France. Nineteenth-century census records, supplemented by marriage records, employment records, contemporary investigations and other documentary evidence, are providing the basis for a great deal of historical, social, economic and demographic research (Wrigley, 1972; Foster, 1974; Lawton, 1978; Hershberg, 1981; Bateman and Weiss, 1981; Hakim, 1982: 82–94; Hareven, 1982).

Administrative records can also provide a key source of data on events or groups too small and scattered or otherwise difficult to trace for national interview surveys to be a realistic possibility. The classic example is the use of data from death registration records for research on suicide (Phillips, 1983; Wasserman, 1984), a topic that could not be studied in any other way, whatever the limitations of the records, with health service records being used to study the somewhat different phenomenon of attempted suicide (Platt and Kreitman, 1985). Administrative records also provide a ready source of data on relatively rare events such as divorce (Leete and Anthony, 1979) and migration (Mueller, 1982) as well as crime, although some of the large scale regular surveys and longitudinal studies are now also providing data on such rare events.

Administrative records are used in their own right, rather than *faute de mieux*, for research on the policy process itself and in evaluation research. In this case records and documents, albeit incomplete accounts, are part of the reality being studied, rather than being regarded as a poor substitute for data that would ideally be obtained in other ways. For example, records provided an appropriate basis for research on racial discrimination in the allocation of public housing (Parker and Dugmore, 1976), and to determine whether homeworkers were less likely to be assessed as legally underpaid than their counterparts working in the employer's workplace (Hakim and Dennis, 1982). Administrative records provide an important basis for assessments of whether an organization is practising discrimination, wittingly or indirectly, with regard to the race or sex of applicants and employees (Chiplin, 1981; Siebert and Sloane, 1981). In the United States, applicant and employee records are frequently a key source of evidence in legal cases on discrimination, with increasingly sophisticated techniques being employed for the analysis of such data in class actions (Ragin *et al.*, 1984).

Studies of organizational policy and decision-making processes shade into general organizational studies in which administrative records can provide an important source of data, especially if they are available for long stretches of time. This type of use is common in case studies, with the analysis of data from records complemented by other research methods, which can provide crucial information for interpreting the records data (as illustrated by Blau, 1963; Wrench and Lee, 1982; Edwards and Scullion, 1984).

When records are available for sufficiently long stretches of time they can provide the time series data needed for quasi-experimental designs which provide 'before' and 'after' measurements without a control group (Campbell and Stanley, 1963: 37–43; Campbell, 1969; Cook and Campbell, 1979: 207–32). For example, records could be used to assess the effect of a change in divorce laws on the divorce rate; Berk and Newton (1985) used police records on wife-battering incidents for a quasi-experimental analysis of the deterrent effects of arrest. Records can also provide data for more general longitudinal studies. Personnel records in private sector corporations and in public sector organizations have been used as the basis for research on internal labour markets: patterns of recruitment, promotion, job moves and quits, and the effects of economic conditions, affirmative action policies, organizational growth and contraction as well as human capital factors on the careers of individuals, or of entry cohorts. A study of careers in the US civil service over the period 1963–77 was based on a one per cent sample of personnel records for federal employees (Grandjean, 1981), while Rosenbaum (1984) used the personnel records of a large American corporation for roughly the same period, 1962–75, to study these questions. Fruin was able to analyse the personnel records of a Japanese company since its incorporation in 1918 up to the 1970s to assess variations over time in the practice of lifetime employment and seniority-based compensation (Fruin, 1978, 1980).

Data from public sector records are sometimes sufficiently extensive in scale to permit area-based studies. Stevens and Willis (1979) combined data from police records and population census statistics to compile arrest rates for whites and ethnic minority groups for police districts, and then studied the ecological correlations of arrest rates. They found a significant association between unemployment and crime among whites, but not among ethnic minority groups, despite higher levels of unemployment among blacks.

Despite international variations in record-keeping systems, it has proved possible to carry out international comparative studies on some topics, such as homicide. Archer and Gartner (1984) compiled an enormous cross-cultural database on criminal violence (homicide, assault, robbery, theft and rape) for over a hundred countries and covering the first three-quarters of the twentieth century, which formed the basis for international studies of the deterrent effect of the death penalty and of whether wars produce a postwar increase in rates of violent crime.

As the last example demonstrates, it can require considerable time and effort to collate very large datasets derived from administrative records. But smaller scale studies can usually be done comparatively quickly and cheaply compared to the resources required for new data collections.

One key disadvantage is that the scope and content of studies are constrained by the nature of the data available from records. Even when relevant records exist, they may not provide the particular items of information required to address the question at issue; information may be present but the definitions and classifications applied may be incompatible with those the researcher wishes to use; there may be large blocks of missing data (which may not matter for administrative purposes but present serious problems for a research analysis); there may be constraints on access, or relevant data may be censored for confidentiality reasons. Whereas with secondary analysis there is a good chance that more than one appropriate dataset might be located, and some secondary analyses have used dozens of previous studies, there is rarely any possibility of locating better alternatives to a set of records that are less than ideal for a study. The design of research based on administrative records involves a large element of knowing what is available, and making the most of it. Opportunistic designs are almost a requirement.

The Nature and Quality of Data from Administrative Records

Some datasets are compiled from records specifically for research purposes, in which case special effort is devoted to ensuring that the information is complete, checking queries or anomalies, and producing documentation for the resulting database. One example is the Aberdeen maternity and neonatal databank initiated in 1948. This has been laboriously compiled from hospital and other records to provide a longitudinal file with an obstetric history and related clinical and social data for each woman resident within the district; it is extensively used for social and medical research on topics related to fertility and pregnancy (Thompson *et al.*, 1981).

More commonly, researchers have to compile their own *post hoc* account of the procedures and methods used to compile and update the records on which a study is based. This account replaces the usual methodological report on how data were specially collected in other types of study, and constitutes the documentation for the dataset extracted from the records. Many of the points to note are of a quite different nature to ordinary research data.

As a general rule, information that is essential or central to the activities of an organization will be more carefully monitored and of better quality than more peripheral items of information. So it is important to identify the primary administrative uses of the records, and which items of data are central, or peripheral, to these purposes. Although distinctions are commonly made between public sector and private sector records, there are also important differences *within* these categories, especially within the public sector, where agency functions are often defined in law. The primary use of records may be for decision-making with reference to *minima* only, such as minimum wages, minimum health and safety standards, and so on; full details will not be recorded for those cases where the minima are exceeded, so the data are truncated. Records kept in the context of implementing rules, regulations or legislation with *universal applicability*, such as car registration, will contain more complete and standardized information on all cases, to ensure consistent and uniform treatment. Other records are kept in the context of *service delivery* activities, where there is no precise, or minimum, entitlement and the nature of the service depends on the individual case, so that information in the records is not standardized and may vary greatly in quantity and detail. The degree of standardization, consistency and quality of information also varies between records that are routinely compiled and those compiled on a one-off basis for some special exercise or study (Hakim, 1983: 490–5).

Distinctions might also be usefully drawn between records kept for internal use by the organization, those kept solely to comply with regulations and legislation, and those used to produce public statements, accounts or statistics; or between items of information supplied by the individual concerned, or by an informant. For example, the quality of information on race or ethnic minority group membership can vary a great deal between record systems according to who supplied the information and whether it was actively used within an affirmative action policy, or whether it was collected solely to comply with some regulation.

Some understanding of the nature and original purpose of any set of records is important not only with reference to the quality, consistency and completeness of the data they provide, but also for the interpretations that can be placed on the results – just as it is crucial to the reading and interpretation of any documentary evidence to know what class of document it belongs to (rule-book, public statement, official record of a meeting, personal account based on recall, public lecture, letter, diary and so forth). Also, formal organizational rules are often supplemented, sometimes even over-written, by informal rules, and such practices may affect the consistency of records over a period of time, over and above any changes to the formal rules about how the records are kept or the activities to which they relate. Obtaining information on how the records were compiled and updated usually requires consultations with the people responsible for the records. This can prove fruitful even when the records are old or historical in nature, as those responsible for them may have relevant documents or an accumulated oral history on how they have changed and developed over time.

There is a conventional view that data from administrative records is seriously deficient, particularly in relation to value-laden topics such as crime. But the problem is less significant than the prejudice assumes. Administrative records provide more reliable information than interview self-reports on some topics, such as hours worked, unemployment, annual earnings and job tenure (Duncan and Mathiowetz, 1984), or visits to the doctor (Siemiatycki, 1979). Case studies of police procedures have shown little or no bias in official crime records (Mawby, 1979; Walker, 1983); careful comparisons of research results using self-reported criminal activity with data from official records have shown far smaller discrepancies between the two types of study than is suggested by the conventional prejudice (Blumstein and Cohen, 1979; Hindelang *et al.*, 1979; Braithwaite, 1981; Thornberry and Farnworth, 1982); and faulty analysis of data from records can produce more unjustified conclusions than the weaknesses of the data themselves (Hakim, 1983: 508–10; Walker, 1983, 1985). The problem, while real, seems to have been exaggerated, and Braithwaite suggests (1981: 46–7) that certain prejudices persist because they are ideologically attractive to both liberal and conservative researchers. So the more informed perspective is that the interpretation of data from records requires great care, and for this it is essential to have detailed knowledge and understanding of the social processes involved in the production of data in records (Walker, 1983).

Record Linkage

Distinctions between types of records, and even between specially collected research data and data from administrative records, can become obscured in datasets created by linking together information from records, the population census and sample surveys. This innovation is facilitated by the computerization of many record systems, allowing linkage to be carried out on a much larger scale than in previous studies, which were based on either manually linking together discrete records, such as marriage, divorce and birth records (Christensen, 1963), or else *ad hoc* linkage of information from survey respondents with data on their incomes, earnings or social security benefits from tax and social security records (Sewell and Hauser, 1975; Moylan *et al.*, 1984).

At the simplest level, discrete records within a single source are linked together to create longitudinal datasets. For example, the US Social Security Administration has for many decades maintained the Continuous Work History Sample (CWHS) which provides a longitudinal file of earnings and benefit histories for a one per cent sample of social security numbers, updated annually. The CWHS is used for internal research on the characteristics of workers covered by social security and how this population has changed with legislative changes. Until 1976, data from the CWHS was released also for external research on work force characteristics, life-cycle earnings, migration, labour force participation and related topics (Traugott and Clubb, 1976: 397; Farkas, 1977; Mueller, 1982; Tanur, 1983: 52).

More complex projects merge data from different sources into a single file, either on an *ad hoc* basis or as a continuing project. The 1973 Current Population Survey–Administrative Record Exact Match Study linked data on income, earnings and benefits from tax and social security records (held by two different agencies) to the March 1973 CPS survey data to create an extremely rich dataset for a nationally representative sample of the population. The file is available for public use and has formed the basis for methodological, cross-sectional and longitudinal studies (Tanur, 1983: 52; Behrman *et al.*, 1983).

In Britain, the Longitudinal Study (LS) links population census records for a one per cent sample of the population with information from other records held in the census office, such as birth and death registration and notifications of cases of cancer. So far information on personal and household characteristics from the 1971 and 1981 Censuses has been added to the file, which is extensively used for research on mortality differentials, supplementing the more restricted studies based on death registration records alone (OPCS, 1973; Brown and Fox, 1984; Fox *et al.*, 1985; see also Hakim, 1982: 43, 71–2).

As principles and rules are evolved to deal with the legal and ethical problems of linking data from disparate record systems and agencies, and as techniques are developed for dealing with the methodological problems (such as the varying units of analysis within record systems), more record linkage projects are being designed (Tanur, 1983: 51–5). One new idea is *synthetic datasets* in which data for *similar* but not identical people would be merged, using the techniques currently employed to impute missing values in survey data. The trouble with this approach is that it can end up begging the very questions that might be addressed in research analyses.

Documentary Analysis

It is even more difficult to generalize about the research uses of individually unique documents than about records-based studies – so much depends on the nature and contents of the documents in question, whether they are subjected to qualitative or quantitative analysis. So only a brief indication of possible research designs is given here.

Documents may be subjected to an *analytical reading*, as illustrated by analyses of political ideologies (Fielding, 1981). Readings of the population census commentaries have provided information on changing conceptions of work and employment, the underlying rationales for occupational classifications, the changing status of particular occupations and trends in occupational segregation (Davies, 1980; Hakim, 1980).

Documents may be subjected to various forms of *content analysis*, some of them using quantitative techniques – for example, to expose the sex role or racial stereotypes contained in children's books, to show how the professional ideologies of scientists are structured to promote and defend their claims to authority, autonomy and resources (Gieryn, 1983), or to assess degrees of bias in media coverage of the news (Glasgow University Media Group, 1976, 1982).

Some documents may be subjected to *quantitative analysis* because they provide information which is itself systematic and quantifiable. For example, the *Dictionary of Occupational Titles* provides various measures of the content, characteristics and skill requirements of occupations, and is used as a source of data on the occupational structure, as distinct from the characteristics of workers within occupations (Cain and Treiman, 1981; Parcel and Mueller, 1983).

Overlaps, Linkages and Combinations

For all their limitations, records-based studies permit quite a range of research designs. Many of the examples given above illustrate overlaps and links with other types of study more commonly based on specially collected research data.

One type of overlap deserves special note. Some surveys are a cross between the postal survey and data extracted from administrative records. National surveys and censuses of employers are often of this type, with self-completion questionnaires sent out to employers who will normally have to extract the relevant data themselves from their own records – for example, on the size and characteristics of their work force, the earnings paid to their employees, or their output and exports. Although these surveys appear, on the surface, to have the characteristics of specially designed research surveys, the data that can be collected are in practice wholly constrained by the nature of employers' personnel records and bookkeeping systems.

Practical Considerations

Some datasets extracted from government records are routinely released for public use; in other cases access may need to be specially negotiated; in yet others laws specifically prohibit the release of such data. The rules on access may change over time, even in relation to a single dataset. For example, the American Tax Reform Act of 1976 prohibited any further release of CWHS data for public use, whereas special arrangements for improving access to the British LS were made in the 1980s. Access to organizational records in the private sector must invariably be negotiated for each study, and rules to protect confidentiality may also need to be agreed.

Whether the required information has to be specially extracted from records or computer files, or is already available as a standard release tape, it is essential that sufficient time and resources are allocated to the tasks of familiarization with the contents, preparation of basic or additional documentation with reference to the specific questions addressed by the study and pertinent data items and, in some cases, sorting out whether missing values can reliably be imputed or estimated. Perhaps the most common mistake is to think of data from records as ready to use research data, whereas they usually require more preparation, care and effort than an equivalent secondary analysis of a research dataset.

Hakim (1983) provides a general review of the methodology and problems of interpretation arising in research analysis of data from administrative records. But problems are often specific to a particular set of records, or to a particular intended use of them. In the absence of detailed guides to the relevant administrative record systems and the data obtained from them (for example Walker, 1981, and other volumes in the Maunder series), consultation with those responsible for the records is frequently required – for example, to check potentially erroneous assumptions.

There are a number of general texts on content analysis and the analysis of documentary evidence (see, for example, Berelson, 1952; Platt, 1981). Flaherty (1979) and Boruch and Cecil (1983) review the legal and ethical considerations raised by this type of study. Although quite a few records-based datasets are now held in archives, replications of the original analyses and secondary analyses are still quite rare (but see Bursik and Webb, 1982; Furet and Ozouf, 1982).

References

Archer, D. and Gartner, R. (1984) *Violence and Crime in Cross-National Perspective*. New Haven, CT: Yale University Press.

Bateman, F. and Weiss, T. (1981) *A Deplorable Scarcity: The Failure of Industrialization in the Slave Economy*. Chapel Hill: University of North Carolina Press.

Behrman, J.R. *et al.* (1983) 'The impact of minimum wages on the distribution of earnings for major race–sex groups: a dynamic analysis', *American Economic Review*, 73: 766–78.

Berelson, B. (1952) *Content Analysis in Communication Research*. Glencoe, IL: Free Press.

Berk, R.A. and Newton, P.J. (1985) 'Does arrest really deter wife battery? An effort to replicate the findings of the Minneapolis spouse abuse experiment', *American Sociological Review*, 50: 253–62.

Blau, P.M. (1963) *The Dynamics of Bureaucracy: A Study of Interpersonal Relations in Two Government Agencies*, 2nd edn. Chicago: University of Chicago Press.

Blaug, M. (1980) *The Methodology of Economics: Or How Economists Explain*. Cambridge: Cambridge University Press.

Blumstein, A. and Cohen, J. (1979) 'Estimation of individual crime rates from arrest records', *Journal of Criminal Law and Criminology*, 70 (4): 561–85.

Boruch, R.F. and Cecil, J.S. (eds) (1983) *Solutions to Ethical and Legal Problems in Social Research*. New York: Academic Press.

Braithwaite, J. (1981) 'The myth of social class and criminality reconsidered', *American Sociological Review*, 46 (1): 36–57.

Brown, A. and Fox, J. (1984) 'OPCS Longitudinal Study: ten years on', *Population Trends*, 37: 20–2.

Bursik, R.J. and Webb, J. (1982) 'Community change and patterns of delinquency', *American Journal of Sociology*, 88 (1): 24–42.

Cain, P.S. and Treiman, D.J. (1981) 'The *Dictionary of Occupational Titles* as a source of occupational data', *American Sociological Review*, 46 (3): 253–78.

Campbell, D.T. (1969) 'Reforms as experiments', *American Psychologist*, 24: 409–29. (Reprinted in J. Bynner and K.M. Stribley (eds), *Social Research: Principles and Procedures*. London: Longman/Open University Press, 1979, pp. 79–112.)

Campbell, D.T. and Stanley, J.C. (1963) *Experimental and Quasi-Experimental Designs for Research*. Chicago: Rand McNally.

Chiplin, B. (1981) 'An alternative approach to the measurement of sex discrimination: an illustration from university entrance', *The Economic Journal*, 91: 988–97.

Christensen, H.T. (1963) 'Child spacing analysis via record linkage: new data plus a summing up from earlier reports', *Marriage and Family Living*, 25 (3): 272–80.

Cook, T.D. and Campbell, D.J.T. (1979) *Quasi-Experimentation: Design and Analysis Issues for Field Settings*. Chicago: Rand McNally.

Davies, C. (1980) 'Making sense of the census in Britain and the USA: the changing occupational classification of the position of nurses', *Sociological Review*, 28 (3): 581–609.

Duncan, G.J. and Mathiowetz, N.A. (1984) *A Validation Study of Economic Survey Data*. Ann Arbor, MI: University of Michigan, Institute for Social Research Survey Research Centre.

Edwards, P. and Scullion, H. (1984) 'Absenteeism and the control of work', *Sociological Review*, 32 (3): 547–72.

Farkas, G. (1977) 'Cohort, age, and period effects upon the employment of white females: evidence for 1957–1968', *Demography*, 14 (1): 59–72.

Fielding, N. (1981) *The National Front*. London: Routledge & Kegan Paul.

Flaherty, D.H. (1979) *Privacy and Government Databanks: An International Perspective*. London: Mansell Scientific.

Foster, J. (1974) *Class Struggle and the Industrial Revolution*. London: Weidenfeld & Nicolson.

Fox, J. *et al.* (1985) 'Socio-demographic differentials in mortality', *Population Trends*, 40: 10–16.

Fruin, W.M. (1978) 'The Japanese company controversy', *Journal of Japanese Studies*, 4: 267–300.

Fruin, W.M. (1980) 'The family as firm and the firm as family in Japan: the case of Kikkoman Shoyu Company Ltd', *Journal of Family History*, 5: 432–9.

Furet, F. and Ozouf, J. (1982) *Reading and Writing: Literacy in France from Calvin to Jules Ferry*. Cambridge: Cambridge University Press.

Gieryn, T.F. (1983) 'Boundary work and the demarcation of science from non-science: strains and interests in professional ideologies of scientists', *American Sociological Review*, 48: 781–95.

Glasgow University Media Group (1976) *Bad News*. London: Routledge & Kegan Paul.

Glasgow University Media Group (1982) *Really Bad News*. London: Writers and Readers Publishing Co-operative.

Grandjean, B.D. (1981) 'History and career in a bureaucratic labour market', *American Journal of Sociology*, 86: 1057–92.

Griliches, Z. (1985) 'Data and econometricians – the uneasy alliance', *American Economic Review*, 75 (2): 196–200.

Hakim, C. (1980) 'Census reports as documentary evidence: the census commentaries 1801–1951', *Sociological Review*, 28 (3): 551–80.

Hakim, C. (1982) *Secondary analysis in Social Research: A Guide to Data Sources and Methods with Examples*. London: Allen & Unwin.

Hakim, C. (1983) 'Research based on administrative records', *Sociological Review*, 31 (3): 489–519.

Hakim, C. and Dennis, R. (1982) *Homeworking in Wages Council Industries: A Study Based on Wages Inspectorate Records of Pay and Earnings*. Research Paper No. 37. London: Department of Employment.

Harbury, C.D. and Hitchens, D.M. (1979) *Inheritance and Wealth Inequality in Britain*. London: Allen & Unwin.

Hareven, T.K. (1982) *Family Time and Industrial Time*. Cambridge: Cambridge University Press.

Hershberg, T. (ed.) (1981) *Philadelphia*. Oxford: Oxford University Press.

Hindelang, M.J. *et al.* (1979) 'Correlates of delinquency: the illusion of discrepancy between self-report and official measures', *American Sociological Review*, 44: 995–1014.

144   Catherine Hakim

Lawton, R. (ed.) (1978) *The Census and Social Structure: An Interpretative Guide to the 19th Century Censuses for England and Wales*. London: Frank Cass.

Leete, R. and Anthony, S. (1979) 'Divorce and remarriage: a record-linkage study', *Population Trends*, 16: 5–11.

Maunder, W.F. (ed.) (1974–85) *Reviews of United Kingdom Statistical Sources*, 17 vols. London: Heinemann; Oxford: Pergamon.

Mawby, R. (1979) *Policing the City*. Farnborough: Saxon House.

Moylan, S., Millar, J. and Davies, B. (1984) *For Richer, for Poorer?* DHSS Cohort, DHSS Social Research Branch Research Report 11. London: HMSO.

Mueller, C.F. (1982) *The Economics of Labor Migration: A Behavioral Analysis*. New York: Academic Press.

OPCS (1973) *Cohort Studies: New Developments*. Studies on Medical and Population Subjects 25. London: HMSO.

Parcel, T.L. and Mueller, C.W. (1983) 'Occupational Differentiation, prestige, and socioeconomic status', *Work and Occupations*, 10 (1): 49–80.

Parker, J. and Dugmore, K. (1976) *Colour and the Allocation of GLC Housing: The Report of the GLC Lettings Survey 1974–5*. Research Report No. 21. London: Greater London Council.

Phillips, D.P. (1983) 'The impact of mass media violence on US homicides', *American Sociological Review*, 48: 560–8.

Platt, J. (1981) 'Evidence and proof in documentary research', *Sociological Review*, 29 (1): 31–66.

Platt, S. and Kreitman, N. (1985) 'Parasuicide and unemployment among men in Edinburgh 1968–1982', *Psychological Medicine*, 15: 113–23.

Ragin, C.C., *et al.* (1984) 'Assessing discrimination: a Boolean approach', *American Sociological Review*, 49: 221–34.

Rosenbaum, J.E. (1984) *Career Mobility in a Corporate Hierarchy*. New York: Academic Press.

Rubinstein, W.D. (1981) *Men of Property: The Very Wealthy in Britain since the Industrial Revolution*. London: Croom Helm.

Sayer, A. (1984) *Method in Social Science: A Realist Approach*. London: Hutchinson.

Sewell, W.H. and Hauser, R.M. (1975) *Education, Occupation and Earnings: Achievement in the Early Career*. New York: Academic Press.

Siebert, W.S. and Sloane, P.J. (1981) 'The measurement of sex and marital status discrimination at the workplace', *Economica*, 48 (190): 125–41.

Siemiatycki, J. (1979) 'A comparison of mail, telephone and home interview strategies for household health surveys', *American Journal of Public Health*, 69: 238–45.

Stevens, P. and Willis, C.F. (1979) *Race, Crime and Arrests*. Home Office Research Study 58, London: HMSO.

Tanur, J.M. (1983) 'Methods for large-scale surveys and experiments', in S. Leinhardt (ed.), *Sociological Methodology 1983–4*. San Francisco: Jossey-Bass, pp. 1–71.

Thompson, B. *et al.* (1981) 'Longitudinal studies in Aberdeen, Scotland', in S.A. Mednick and A.E. Baert (eds), *Prospective Longitudinal Research*. Oxford: Oxford University Press, pp. 60–76.

Thornberry, T.P. and Farnworth, M. (1982) 'Social correlates of criminal involvement: further evidence on the relationship between social status and criminal behaviour', *American Sociological Review*, 47: 505–18.

Traugott, M.W. and Clubb, J.M. (1976) 'Machine-readable data production by the federal government', *American Behavioral Scientist*, 19 (4): 387–408.

Walker, M.A. (ed.) (1981) *Crime Statistics*. Oxford: Pergamon.

Walker, M.A. (1983) 'Some problems in interpreting statistics relating to crime', *Journal of the Royal Statistical Society*, Series A, 146 (3): 281–93.

Walker, M.A. (1985) 'Statistical anomalies in comparing the sentencing of males and females', *Sociology* 19: 446–51.

Wasserman, I.M. (1984) 'Imitation and suicide: a re-examination of the Werther effect', *American Sociological Review*, 49: 427–36.

Wrench, J. and Lee, G. (1982) 'Piecework and industrial accidents: two contemporary case studies', *Sociology*, 16: 512–25.

Wrigley, E.A. (1972) *Nineteenth Century Society: Essays in the use of Quantitative Methods for the Study of Social Data*. Cambridge: Cambridge University Press.

13

How Official Statistics are Produced: Views from the Inside

Government Statisticians' Collective

There is little awareness, except on the part of those directly involved, of the ways in which official statistics are produced. Reasons for this neglect include the legally enforced secrecy, except for literature officially published, in which all Government operations are shrouded; the conventions of academic writing which in all fields tends to obscure the muddled and makeshift nature of what really happens; and a general lack of interest in a matter usually assumed to be of trivial importance. Yet an awareness of this labour process, and of the state institutions in which it takes place, is crucial to understanding the meaning of official statistics. We provide here an account of this process and of its implications. We also hope to communicate a little of what statistical work feels like, as we and our colleagues experience and have experienced it.

The Government Statistical Service (GSS)

Official statistics are produced primarily to provide the information required by administrators, 'mandarins' (the very highest civil servants) and ministers in government departments. A secondary function of increasing importance is the provision of an information service to industry and commerce. On the first page of *Government Statistics: A Brief Guide to Sources* (CSO [Central Statistics Office], 1977), we read: 'The GSS exists first to serve the needs of modern government. But much of the information it compiles is readily usable by business management, particularly in marketing, and indeed large parts of the system have been shaped with this in mind.' An even clearer indication of these priorities is provided in the booklet *Profit from Facts* (CSO, 1973), produced for and issued free to businesses (see also Stibbard, 1972).

From J. Irvine, I. Miles and J. Evans (eds), *Demystifying Social Statistics*, Pluto Press, London, 1979, pp. 130–51.

Academic researchers and other users of published data are, not surprisingly, assigned the lowest priority of all in GSS planning.

The GSS was created as a distinct section of the Civil Service in 1941. Wartime planning had necessitated more direct state control of the economy, and thus a firm quantitative base for government decision-making. Harold Wilson fondly recalled the heroic improvizations of those years in his 1973 Presidential Address to the Royal Statistical Society (Wilson, 1973). After the war, extensive government activity continued with the mixed economy and the welfare state: the GSS consequently expanded at a phenomenal rate, doubling in size every seven or eight years.

This expansion continued through the 1960s, especially under the enthusiastic patronage of Prime Minister Wilson, who had (as did Heath) a close relationship with the head of the GSS, Claus Moser. The GSS was to be part of the 'white heat of the technological revolution', which the Labour government hoped would modernize the British state and economy, and make British capital more competitive against its overseas rivals. Certain politicians and officials have seen statisticians as a new innovating influence in the fusty, out-of-date atmosphere of Whitehall.

As with all government expenditure in the present colder economic climate, so also for the GSS: the party is over. Its growth has levelled off at about 550 professional staff, and 7,000 in all, including all types of support staff (see Pite, 1975, on the allocation of staff; Moser, 1973, is of interest though out-of-date). The end of GSS expansion has been felt by statisticians in increasing work pressures and declining promotion prospects.

Moser's good relations with Wilson and Heath not only promoted the quantitative growth of the GSS, but also secured for it greater prestige and influence than are enjoyed by the statistical services of most countries. Whereas most countries and international organizations have giant central offices for statistics – 'statistics factories', such as 'Statistics Canada' and the 'Statistical Office of the European Communities' – isolated from centres of power,[1] the GSS is relatively decentralized and less isolated. Notwithstanding recent moves in the direction of more centralization, it is likely to remain so.[2]

In large part, the GSS is constituted by the Statistics Divisions (or, in some cases, combined Statistics and Economics Divisions) of which there is one or more in most government departments. Statisticians advise administrators – and, mainly through them, ministers – and often work closely with administrators in the formulation of policy. In addition, there are three statistical agencies outside the departments: the Central Statistical Office, the coordinating centre of the GSS whose Director also heads the GSS, and which is directly under the Cabinet Office and thus the Prime Minister; and, of lesser importance, the Business Statistics Office, and the Office of Population Censuses and Surveys (OPCS), which includes a semi-autonomous Social Survey Division. This division, not usually considered part of the GSS, is commissioned by government departments to conduct surveys for them (on, for example, family expenditure or alcoholism).

Thus decentralization to the departments is combined with some central co-ordination – an attempt to enjoy the best of both worlds. Statisticians are regarded as having a 'dual loyalty': their lines of command run, via the heads of statistics branches, up the departmental hierarchies, while at the same time they have links (which, in practice, may be highly attenuated) with the rest of the GSS, and with the statistical profession as a whole.

In contrast to the many Civil Service specialists (scientists, architects, surveyors, meteorologists, etc.) concerned only with technical tasks, statisticians are often in positions which bridge the gap between technical problems (sample design, computing, etc.) and administration and policy-making. They are closely integrated into the bureaucratic machine. They share the salary and promotion structure of the administrators – a more favourable one than most other specialists (including, to touch a sore point, the Research Officers of the OPCS Social Survey Division). For rank, or grade, is a pervasive and oppressive influence in the Civil Service, and, if statisticians are to be listened to, their rank must correspond with that of the administrators they work with. These circumstances they share only with economists.

Most members of the public who come into contact with the GSS do so through inclusion in the surveys and censuses carried out by OPCS. Apart from such special surveys, government statisticians work on a great variety of projects with specific purposes.

For example, they design and operate statistical computer models with purposes ranging from the projection of economic and population trends (Treasury, OPCS), the analysis of the supply of teachers (Department of Education and Science), the examination of energy policies (Department of Energy), the allocation of Rate Support Grant to local authorities (Department of the Environment), the planning of manpower systems (Civil Service Department) to the control of inventories of military equipment (Ministry of Defence). Unfortunately, even when details of such models are published in technical journals, there is often no public or academic discussion of them, in spite of the importance of their applications. We can cite the calculation, on a very dubious basis, of the 'needs element' of the Rate Support Grant, which determined the distribution of £3,700 million to local authorities in 1977–8.

However, the largest part of government statistical work is the continuous routine data collection and processing in the departments. In several, this involves extensive use of computers.[3] It is to some typical examples of such work that we now turn. Let the reader judge whether these are appropriate examples of the 'varied and interesting work' advertised in the Civil Service Commission recruitment pamphlet, *Statisticians in Government Service* (1974: 15).

The Process of Production of Statistics[4]

The most crucial documents in the whole process of producing statistics are the *forms*, or *returns*, sent out by the government department (not necessarily by the statisticians) to the organizations from which information is needed: for example, to the offices of business firms, local tax offices, police stations, employment exchanges and local authority social services departments. The unfortunate people given the job of filling in these forms collect (or sometimes invent) and record the requisite information with varying degrees of accuracy and comprehensibility. While some forms are specially designed for statistical purposes, others have a completely different primary purpose – claims for grants, say, or National Health Service records – and provide statistical information only as a by-product.

The completed forms are typically posted, or ferried by van, to a data processing and computer centre in a provincial town. Medical certificates, for example, end up in Newcastle, and Population Census forms in Titchfield. This centre will form part of the statistics branch (or division or organization) of the department concerned. The work of statisticians, usually located in London offices, and that of technical staff at the computer centre, is co-ordinated by telephone and travel between the centre and the departmental office. It is the statisticians' job to order, analyse and interpret computer output so as to meet the requirements of the departmental administrators for information, and to compile statistical volumes and reports.

It is useful at this point to consider in more detail the division of labour between the different types of staff involved. Figure 1 shows the hierarchical structure of a statistics branch (including a computer centre) in a government department, and the main lines

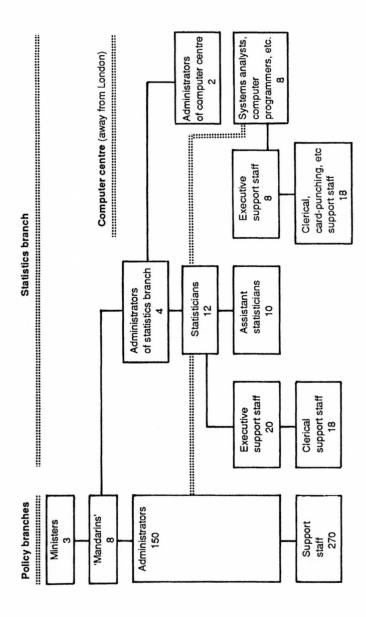

Figure 1 *Structure and relationships of a large statistics branch containing a computer centre in a government department*

of communication and command within it, and between it and the administrative and policy-making sector of the department. The size of statistics branches varies considerably: the example shown here is of a large branch with a staff of 100. [. . .]

The Cycle of Statistical Production

Within this structure, statistics are produced in a cyclical process. Under the influence of departmental policy, as formulated by its ministers, mandarins and administrators, and drawing on their own experience, the statisticians elaborate and revise the concepts and procedures for categorizing and measuring the matters of concern to the department. These form the basis on which statisticians, computer specialists and supervisory staff design, adjust and maintain the entire statistical production system.

Such a system is often extensive and unwieldy. To change it, except very gradually, is often difficult and disruptive of work schedules. Thus, once a statistical system has been designed and is in operation, revision of its concepts and organization in the light of experience and of changing requirements is likely to be slow. Figure 2 indicates the stages in which statistics are produced, which staff are responsible for each stage, and how the stages interconnect. The sequence shown by arrows is one of influence (in practice, often a two-way influence) rather than of time, or of workflow. All stages may occur simultaneously.

At the base of both the process and of the hierarchy, subordinate staff perform routine clerical and data processing tasks of many kinds, such as form-filling, coding and card-punching. The end-results of their work, in the form of computer output, are analysed and interpreted by statisticians, and used by administrators, mandarins and ministers in the department, and in other departments, to develop and justify policies.

The 'attitudes' of different layers of staff to their work, shown in Figure 2, whilst being simplified representations, are nevertheless worth recording on this understanding. Administrators are not all cynical – some really believe in 'serving the state', or even 'reforming society'; while cynicism may be found among routine employees, as well as naive commitment or indifference to their work. Powerful influences, however, do tend to structure attitudes in the directions shown. For example, the higher placed people are in the hierarchy, the more information they have about the real rationale for policies (often so different from those publicized), and the more useful cynicism is in adapting to this information.

By 'professionalism' is meant the ethos by which professional

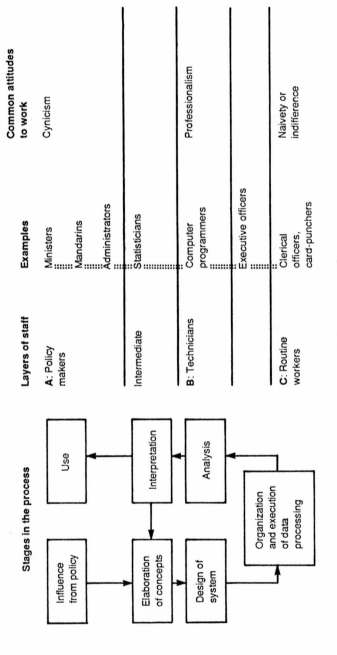

Figure 2 *The cycle of statistics production in a typical government department*

workers try to maintain a certain independence, and standards of competence, accuracy and integrity, within their own narrow technical sphere, while carefully abstaining from questioning, or taking responsibility for, the ends to which their skills are used. Statisticians, working in closer contact with administrators than most other professional staff, retain only an attenuated professional ethos, and partly come to share the attitudes of administrators.

In the rest of this article we consider in turn the stages of statistics production indicated in Figure 2.

The 'Elaboration of Concepts' Stage

There is no one set of methods and concepts which must be used to make sense of our social environment and to gather and assimilate information about it. The methods and concepts developed and used for official statistics are shaped by the sorts of policies powerful people in the state wish to consider and by the concerns which preoccupy them. These concerns determine, at least partly, which phenomena are to be investigated as 'social problems', and which neglected.

[. . .]

Isolated critiques of specific areas of statistics generally fail to expose the deeper influences of the social order on the range of issues considered in official statistics and the treatment of these issues. It is extremely difficult, if not impossible, to make a really radical criticism of society using available statistical sources, which imprison us in the concepts and concerns that dominate official political and economic life. Yet, unless we are prepared to abandon quantification altogether, we have no choice but to use government sources, as only the state has the power and resources to produce statistics on such a large scale.

We consider two examples of such difficulties. The first arises in the definition of geographical regions. The regions of England to which statistics relate are standardized – North-East, North-West, Midlands, etc. This makes it difficult to compare regions constructed on different criteria, for example, coastal, lowland, mountain, etc. And virtually all statistics relate to particular nation-states, while in developing a critique of the nation-state as an institution, we may well need to study regions whose boundaries do not coincide with national frontiers.

The second example concerns statistics of production and distribution. Overwhelmingly these are collected and presented in money terms, a consequence of production and distribution being determined by the imperatives of buying and selling on world markets, rather than by the direct assessment of human needs. This poses enormous problems if we seek to analyse the use for different economic purposes of given raw materials, productive capacities or labour time. How can we find out how many tonnes of aluminium, millions of person-days, or items of electronic control equipment are squandered by British capitalism (as well as other capitalist and bureaucratic societies) on war preparations, protection of property and non-productive activities (advertising, banking, accounting, political and religious rituals, etc.), and thus develop alternative plans for these resources?[5] One is not able to 'profit from facts' in carrying out such forms of quantitative assessment.

Practical constraints reinforce the conservatism of statistical systems. Conventions on how to handle data, even when they are generally admitted to be inappropriate, are retained – from inertia, from the desire to maintain the consistency and comparability of statistics over different areas and over time, and in view of the costs and difficulties of change. For example, only extremely serious reasons could conceivably impel fundamental change in the vast and complex classification system of firms and industries which is the *Standard Industrial Classification*, given the great problems and costs of discontinuity in processing, analysis and interpretation. In fact, the revisions being undertaken in the late 1970s have no theoretical rationale, but are aimed at achieving consistency with the classification used by the EEC.

Even seemingly harmless conventions may have implications deserving some thought. What value judgements are hidden, for instance, in such routine decisions as those to treat a part-time worker as equal to one-half of a full-time worker, a child as one-half of a person, or a bathroom as one-half of a room? There are also less structural aspects of statistical conservatism. For example, some figures are not needed for action, but nevertheless continue to be collected, almost as a matter of tradition.

A further important problem arises when statistics are produced as by-products of administrative systems existing mainly for other purposes. Many regular official statistics are in fact produced in this way. Examples are Inland Revenue estate duty statistics being used to derive statistics on the distribution of wealth (see Hird and Irvine, 1979; and Atkinson, 1974); unemployment statistics being based on the records kept by employment exchanges (see Hyman and Price, 1979), and homelessness statistics being based on the records kept by local authorities on those who apply to them for help.

What such statistics tend to monitor is not so much the social conditions of wealth, unemployment or homelessness, but rather the operations of the state agencies responsible for dealing with the matter. Wealthy people who avoid estate duty through timely gifts to relatives, unemployed married women who do not register at the employment exchange (because they are not eligible to claim benefits), and homeless people who do not apply to local authorities for help (knowing that they do not fall into a category of people which the authority is prepared to help) are ignored by the agencies and thus structurally excluded from the statistics. The consequence, often very convenient to the state, is a lack of reliable information on social problems about which little or nothing is being done.

An excellent example of this phenomenon is provided by an account in *Statistical News* of a new system of statistics on homelessness (Morrison, 1976). (It should be noted that the new system is in fact a considerable improvement on the old one.) The statistics are derived from computer analysis of forms sent in (sometimes) by local authorities, recording applications for help made to them and how such applications have been dealt with.[6] Morrison tells us:

> Some homeless households, after the Authority has accepted responsibility, make no further contact or leave temporary accommodation provided without contacting the Authority; if no further contact is made during the following six months, it is assumed that they are no longer homeless, and a 'permanent solution' is recorded. Although when contact is lost this is recorded as a 'permanent solution', this is partly a matter of statistical convenience; *it is permanent in the sense that the case is now closed.* If the household re-applies at a later date, this is treated as a new case; to do otherwise would make the statistical system too complex. (our emphasis)

and

> The statistics reflect the practices of individual Local Authorities in their dealings with the problem of homelessness as manifested in the applications they receive and the actions they are able to take. It is recognised that there are some shortcomings in the new system (of statistics), particularly since this is an area where there are no clear and unequivocal definitions. For example, those households who approach the Local Authority and do not fall into one of the groups which it is the policy of that Local Authority to help often never reach the stage of making a formal application.[7] Local Authority officers are understandably reluctant to ask for detailed information from someone they know they will be unable to help. The collection of information on those without shelter who did not contact the Local Authority would be even more difficult; it is extremely doubtful whether a comprehensive set of statistics could be maintained on those people.

The 'Design of System' Stage

A vast clerical operation exists to distribute and collect forms, to check and clarify information on incoming forms, to convert it into a form which the computer can handle (that is, computer codes punched on computer cards), and to perform related tasks. This operation must be maintained and adjusted to changing circumstances and requirements. In these jobs – which include the design of forms, the specification of processing instructions, the supervision of processing staff, and the organization of the channels through which paper flows – both statisticians and supervisory staff (in small operations the same person may well be both) play a part. The problem of organization is more complicated for those systems where the documents used do not have solely statistical functions but are first used outside the statistics organization for other purposes.

Also included in this stage are the organization of the operations of the computer centre and the development by computer specialists of computer programs and systems to handle the computer processing of the data, and to produce tabulations and other output for analysis.

The 'Data Processing' Stage

The data to be processed are usually taken from a set of forms completed in commercial or government offices, offices in which such form-filling tends to be the lowest priority. One indication of this prioritization is the 'statistics strike', a mild kind of industrial action, in which forms are not completed. Such a strike paralysed the statistical organization of the Department of Employment from August 1976 to January 1977, as many pages of the *Department of Employment Gazette* for those months made clear. Admittedly, the world did not come to an end as a result.

The annoying chore of form-filling tends to be shoved on to the least knowledgeable or least competent clerical staff, or simply on to whomever happens to be available at the time, although forms are often not designed with such people in mind. Thus forms are often not completed fully, accurately or even comprehensibly, and at busy times perhaps not dealt with at all. Sending incomplete data is especially tempting when there is no way for the collectors to tell whether the data are complete or not (as in the case of the local authority returns on homelessness).

Businesses are urged to co-operate by drawing their attention to the profit they may derive from the statistics to which they contribute. However, many types of data (for example, on industrial accidents) can be neglected or falsified without risk of discovery. Nor do guarantees of confidentiality necessarily prevent falsification of returns. One of our correspondents wrote of his experience in a large company: 'I was pressed time and again to use false figures for turnover, cost of raw materials, etc., for fear of the taxman. They did not realize that the taxman would never see the forms – or so I hoped. I fought bitter battles, and once threatened to give notice to prevent the fraud. I know that others do not have the power to do this, or do not care.'

The data processing stage is marked above all by tedium. The DHSS computer centre handles millions of medical certificates per year, the Inland Revenue centre millions of forms from tax offices. Storeroom attendants spend their days keeping track of the bundles of paper taken to and from the long dusty, shelves. Clerks sit in rows in large open-plan rooms (designed so that everyone is visible to the supervisor) and sort out the forms into categories, or put every nth form aside for processing of a sample. Others translate the scrawl on the forms into computing codes, written on coding sheets in accordance with prepared coding instructions. From these the 'card-punch girls' – it's 'women's work', of course – punch out computer cards on rows of machines hammering out like very loud typewriters, and the cards are fed, after checking, into the hungry jaws of the computer's card-readers. Supervisors make spot-checks and try to keep to schedule. All to the sound of soft piped pop music, year after year. The computer, supposed to usher in an age of automated freedom from clerical toil, has so far merely raised the productivity of boredom, and added new varieties of routine work to the old ones.

[. . .]

From the time when figures are first entered on a form in a local Government or business office, until the statistics are published in statistical volumes and reports, data processing is highly sensitive to many mundane sources of error – misunderstood instructions on forms, misreading of hastily written figures, misplacing a decimal point, losing one's place in copying, accidental 'corruption' of data in computer files, or printing errors. It is quite possible for a mistake anywhere along the line to go undetected and work its way through into published figures. Once in a while such a case emerges into the glare of publicity, giving newspaper cartoonists a chance to re-use their civil servant caricatures.

One example was when, following the accidental omission of a zero by an Olivetti employee reporting the firm's exports, an underestimate of national exports (and thus an overestimate of the excess of imports over exports) generated a phoney balance of payments crisis. Another was when the trade figures went haywire over a period of many months because a clerk at one point copied two lines of figures onto a coding sheet in the wrong order. (The first assumption, as reported in the press, was that it was the fault of an excessively complex computer program for carrying out seasonal adjustments on the figures.) A major error in Home Office migration figures resulted from accidentally counting the same set of movements twice.

High-level post-mortem investigations are usually held when such large errors in politically important statistics come to light. (Less important errors may never come to light, since many statistics never come under critical scrutiny.) Statistics administrators respond by making pleas for simpler, less error-prone procedures, and for more effective checking arrangements. But such expedients have limited potential: everything cannot be checked and cross-checked, and the person doing the checking may well repeat the errors of the person being checked.

Serious errors would certainly occur less often if staff had the ability to recognize figures as implausible and the initiative then to get them sorted out. Yet the necessary knowledge of the subject matter is rarely available to clerical staff, while initiative is discouraged by the clearly defined roles of the hierarchical division of labour, in the interests of control and uniformity of processing.[8] Clerks are supposed to refer anomalies and ambiguities in the data to their supervisors, but it takes initiative and knowledge to realize that something needs questioning. Even the best writer of instructions cannot foresee all sources of confusion and misunderstanding, or be able to guard against them. For example, an empty box on a form (especially on a poorly designed form) may mean 'no', 'none', 'don't know', 'won't tell', 'does not apply' or 'forgot to fill in this box'. The differences between these meanings are crucial, and it would be very difficult to give precise advance instructions on how to resolve the ambiguity.

Automatic checks of the internal consistency and plausibility of data can often be programmed into the processing of computer data files, although it is impossible within the computer to check other aspects of data quality: to spot consistent errors or incorrect but plausible data. The computer can check whether values are in a given range, whether two figures add up to a third, and so on. For example, in a survey of household accommodation, the computer might be programmed to draw attention to, or reject, cases where the number of toilets was recorded as less than zero, more than six, or more than one-half of the total number of rooms.

But, even when a comprehensive series of such checks is built in, it cannot even detect *all* implausible, let alone plausible but invalid, data. To take the case mentioned of a tenfold under-recording of Olivetti exports, the recorded figure was within a plausible range of values for firms in general; it needed someone with a knowledge of the export activities of different firms to spot that it was an unlikely figure for Olivetti in particular. In the last resort, therefore, the crucial check must be that of use.

The extent of the inaccuracy introduced by these problems depends, among other things, on how 'close to the data' the statisticians are: that is, on how far they are able, or inclined, to involve themselves effectively in the details of data processing. To minimize such problems, they need to spend a day doing each of the processing jobs in the system – a rare practice!

A final key factor is the attitude of processing workers to their work. Statisticians are forced, by the responsibility imposed on them, to care about the reliability of data. But there is no good reason why a clerical officer should worry. Many staff are, nevertheless, painstakingly conscientious about such things. (Indeed, among the older generation of civil servants, there are those prepared to work unpaid overtime and take work home; this work ethic, though, seems to be on the decline.) But those who are indifferent – either sinking into tedium-induced stupor, or concentrating on conversation with others (where conditions allow this), or on daydreams – are engaged in passive resistance to their work situation, a work to rule.

Thus those who call, for whatever reason, for more timely, comprehensive, useful or reliable statistics should remember that, under present conditions, they thereby call for more stress on, and regimentation of, statistical workers.

The Stages of 'Analysis, Interpretation and Use'

Many computer tabulations are produced on a regular schedule for use in published statistical volumes, or for reference by statisticians as needed. Other output is ordered, or obtained through computer terminals, by statisticians for special purposes. They select what is needed, analyse it and interpret its meaning for administrators or enquirers.

If co-ordination between statisticians and computer staff has been inadequate, statisticians may at this stage find themselves unable to carry out desired analyses, for reasons such as the way the data are stored in the computer.

The best use possible has to be made of whatever data are

available. As administrators are reluctant to accept that whatever information they require may not be available, 'guesstimates' are often provided where reliable estimates are impossible, however doubtful the assumptions made to derive them. The requirement for clear-cut conclusions, the pressure of work and the petrification of the original theoretical knowledge of the statistician, encourage such misleading practices as the automatic mechanical use of (perhaps inappropriate) significance tests at 95 per cent level of significance – without the proviso, however, that 1 in 20 of results so obtained is expected to be incorrect. (The easy availability of standard tests on computer programs and packages is a standing invitation to such procedures.)

Another problem which statisticians face in presenting statistics for the use of mandarins and administrators is the latter's preference for figures which are easy to remember, have straightforward meanings and are not subject to frequent revision. An apocryphal story relates that after the war Sir Godfrey Ince, then Permanent Secretary at the Ministry of Labour and National Service, complained about the changes in the figures of unemployed: once he had learned to remember them, they should not be changed at such frequent intervals.

Under the pressure of schedules for the production of statistics, statisticians usually lack enough time also to analyse and interpret them thoroughly. However, in those places where different people are made responsible for production and for interpretation (for example, Department of Industry statisticians interpret statistics produced by the Business Statistics Office, and economists interpret statistics in several Departments – a smouldering demarcation dispute), misunderstandings and failures of communication, as well as friction and frustration, are much greater.

Much statistical material is published in official publications, and much more remains unpublished in order to keep down the bulk and cost of publications. It is often possible to obtain unpublished or not yet published data, and – for a price – even to obtain specially produced tabulations of unpublished data; for example, Census data for small areas. In general, the more acceptable are enquirers' political and academic credentials, and the more trustworthy they are regarded by a Department, the more co-operative the Department will be in releasing information to them. One of the constraints is that it should not be possible to identify from released data individual households or firms, though in practice it sometimes is.[9]

There is, however, a certain amount of unpublished data which is considered politically sensitive. Even trusted contacts of a

Department will find it difficult to get hold of such material, meeting with evasion, claims of ignorance, and – as a last resort – outright refusal. 'When in doubt, say nowt' is the course often recommended to civil servants in such situations.

Although we have tried to correct the balance in the way official publications are usually uncritically accepted, by concentrating on difficulties and problems, the extent to which official statistics are unreliable should not be exaggerated. In many areas they are an important source of information, if examined critically, and, where possible, used in conjunction with other evidence. It is especially important that they should be interpreted in the context of the assumptions, definitions and methods of collection on which they are based, and GSS publications generally describe these, at least to some extent.

However, administrators, mandarins, politicians, social scientists and the mass media tend to disregard this small print. Misinterpretation of statistics, accidental or deliberate, in the form in which they reach a wide public, is common. As secrecy about what they learn in the course of official duty, and abstention from public controversy, are conditions of employment for civil servants, the former backed up by the all-encompassing provisions of the Official Secrets Act, Government statisticians are unable (except occasionally with special permission) to protest publicly at such misinterpretation.

Due to the enforced secrecy in which such practices take place, it is difficult to assess the extent of deliberate manipulation of statistics for political purposes.[10] Serious manipulation, however, seems to be rare except in a few sensitive areas (such as the concealment of staffs, budgets and even existence of the security services and of Government Communications Headquarters). Wages and prices statistics, because of their importance in justifying and implementing wages policies, are also susceptible to manipulation under pressure from the Treasury.[11]

Although statisticians are prevented from protesting publicly at such practices, it is open to them to protest internally, to seek the support of GSS superiors against administrators, and in the last resort to resign and look for a new job. People vary in how far they are prepared to stick their necks out in such circumstances. Collective protest is very unlikely for a host of reasons: the isolated situation of statisticians (in their work and even physically), the competitive structure of the hierarchy, and – perhaps most important of all – the fears, customs and attitudes of the milieu. The likelihood of success in internal individual protest will depend on the power of the opponent: it is easier to protest about the speech of a politician seeking party-political advantage than it is to protest about matters whose necessity is advocated by mandarins.

As the outright falsification of figures is risky, it is very rare. More common tactics include non-publication ('the truth, nothing but the truth, and as little of the truth as possible'), delay of publication (such as the six-month delay of 'race' statistics by Crossman, who feared the reaction to projections of the number of 'immigrants'), misleading or inadequate commentaries on published figures (for example, in order to be 'optimistic' about the economic situation), and 'massage'.

Massage is the manipulation of the way figures are derived or presented in order to create desired impressions. It covers a continuum of deception ranging from the choice of the most presentable of several equally accurate modes of presentation, to subterfuges which, in practice at least, amount to falsification. We mention four types of massage:

1. *Changing the definitions of terms* in order to create a desired effect. The unemployment figures reported over the years in the *Department of Employment Gazette* reflect a successive narrowing of the definition of unemployment, to keep figures down – with regard to the inclusion or exclusion of such groups as married women, school-leavers, people out of work for short periods and part-time workers.

2. *Unjustifiable extrapolation of trends.* For example, Chancellor of the Exchequer Healey claimed in an election campaign that inflation was running at 8½ per cent per year. He could claim to be right only by ignoring seasonal adjustment and extrapolating from a short untypical part of the year; the rate of inflation at the time, taken over any reasonable period, was much higher.

3. *Manipulation of adjustments.* Here advantage is taken of the practice of adjusting figures so as to reduce the impact on them of atypical circumstances at the time of collection. An example has been the selective application, under pressure from the Treasury, of adjustments to the Retail Price Index, made with the purpose of reducing the impact on the Index of rapid fluctuations in the prices of eggs, fresh vegetables and other perishable foodstuffs, *when and only when such adjustments served to depress the Index.*

4. *Manipulation of categories.* The categories into which items (foods, people, or whatever) are divided may be chosen in order to clarify or in order to obfuscate. A relatively small group of items, which is nevertheless of interest, may be included in a larger category, or in a rag-bag category marked 'other' or 'miscellaneous' for the purpose of concealment. Thus are

concealed, for example, the staffs and budgets of secret agencies, and the embarrassing survival in a handful of villages of all-age schools.

Conclusion

We have not in this article aimed at a comprehensive overview of the government statistical system. But we hope we have focused the mind of the reader on the fact that statistics do not, in some mysterious way, emanate directly from the social conditions they appear to describe, but that between the two lie the assumptions, conceptions and priorities of the state and the social order, a large, complex and imperfectly functioning bureaucracy, tonnes of paper and computing machinery, and – last but not least – millions of hours of human grind.

Notes

1. Policy Departments in fact try to overcome this situation by such subterfuges as employing their own statisticians disguised as 'economists' (as in Holland).
2. The question of centralization is linked to the controversy over the possible linkage of data banks held in the computers of different departments (see *Financial Times*, 18 October 1977: 'Society today – awesome model for government statistics: building in the safety devices', by Joe Rogaly).
3. For example, Business Statistics Office (computer centre at Swansea); Civil Service Department (Chessington, Surrey); Ministry of Defence (London); Department of Education and Science (Darlington); Department of Health and Social Security (Newcastle); Board of Inland Revenue (Worthing); OPCS (Titchfield, Hants); Scottish Office (Edinburgh).
4. We pay no attention to technical problems of statistical work such as bias and sampling error. Though important, many texts on survey methods (Moser and Kalton, 1971) deal with them. Such texts also deal with the pitfalls of form design (see also the booklet *Ask a Silly Question!* issued by the CSO Survey Control Unit, 1976).
5. For contrasting monetary and material approaches in the field of input–output analysis, see Berman (1968), and Roberts (1976), respectively. In the wake of problems over the supply of natural resources, studies such as Roberts' have begun to attract attention.
6. For a useful attempt to interpret the meaning of homelessness statistics, see Bailey (1977: ch. 2).
7. Single people are rarely helped.
8. In these and many other ways are the inefficiencies of hierarchy and the division of labour revealed. Many support staff lack the confidence to point out an error made by a superior, for example, or even underestimate their own intelligence.
9. The rights of privacy on the whole safeguarded by this and other rules of confidentiality are at least as much concerned with protecting the affairs of powerful companies from public scrutiny as they are with protecting ordinary

citizens. The collection of statistics, in which the identity of individuals is of no interest, is a relatively minor threat to privacy. The publicity about it, culminating in the mild public hysteria of the Census period, contrasts intriguingly with the media's acceptance of the *real* power which employers, schools, credit agencies, security services, etc. derive from detailed non-statistical information on millions of specific individuals (see Hewitt, 1977).

10. Secrecy extends even to refusal of permission to publish academic papers whose political implications are unwelcome. The suggestion by a government statistician (Nicholson, 1975) of a more 'democratic' prices index which, unlike existing ones, would give equal weight to the expenditure of each household in the sample on which the index was based, was published after an enforced delay of 20 years.

11. Those exerting pressure on statisticians do sometimes have valid points to make, which the statisticians have neglected.

References

Atkinson, A.B. (1974) *Unequal Shares: Wealth in Britain*. Harmondsworth: Penguin.

Bailey, R. (1977) *The Homeless and the Empty House*. Harmondsworth: Penguin.

Berman, L.S. (1968) 'Developments in input–output statistics', *Statistical News* (CSO), 3 (November).

CSO (Central Statistical Office) (1973) *Profit from Facts*. London: HMSO.

CSO (Central Statistical Office) (1976) *Ask a Silly Question!* Survey Control Unit. London: HMSO.

CSO (Central Statistical Office) (1977) *Government Statistics: A Brief Guide to Sources*. CO:CSO Section. London: HMSO.

Civil Service Commission (1974) *Statisticians in Government Service*. London: HMSO.

Department of Employment, *Department of Employment Gazette* (monthly).

Hewitt, P. (1977) *Privacy: The Information Gatherers*, London: National Council for Civil Liberties.

Hird, C. and Irvine, J. (1979) 'The poverty of wealth statistics', in J. Irvine, I. Miles and J. Evans (eds), *Demystifying Social Statistics*. London: Pluto Press.

Hyman R. and Price, B. (1979) 'Labour statistics', in J. Irvine, I. Miles and J. Evans (eds), *Demystifying Social Statistics*. London: Pluto Press.

Morrison, H. (1976) 'New system of statistics on homelessness', *Statistical News* (CSO), 35 (November).

Moser, C.A. (1973) 'Staffing in the Government Statistical Service', *Journal of the Institute of Statisticians*, 1.

Moser, C.A. and Kalton, G. (1971) *Survey Methods in Social Investigation* 2nd edn. London: Heinemann.

Nicholson, J.L. (1975) 'Whose cost of living?', *Journal of the Royal Statistical Society*, Series A., 138 (4).

Pite, J.C. (1975) 'The deployment of staff in the Government Statistical Service', *Statistical News* (CSO), 30 (August).

Roberts, N. (1976) 'Energy balances', *Statistical News* (CSO), 35 (November).

Royal Statistical Society, *News and Notes* (monthly).

Stibbard, P.J. (1972) 'Use of official statistics in firms and *Profit From Facts'*, *Statistical News* (CSO), 17 (May).

Wilson, J.H. (1973) 'Statistics and decision-making in government – Bradshaw revisited: the Address of the President (with Proceedings)', *Journal of the Royal Statistical Society*, Series A, 136 (1).

14

'It's Great to Have Someone to Talk to': Ethics and Politics of Interviewing Women

Janet Finch

The issues which I discuss in this chapter have been raised by my own experience of doing social research of a qualitative variety. In particular, my experience of interviewing has raised a combination of methodological, personal, political and moral issues, upon which I find it necessary to reflect both as a sociologist and as a feminist. These issues have become focused by considering the extreme ease with which, in my experience, a woman researcher can elicit material from other women. That in turn raises ethical and political questions which I have found some difficulty in resolving. One reason for this difficulty is, I shall argue, that discussions of the 'ethics' of research are commonly conducted within a framework which is drawn from the public domain of men, and which I find at best unhelpful in relation to research with women.

I shall illustrate and discuss these issues by drawing upon two studies in which I was the sole researcher, and did all the interviewing myself. These are firstly, a study of clergymen's wives and their relationship to their husband's work, which was based on interviews with 95 women; secondly, a study of 48 women (mostly working class) who were running and using preschool playgroups. In both cases, the interviews were arranged in advance. I contacted prospective interviewees initially by a letter which introduced myself and the research, then made an appointment to interview them in their homes at a pre-arranged time. All the interviews were tape recorded unless the interviewee requested otherwise, and were based on a list of questions to be covered during the interview, rather than upon a formal questionnaire. In the study of clergymen's wives, the interview was the first occasion on which we met. In the playgroup study, I had met some (but not all) of the interviewees during the preceding two years, when I had made observational visits to the playgroups themselves.

From C. Bell and H. Roberts (eds), *Social Researching: Politics, Problems, Practice*, Routledge, London, 1984, pp. 70–87.

The Woman-to-Woman Interview

Both the clergymen's wives and the playgroups studies were concerned entirely with women; in both I used qualitative techniques including in-depth interviewing; and in both I talked to women in their own homes about aspects of their lives which centrally defined their identities as women – marriage, motherhood and childrearing. My consciousness of the special character of a research situation in which women talk to another woman in an informal way, and about these issues, was heightened by reading Ann Oakley's (1981) discussion of interviewing women. Oakley takes the view that formal, survey-type interviewing is unsuited to the production of good sociological work on women. She prefers less-structured research strategies which avoid creating a hierarchical relationship between interviewer and interviewee. That sort of relationship, she argues, is inappropriate for a feminist doing research on women, because it means that we objectify our sisters.

I share Oakley's preference on both methodological and political grounds, and my own research has all been of the type which she recommends. I have also found, quite simply, that it works very well. Initially I was startled by the readiness with which women talked to me. Like every other researcher brought up on orthodox methodology textbooks, I expected to have to work at establishing something called rapport (Oakley, 1981). In my experience, such efforts are normally unnecessary when interviews are set up in the way I have described. Women are almost always enthusiastic about talking to a woman researcher, even if they have some initial anxieties about the purpose of the research or their own 'performance' in the interview situation. Their intentions are apparent, simply from the hospitality which one characteristically receives – an aspect of the research experience which Oakley (1981) notes is seldom mentioned in reports. In my study of clergymen's wives, I was offered tea or coffee, and sometimes meals, in all but two instances; the same happened in the majority of interviews in my playgroup study. One is, therefore, being welcomed into the interviewee's home as a guest, not merely tolerated as an inquisitor. This particular contrast was demonstrated to me in graphic form when I arrived at one interviewee's home during the playgroup study, only to find that she was already being interviewed by someone else. This seemed like the ultimate researcher's nightmare, but in the end proved very much to my advantage. The other interviewer was in fact a local authority housing visitor, who was ploughing her way through a formal questionnaire in a rather unconfident manner, using a format which required the respondent to read some questions from a card ('Do you receive any of the benefits listed on card G?', and so on). My presence during this procedure must have been rather unnerving for the housing visitor, but was most instructive for me. I recorded in my fieldnotes that the stilted and rather grudging answers which she received were in complete contrast with the relaxed discussion of some very private material which the same interviewee offered in her interview with me. My methodological preferences were certainly confirmed by this experience.

I claim no special personal qualities which make it peculiarly easy for me to get people to talk, but women whom I have interviewed often are surprised at the ease with which they do talk in the interview situation. One woman in my playgroup study (who told me that she was so chronically shy that when she had recently started a new job it had taken her a week to pluck up courage to ask how to find the toilet), said after her interview that she had surprised herself – it had not really felt, she said, as if she was talking to a stranger. Another woman in this study said that she found me an easy person to talk to and asked, 'Where did you get your easy manner – did you have to learn it or is it natural?' I quote these instances not to flaunt my imputed skills as an interviewer, but as instances which demonstrate a feeling which was very common among the women I interviewed in both studies – that they (often unexpectedly) had found this kind of interview a welcome experience, in contrast with the lack of opportunities to talk about themselves in this way in other circumstances. Some variation on the comment 'I've really enjoyed having someone to talk to' was made at the end of many interviews.

How far does this experience simply reflect the effectiveness of in-depth interviewing styles *per se*, and how far is it specific to women? It seems to me that there are grounds for expecting that where a woman researcher is interviewing other women, this is a situation with special characteristics conducive to the easy flow of information. Firstly, women mostly are more used than men to accepting intrusions through questioning into the more private parts of their lives, including during encounters in their own homes. Through their experience of motherhood they are subject to questioning from doctors, midwives and health visitors; and also from people such as housing visitors, insurance agents and social workers, who deal principally with women as the people with imputed responsibility for home and household. As subjects of research, therefore, women are less likely than men to find questions about their lives unusual and therefore inadmissible. Secondly, in the setting of the interviewee's own home, an interview conducted in an informal way by another woman can easily take on the character of an intimate conversation. The interviewee feels quite comfortable with this precisely because the interviewer is acting as a friendly guest, not an official inquisitor; and the model is, in effect, an easy, intimate relationship between two women.

Thirdly, the structural position of women, and in particular their consignment to the privatized, domestic sphere (Stacey, 1981), makes it particularly likely that they will welcome the opportunity to talk to a sympathetic listener. The experience of loneliness was common to women in both my studies. The isolation of women who are full-time housewives has been well documented by Dorothy Hobson, in a study of women whose circumstances were very similar to those in my playgroup study (Hobson, 1978, 1980). The loneliness experienced by clergymen's wives is less obvious at first sight, but in fact it has a very special character. Many of them adopt a rule that they should have no friends in the locality, for fear that they might harm their husband's work by being seen as partisan (for discussion, see Finch, 1980). The consequences of this were described to me by one Methodist minister's wife as,

> I agree if it's going to hurt people, if it's going to harm her husband's ministry, it's better not to have friends nearby. But I think it's terribly difficult, because I think a woman needs a particular friend. I've always tried not to make particular friends but as I say, you can't help being drawn to some people. But as I say, I try not to show it. I never sit beside the same person in a meeting. I never visit one more than anybody else.

The friendly female interviewer, walking into this situation with time to listen and guarantees of confidentiality, not surprisingly finds it easy to get women to talk. In one instance, a clergyman himself thanked me for coming to interview his wife because, he said, *he* felt that she needed someone to talk to. It is not, however, only in the few cases where one is clearly being used as a social worker that women's need to talk is apparent. Almost all the women in my two studies seemed to lack opportunities to engage collectively with other women in ways which they would find supportive, and therefore they welcomed the opportunity to try to make sense of some of the contradictions in their lives in the presence of a sympathetic listener. There seems no reason to doubt that most women who similarly lack such opportunities will also find such an interview a welcome experience.

For these three reasons, the woman-to-woman interview (especially when conducted in the settings and in the ways I have described) does seem to me to be a special situation. This is not to say that men can never make good interviewers, although practice in research teams does suggest that research directors often regard women as especially suited to this task, as Scott (1984) points out. Men, as social workers or as counsellors, for example, can be very effective in getting both women and men to talk about intimate aspects of their lives. But systematic comparisons of men and women interviewers, in a range of research situations, are not possible because we lack sufficient studies or accounts of the research process which consider the relationship of the gender of the interviewer to the research product. That is an interesting and important methodological issue; but my point about the special character of the woman-to-woman interview is as much political as methodological, and has particular resonance for any sociologist who is also a feminist. However effective a male interviewer might be at getting women interviewees to talk, there is still necessarily an additional dimension when the interviewer is also a woman, because both parties share a subordinate structural position by virtue of their gender. This creates the possibility that a particular kind of identification will develop.

In my own research experience, I have often been aware of such an identification, as women interviewees have begun to talk about key areas of their lives in ways which denote a high level of trust in me, and indicate that they expect me to understand what they mean simply because I am another woman. One example taken from each of my studies – both concerning the interviewee's experience of marriage – should serve to illustrate this. The first extract comes from the interview with the wife of an Anglican clergyman, living in a huge and decaying vicarage, in a mill village on the Yorkshire moors:

> One big problem in being a clergy wife I feel is, at the odd time which happens in every marriage – and it happens in clergy marriages as much as it happens outside – is that when you get the big bang in a marriage, when you get some sort of crisis, and I don't think a marriage ever gels until you've had a crisis in a marriage, where do you go for advice? If you're like me, you can't ask your mother because it's an admission of defeat that you have a problem – a big enough problem to seek advice on – in your marriage. You can't ask the vicar or the vicar's wife because you are, by definition, criticising his curate. You cannot ask the bishop or the archdeacon because, again, you are casting some sort of slight on one of his priests who cannot manage his own marriage. So who do you ask?
>
> I was very fortunate in that I knew the widow of a clergyman who had no sort of direct tie with the church but had sort of been through the lot herself and could help me. I find this sort of person invaluable, but how many people manage to find her? Other than that, just who do you go to?

The second illustration is from the interview with a 24-year-old mother of two daughters under school age, living on a run-down council estate on the edge of an east Lancashire town:

> *Self*: I know that the children are sort of small at the moment, but do you ever have any sort of hopes or dreams about what they might do when they grow up?
>
> *Interviewee*: Yes, I'm always – Don't get married for a start. [*To child*] Not to get married, are you not! And have a career, with some money. And don't have a council house. Bet there's no such thing as council houses when they get older. But I don't want them to get married.
>
> *Self*: No?
>
> *Interviewee*: No but I don't, because I think once you get married and have kids, that's it. To a lot of women round here – when you see them walking past – big fat women with all their little kids running behind them. And I think, God. That's why I want to go to College and do something. But fellas don't see it like that, do they? Like, he thinks it's alright for me just going back to work in a factory for the rest of my life, you know. But I don't want that. [*To child*] You have a career, won't you? Prime Minister, eh?

Comments of this kind – albeit very differently conceptualized and articulated – would not have been elicited in a formal questionnaire nor if I, as interviewer, had been attempting to maintain an unbiased and objective distance from the interviewees. Nor, I suggest, would they have been made in the same way to a male interviewer. Comments like 'fellas don't see it that way, do they?' and 'you can't ask your mother because it's an admission of defeat' indicate an identification between interviewer and interviewee which is gender specific.

That identification points to a facet of interviewing which I experienced strongly and consistently throughout these two studies: namely that the ease with which one can get women to talk in the interview situation depends not so much upon one's skills as an interviewer, nor upon one's expertise as a sociologist, but upon one's identity as a woman. In particular, I found that there was some unease in the interview situation if an interviewee was in some doubt about how to place me in relation to the crucial categories of marriage and motherhood. For example, during the three years when I was conducting the observational and interview phases of the playgroup study, I changed both my name and address. With several women who ran the playgroups, I noted some hesitation in their approach to me (comments like, 'You've moved, have you?') until I clarified that this was indeed because my marriage had ended. Other researchers have similarly reported that interviewees wanted to 'place' them as women with whom they

could share experiences (Hobson, 1978; Oakley, 1981). Male interviewers of course may also be 'placed' (by their occupational or
family status, for example). But again, being 'placed' as a woman
has the additional dimension of shared structural position and
personal identification which is, in my view, central to the special
character of the woman-to-woman interview.

The Basis of Trust and its Exploitative Potential

From an entirely instrumental point of view as a researcher, there
are of course great advantages to be gained from capitalizing upon
one's shared experiences as a woman. The consequences of doing
so can be quite dramatic, as was illustrated to me in my study of
clergymen's wives. As an anxious graduate student, I agonized over
the question of whether I should reveal to my interviewees the
crucial piece of information that I myself was (at that time) also
married to a clergyman. Wishing to sustain some attempt at the
textbook, 'unbiased' style of interviewing (which Ann Oakley,
1981, has so effectively exposed for the sham it always was), I
initially merely introduced myself as a researcher. I found however,
that before I arrived for the interview, some people had managed
to deduce my 'true' identity. The effects of this unmasking so
clearly improved the experience for all concerned that I rapidly
took a decision to come clean at the beginning of each interview.
The consequence was that interviewees who had met me at the
front door requesting assurances that I was not going to sell their
story to a Sunday newspaper, or write to the bishop about them,
became warm and eager to talk to me after the simple discovery
that I was one of them. Suspicious questions about why on earth
anyone should be interested in doing a study of clergymen's wives
were regarded as fully answered by that simple piece of information. My motives, apparently, had been explained. I rapidly found
this a much simpler strategy than attempts to explain how intellec-
tually fascinating I found their situation. The result of course was
that they talked to me as another clergyman's wife, and often they
were implicitly comparing their own situation with mine. The older
women especially made remarks such as 'possibly you haven't
come across this yet' or 'of course I suppose it's a bit different for
you younger ones now'. The general tone of these interviews often
made me feel that I was being treated as a trainee clergyman's
wife, being offered both candid comment and wise advice for my
own future benefit. In several cases the relationship was reinforced
by gifts given to me at the end, and I became quite good at predic-
ting those interviews where the spoils were likely to include a

chocolate cake or a home-grown cabbage as well as the tapes and fieldnotes.

One's identity as a woman therefore provides the entrée into the interview situation. This obviously was true for me in a rather special way in my study of clergy wives, but that does not mean that only interviewers whose life circumstances are exactly the same as their interviewees can conduct successful interviews. It does mean, however, that the interviewer has to be prepared to expose herself to being 'placed' as a woman and to establish that she is willing to be treated accordingly. In the case of my playgroup study, my life situation was rather different from my interviewees': I did not have young children, and by the end of the study I was not married either. However, this seemed no real barrier to encouraging women to talk freely in the interviews. In the previous two years, through my visits to the playgroups, I had already established myself as a figure on their social scene, and they had taken the opportunity to make key identifications of me as a woman. Once these identifications are made, it does indeed seem the easiest thing in the world to get women to talk to you.

The moral dilemmas which I have experienced in relation to the use of the data thus created have emerged precisely because the situation of a woman interviewing women *is* special, and is easy only because my identity as a woman makes it so. I have, in other words, traded on that identity. I have also emerged from interviews with the feeling that my interviewees need to know how to protect themselves from people like me. They have often revealed very private parts of their lives in return for what must be, in the last resort, very flimsy guarantees of confidentiality: my verbal assurances that the material would be seen in full only by me and the person transcribing the tapes, and that I would make any public references to them anonymous and disguised. These assurances were given some apparent weight, I suppose, through my association with the university whose notepaper I used to introduce myself. There were, in fact, quite marked differences in the extent to which my various interviewees requested such guarantees. None of the working-class women in my playgroup study asked for them, although one or two of the women in my middle-class comparison playgroup did so. A number of clergymen's wives asked careful questions before the interview, but I found that they were easily reassured, usually by the revelation that I too was a clergyman's wife, rather than by anything I might have tried to indicate about the professional ethics of a sociologist. With them, as with the women in the playgroup study, it was prin-cipally my status and demeanour as a woman, rather than anything to do with the research process, upon which they based their trust in me. I feel certain that *any* friendly woman could offer these assurances and readily be believed.

There is therefore a real exploitative potential in the easily established trust between women, which makes women especially vulnerable as subjects of research. The effectiveness of in-depth interviewing techniques when used by women researchers to study other women is undoubtedly a great asset in creating sociological knowledge which encompasses and expresses the experiences of women (Oakley, 1981). But the very effectiveness of these techniques leaves women open to exploitation of various kinds through the research process. That exploitation is not simply that these techniques can be used by other than *bona fide* researchers: but it is an ever-present possibility for the most serious and morally upright of researchers, feminists included. It seems to me that the crux of this exploitative potential lies in the relationship established between interviewer and interviewee. I would agree with Oakley that the only morally defensible way for a feminist to conduct research with women is through a non-hierarchical relationship in which she is prepared to invest some of her own identity. However, the approach to research – and particularly to interviewing – which this requires can easily be broken down into a set of 'techniques', which can then be divorced from the moral basis in feminism which Oakley adopts. These techniques can be used to great effect to solicit a range of information (some of it very private), which is capable of being used ultimately against the interests of those women who gave it so freely to another woman with whom they found it easy to talk. The prospects for doing that clearly are magnified when (as is so often the case) women interviewers are not themselves the people who will handle and use the data they have created. In those circumstances, women interviewers and research assistants may find that the material which they have created is taken out of their control, and used in ways of which they do not approve and which seem to them to be against the interests of the women whom they interviewed. I have never been in that situation, but I have found that the issues are by no means avoided in research settings such as I have experienced, where I was both interviewer and sole researcher.

Ethics, Morals and Politics in Research

Moral dilemmas of the kind to which I allude are commonly discussed in research textbooks under the heading of 'ethics'. These debates have been well summarized by Barnes (1979). They are formulated in terms of the rights to privacy and protection of those being researched, which are sometimes thought to be assured by adherence to a code of professional ethics. So, are the moral dilemmas raised when women interview women to be resolved by a greater sensitivity to women's right to privacy? Or perhaps a special code of ethics for feminists to adopt if they choose? I think not. I find the terms in which these debates about ethics are constituted unhelpful in relation to women, and it is instructive that the issue of gender is rarely mentioned. Barnes's own discussion conceptualizes it as an issue of the rights of the 'citizens' – certainly an advance upon the term 'subject' or even 'respondent' for the people being researched. None the less, 'citizen' is a concept drawn from the public domain of men, in particular from the political arena, from which women have always been excluded (Stacey and Price, 1980), and it implies a framework of formalized rights and obligations, along with procedures of legal redress. Women are unlikely to feel comfortable with such procedures, and do not necessarily have access to them. Barnes is, however, reflecting the essentially male paradigms in which most debates about 'ethics' are conducted. For example, most such discussions tend to focus upon the point of access or of data collection rather than upon the use of the material. These discussions implicitly assume that research 'citizens' can *anticipate* potentially harmful uses to which such data can be put, and take action accordingly. Most women are unlikely to be in a position where they can anticipate the outcome of research in this way, since they have little access to the public domain within which the activity of research can be contextualized. When discussing ethical issues about the use of research data, Barnes argues that the tension is between, on the one hand, the desire of citizens to protect their own interests in the short term, and, on the other hand, the long-term interests of sustaining informed criticism in a democratic society, which suggest that the results of research should be published whatever they are. Presumably few male research subjects are wildly enthusiastic about having their short-term interests sacrificed to this latter aim, but women are especially vulnerable. The 'democratic society' where this critical discourse is conducted is of course the public domain of men, where the 'debate' is largely conducted *by* men, in their own terms. As Hanmer and Leonard (1984) point out, the specific interests of women are unlikely to be voiced there and therefore little protection is available to women once the outcome of research has entered the public 'debate' at that level. The sociologist who produces work about women, therefore, has a special responsibility to anticipate whether it could be interpreted and used in ways quite different from her own intentions [. . .]

This highlights a point which is often overlooked in discussions of research ethics, but which is crucial to a feminist doing research on women: namely that collective, not merely individual, interests are at stake. The latter may be relatively easily secured with guarantees of confidentiality, anonymity, codes of ethics and so on. It is far more difficult to devise ways of ensuring that information given so readily in interviews will not be used ultimately against the collective interests of women.

In both my playgroups and clergymen's wives studies, I was very aware that aspects of my data could be discussed in such a way as potentially to undermine the interests of wives and mothers generally, if not necessarily the specific people I had researched in a direct way. For example, many clergy wives expressed satisfaction and contentment in living lives centred around their husband and his work (in which they essentially acted as his unpaid assistants). This could be used to argue that *most* women would be much happier if only they would accept subordinate and supportive positions instead of trying to establish greater independence from their husbands. My developing commitment as a feminist made me very unwilling to see my work used to support such a conclusion. Similarly, in my playgroup study, the character of the playgroups which I was studying certainly was in most cases wildly divergent from bourgeois standards of childcare and preschool developmental practice. This evidence, I feared, could be used to reinforce the view that working-class women are inadequate and incompetent child rearers. Again, I felt that I was not willing to have my work used to heap further insults upon women whose circumstances were far less privileged than my own, and indeed for a while I felt quite unable to write *anything* about this aspect of the playgroup study.

In both cases, my commitments as a feminist raised moral questions for my work as a sociologist. In both cases, however, the consequences were that I was pressed into looking more carefully at my data, into thinking through the dilemmas I had raised for myself as intellectual as well as moral issues, and into contextualizing my problem in ways which I might not otherwise have done. In both cases, I eventually resolved the moral issues sufficiently to be able to write about these studies.[1] Briefly, in the case of the clergymen's wives, I found that I had to look more closely at the structural position in which these women were placed, and to make a clear distinction between structural position and women's own experience of it. This enabled me to see that evidence of women successfully accommodating to various structural features of their lives in no way alters the essentially exploitative character of the structures in which they are located. In the case of the playgroups study, I eventually saw that I should really be taking more account of the culture and character of the formal educational system, for which the playgroups were intended (in the eyes of the mothers who used them) as a preparation. Rather than focusing on the apparent inadequacies of the groups run by working-class women, I needed to locate the disjuncture between playgroups and schools as part of the continuing cultural imperialism of bourgeois practices within formal schooling itself. In neither case would I claim to have found perfect solutions to the dilemmas which my own work raised for me. But, given that the period covered by these studies was also a period when my own commitment to feminism was developing, partly as a result of radical changes in my own life, they were quite simply the best solutions I could manage at the time. I am also certain that in the process, I was producing better sociology.

The dilemmas which I have encountered therefore raise the possibility of betrayal of the trust which women have placed in me when I interviewed them. I do not really mean 'betrayal' in the individual sense, such as selling the story of someone else's life to a Sunday newspaper. I mean, rather, 'betrayal' in an indirect and collective sense, that is, undermining the interests of women in general by my use of the material given to me by my interviewees. It is betrayal none the less, because the basis upon which the information has been given is the trust placed in one woman by another. In such a situation, I find sanitized, intellectual discussions about 'ethics' fairly irrelevant. I have preferred to call my dilemmas 'moral' ones, but in fact they are also, it seems to me, inherently political in character. They raise the 'whose side are we on?' question in a particular form which relates to gender divisions and to the study of women in that context.

It has become commonplace in discussions of research ethics to distinguish between research on powerless social groups (where rights to privacy, protection, and so on, are of great importance) and research on the powerful, where such considerations can be suspended, on the grounds that the groups concerned already have enough privileges or are well able to protect themselves, or have exposed themselves to legitimate scrutiny by standing for public office (Barnes, 1979; Bulmer, 1982). If one takes the view that the powerful are fair game for the researcher, then the issues of gender inevitably must be raised: in a patriarchal society, women are always relatively powerless. Women, therefore, with perhaps very few exceptions, can never be regarded as fair game. Further, precisely because issues of power are central to gender relations, one cannot treat moral questions about research on women as if they were sanitized 'ethical issues', divorced from the context which makes them essentially political questions.

A feminist sociologist of course will be 'on the side' of the women she studies. This stance is entirely consistent with major traditions in sociological research, in which – as has been acknowledged from Becker onwards – the sociologist sides with the underdog (*sic*) (Becker, 1967; Gouldner, 1973; Barnes, 1979). One essential difference, however, is that a feminist sociologist doing research on women actually shares the powerless position of those she researches, and this is often demonstrated in the research context itself, for example through the under-representation of women in the institution which sponsors the research, and their location often at the most junior levels in her department, her section, or the research team. This experience of shared powerless-ness between researchers and researched is seldom paralleled for men unless they are, for example, black sociologists doing work on race, or diabled sociologists researching disability. Siding with the people one researches inevitably means an emotional as well as an intellectual commitment to promoting their interests. How else can one justify having taken from them the very private information which many have given so readily? I find rather unconvincing an argument which says that I should be content with having added to the stock of scientific knowledge. Rather, I would endorse Oakley's position that, as a feminist and a sociologist, one should be creating a sociology *for* women – that is a sociology which articulates women's experiences of their lives – rather than merely creating data for oneself as researcher (Oakley, 1981). How far this has been accomplished is the criterion which I would apply to my own sociological work on women, and to that of other people. This seems to me a more fruitful way to address the moral and political dilemmas I have identified than, for example, writing a separate code of ethics for feminists to follow.

This moral and political position which I (and other feminist researchers) have adopted may provoke the charge that we are not serious sociologists, but merely using our work to promote our politics. Our credibility may be questioned by those who see feminist (and indeed similar) commitments as incompatible with good academic work. Helen Roberts already has produced a convincing answer to such charges, showing that a commitment to taking people's experiences seriously *is* essentially a political activity but is not peculiar to feminist sociologists, nor do we become less professional or rigorous as a result (Roberts, 1981).

Indeed, it seems clear to me that *all* social science knowledge is intrinsically political in character (Bell and Newby, 1977), and is undertaken from a standpoint which embodies some material interests, whatever the claims of the researcher. As Maureen Cain and I have argued elsewhere, this does not mean that the knowledge we produce cannot be evaluated and appraised by others. Indeed, recognizing the intrinsically political nature of both theory and data means that the sociologist has a great responsibility to be open and scholarly about her procedures and her conclusions (Cain and Finch, 1981). It does mean, however, that sociologists who are also feminists need not be defensive about the relationships of our political commitments to our work, nor embarrassed when we resolve the moral dilemmas which it raises by frankly political stances. In so doing, I would argue, not only do we avoid compromising our feminism, but we are likely to produce more scholarly and more incisive sociology.

Notes

The study of clergymen's wives was undertaken for my PhD, partly funded by an SSRC studentship. The fieldwork was undertaken mainly in West Yorkshire between 1971–3, and covered wives of ministers in four denominations. An account of the study and my conclusions can be found in Spedding (1975) and Finch (1980). The playgroup study was funded by an SSRC grant, and was conducted in Lancashire between 1978 and 1980. It was a study, based on two years' observation followed by interviews, of five self-help playgroups, four of which were in inner urban areas or on council estates, and the fifth was a comparison group in a middle-class suburb. An account of this study can be found in Finch (1981, 1983b, 1983c).

1. Discussion of the points referred to briefly here can be found in Finch (1980, 1983a 1983c) for issues arising from the clergymen's wives study; and Finch (1981, 1983b) in relation to working-class women and preschool playgroups.

References

Barnes, J. (1979) *Who Should Know What?* Harmondsworth: Penguin.

Becker, H. (1967) 'Whose side are we on?', *Social Problems*, 14: 239–47.

Bell, C. and Newby, H. (1977) *Doing Sociological Research*. London: Allen & Unwin.

Bulmer, M. (ed.) (1982) *Social Research Ethics*. London: Allen & Unwin.

Cain, M. and Finch, J. (1981) 'Towards a rehabilitation of data', in P. Abrams, R. Deem, J. Finch and P. Rock (eds), *Practice and Progress: British Sociology 1950–1980*. London: Allen & Unwin.

Finch, J. (1980) 'Devising conventional performances: the case of clergymen's wives', *Sociological Review*, 28 (4): 851–70.

Finch, J. (1981) *Working Class Women and Preschool Playgroups*. Report to the Social Science Research Council.

Finch, J. (1983a) *Married to the Job: Wives' Incorporation in Men's Work*. London: Allen & Unwin.

Finch, J. (1983b) 'Dividing the rough and the respectable: working class women and preschool playgroups', in E. Gamarnikov *et al.* (eds), *The Public and the Private*. London: Heinemann.

Finch, J. (1983c) 'A first class environment? Working class playgroups as preschool experience', *British Education Research Journal*, November.

Gouldner, A. (1973) 'The sociologist as partisan', in his *For Sociology: Renewal and Critique in Sociology Today*. London: Allen Lane.

Hanmer, J. and Leonard, D. (1984) 'Negotiating the problem: the DHSS and research on violence in marriage', in C. Bell and H. Roberts (eds), *Social Researching*. London: Routledge & Kegan Paul.

Hobson, D. (1978) 'Housewives: isolation as oppression', in Women's Studies Group, Centre for Contemporary Cultural Studies, *Women Take Issue: Aspects of Women's Subordination*. London: Hutchinson.

Hobson, D. (1980) 'Housewives and the mass media', in S. Hall, D. Hobson, A. Lowe and P. Willis (eds), *Culture, Media, Language*. London: Hutchinson.

Oakley, A. (1981) 'Interviewing women: a contradiction in terms', in H. Roberts (ed.), *Doing Feminist Research*. London: Routledge & Kegan Paul.

Platt, J. (1981) 'Interviewing one's peers', *Sociology*, 15 (2): 75–91.

Roberts, H. (ed.) (1981), *Doing Feminist Research*. London: Routledge & Kegan Paul.

Scott, S. (1984) 'The personable and the powerful: gender and status in sociological research', in C. Bell and H. Roberts (eds), *Social Researching: Politics, Problems, Practice*. London: Routledge & Kegan Paul.

Spedding, J. (1975) 'Wives of the clergy', PhD thesis, University of Bradford.

Stacey, M. (1981) 'The division of labour revisited, or overcoming the two Adams', in P. Abrams, R. Deem, J. Finch and P. Rock (eds), *Practice and Progress: British Sociology 1950–1980*. London: Allen & Unwin.

Stacey, M. and Price, M. (1980) *Women, Power and Politics*. London: Tavistock.

15

Observation and the Police: The Research Experience

Maurice Punch

1. Introduction

My first murder – this is not, I hasten to add, a confession – was that of a young woman whose suspected infidelity had caused her husband to stab her to death. That evening I had arrived at Police Headquarters in Amsterdam for a night duty with a young inspector who was responsible for supervising major incidents in the town. Almost immediately we were called to a suspected murder which involved a long interrogation of an English suspect (which I helped to translate) and the dragging and searching of a canal by divers for the body. It was a bitterly cold night and the eye-witness account of the alleged murder became increasingly discredited as old bicycles, but no body, were brought to the surface. After several hours of interrogations and a long period of standing by the canal the suspect was sent home and we sat down for a welcome cup of coffee at about four o'clock. Immediately the telephone rang and the inspector said, 'It looks like a murder in Amsterdam-South.'

We drove through the slumbering city to a quiet and respectable street where the only indicator of trouble was the patrol-car parked outside a neat row of low-rise flats. We climbed the stairs, met the two policemen who had been first on the scene, and entered a small flat, conspicuously clean, like most Dutch homes. The gas-fire was still burning, a woman's clothes were tidily folded over the back of the chair, and there were mementoes from Sicily on the shelves and wedding and family photos on the walls. The bedroom door was slightly ajar and a bare foot was visible on top of the bed. The inspector entered the room and returned to talk in a hushed voice to the policemen. Steeling myself against an innate fear of death I entered the bedroom. A young, attractive woman in pyjamas lay

From *Policing the Inner City: A Study of Amsterdam's Warmoesstraat*, Macmillan, London, 1979, pp. 1–18.

on her back on top of the bed with her legs slightly drawn up and her arms spread wide. Her open eyes stared glassily like those of a stuffed animal. There were stab wounds in her stomach, neck and face and the sheets and walls were spattered with blood. The holes in her neck were a brown-purple colour with surprisingly little blood around them while a slit on her upper lip made it appear as if she was grinning. With only the hiss of the gas-fire breaking the silence we waited for the other services to arrive.

The husband had discovered some evidence of his wife's unfaithfulness and had stabbed her about thirty times with a stiletto. He then phoned the police and brought his two children downstairs to a neighbour and began walking to the station, but was intercepted by a patrol-car on his way. Below there was an attractive little girl of three and a boy of about nine. The little girl cried when she saw the uniforms and the inspector went down on his haunches and started talking kindly to her. 'Mummy is dead,' she said. Upstairs, the reverential silence in the flat was soon broken. A procession of people arrived – two detectives, two ambulancemen, a doctor, a photographer, and an officer from the detective branch – and joined the four people already there (the two patrolmen, the inspector and myself). Each new arrival introduced himself and shook hands and the conversation became less stilted and more jovial as old acquaintances met up and began to chat amicably. Each newcomer went casually to inspect the body and then the routine surrounding a murder – the removal of the body to the morgue for an autopsy and the bringing of the children to relatives – took over from the particular circumstances of the case. We went to the station and opened the spy-hole in the cell door; the husband raised a weary head from beneath the blankets. He looked quite ordinary. I went home and slept until mid-afternoon. When I woke up I felt ill and went to the toilet where I was sick.

This incident was part of a study carried out with the Amsterdam Police in several periods between 1974 and 1976. The original orientation of the research was to use the approach of Reiss (1971), in his observational study of police–citizen contacts in three high-crime-rate areas of American cities, as an entrée to police work in the city-centre of Amsterdam. But, in a sense, that initial goal was merely a peg on which to hang a diffuse, long-standing interest of mine in the police. This interest had been stimulated by contact with policemen who came to study at my university in England. I found them practical, realistic, humorous and refreshing, and developed a certain affinity with them. Increasingly I turned towards an academic interest in the police and, initially, that was focused on the 'social' role of the police (Punch and Naylor, 1973).

Twice I attempted to carry out projects with the local police, but on both occasions I encountered a negative response from the academic watchdogs of the Home Office who control all research proposals on the police. I was disappointed by the lack of response and decided that The Netherlands might prove a more suitable climate for research, partly because each force makes its own decisions regarding research. In 1973 I had spent a half-year in The Netherlands on a Nuffield Fellowship and had begun to learn Dutch (assisted by my wife, who is Dutch).

Through informal contacts, namely mutual acquaintances in the International Police Association, I was able to spend a couple of weeks with two experienced beat officers who operated in the experimental role of 'community relations officers' in a working-class area of Rotterdam (Punch, 1974a,b). This got the ball rolling and one influential contact which was made in this period was with the psychologist, Dr Tom Fris, who worked for the Amsterdam Police. I planned to return to The Netherlands in the summer of 1974 with the help of a Leverhulme Fellowship, and asked Fris if he could arrange for me to spend one month on patrol with the uniformed branch in the city-centre of Amsterdam. I emphasized the city-centre because I knew the stations there were busy. Given my limited time, I wanted to observe as much as possible and had little inclination to spend my time in a sleepy suburb with traffic accidents and violations as the major diversions from tedium and drinking coffee. Like many foreigners in The Netherlands I tend to see it as a one-city society, with Amsterdam standing out as worldly and cosmopolitan compared to the stiffness of The Hague, the vulgarity of Rotterdam, and the suffocating provincialism of the smaller cities. And there is one police station in Amsterdam which everyone has heard of and which is strategically placed in the heart of the thriving inner city. Instinctively that was where I wanted to be.

Clearly, the influential middle-man role of a social scientist within the police apparatus greatly facilitated my access (cf. Fox and Lundman, 1974). The fact that I was a foreigner was also doubtless an advantage in gaining entry. I was a visiting academic, seemingly a bird of passage, whose intention was to publish in English. In any event, it was not necessary, given my previous police contacts, to establish my bona fides and my request was handled through the police hierarchy by Fris. When I arrived in The Netherlands he had arranged a station, a group which I would be attached to, and a policeman 'mentor' who would take me in tow so that I would not have to work with too many different people. My involvement in a cross-cultural study of a police force was something of a moral apprenticeship in the virtues and value of field-work. Here I should like to employ that experience to clarify some salient issues in the observational study of the police and in the use of qualitative methods.

2. Observation and the Police

The police are often held to be the most secluded part of the criminal justice system (Skolnick, 1975: 14). Like other agencies of social control and like some client-serving bureaucracies, the police organization erects barriers against prying outsiders and endeavours to present a favourable image of itself to the extent of mystifying and even falsifying accounts for public consumption (Manning, 1974a). These structural features of isolation and secrecy, coupled with the intrinsic dangers of police work, help to form an occupational culture which is solidaristic, and wary of non-initiates (Westley, 1970). The researcher's task becomes, then, how to outwit the institutional obstacle-course to gain entry and how to penetrate the mine-field of social defences to reach the inner reality of police work. Prolonged participant observation seems to me to be the most appropriate, if not the sole, method for achieving these ends. This becomes even more likely when we examine the nature of police work.

The essence of uniformed police work is relatively solitary patrolling, free of direct supervision, with a high degree of discretion, in face-to-face interaction with the public, and with decision-making behaviour that is frequently not reviewable. Quinney (1970: 114) states, 'Most of the operating policies of the police are beyond public scrutiny; that is, they are secretive and known only to the police themselves.' Only observation can tap that initial encounter on the streets, or in a private dwelling, with all its implications for the individual citizen concerned and for his potential passage through the criminal justice system. Indeed, the theoretical developments in this area over the past decade have accentuated the need for carefully sketched ethnographies of police–citizen encounters. The insights of deviancy and labelling theory have helped us to focus on the transactional and socially created nature of law-enforcement – so that even when the actors are unlikely to be nominated for Oscars and when their scripts are hackneyed and stereotyped, the spotlight has been turned on the *drama* of police work (Manning, 1974b).

This perspective of mine is strengthened as I am a foreigner working in a Dutch environment. One almost senses a latent hostility among Dutch sociologists against field-work as if they are frightened of involvement in society or feel incapable of taking the role of the other, so that they use their research instruments as a protective barrier to preserve unsullied their self and their ideology (this does not apply to anthropologists; cf. Brunt, 1975). Dutch criminology in particular seems to be dominated by a dehydrated fifties positivism. In contrast, Anglo-American sociology and criminology have to a degree been influenced by the rediscovery of the Chicago School, by the work of ethnographers of deviancy, and by the frontal attack on positivistic methods (Becker, 1970; Faris, 1970; Phillips, 1973). These intellectual forces have helped to re-accentuate interactionism and to reaffirm the value of participant observation. Although observation has been a key technique in most of the standard police studies, there has not been a great deal written about the problems of observing police work except for Manning (1972) and van Maanen (1975).

There were a number of reasons why I used observational techniques. Firstly, when I began this study there was little or no previous Dutch research on the police to guide me; my models then were Anglo-American studies based largely on observation. Secondly, I was conscious of the ecological nature of police work, with Bittner's (1967) analysis of 'peace-keeping on skid-row' fresh in mind, and felt that the inner city had to be experienced at first hand. The members of the Chicago School were great pounders of the streets, and police patrols on foot took me slowly around the narrow streets of the Amsterdam red-light district and into bars, cafés, opium dens, gambling saloons, communes, houseboats, brothels, sex-cinemas, porn shops and private clubs. Thirdly, I was interested in police–citizen encounters on the streets and these could only be witnessed *in situ*. Fourthly, my desire to penetrate the social world of the policemen meant that I wanted to see their 'backstage' performances (Goffman, 1959) – inside the station, away from the public, relaxing in the canteen, taking time off when on duty, socializing with them outside of duty and out of uniform. Fifthly, and finally, I rejected more structured techniques as unable to penetrate to where the 'action' is (Goffman, 1972), and mistrusted them as likely to provide unreliable guidelines to actual behaviour.

The essence of participant observation is the prolonged participation of the researcher in the daily life of a group (though not necessarily *as a member* of the group) and his or her attempt to empathize with the norms, values and behaviour of that group (Becker, 1970). As such the researcher becomes his own research instrument and is necessarily involved in a social relationship with the subjects of his research. It is perhaps not surprising, then, that people who research the police generally end up with more positive attitudes to the police as they come to perceive policemen as workers coping with client emergency, an imperfect legal system, pressures to accept gratuities, and the necessity of conforming to the informal colleague code (Punch, 1976a: 22). A number of academics have actually worked in uniform as policemen – I know of Kirkham (1976) and Buckner (1967) in America, Toebosch (1975) in The Netherlands, and Kurzinger (Punch, 1976a: 16) in West Germany. For example, in the much-publicized case of Kirkham in Florida, he became a police officer for six months and reports a personality change that fundamentally altered him (1974: 129). Kirkham seems to have 'gone native' and to have over-identified with the policeman's role, although it may be that he is just more honest and open about the unexplicated strains of field-work (Clarke, 1975).

Rubinstein (1973), on the other hand, went almost to the point of becoming a policeman – he worked as a crime reporter, completed the police training, and rode as an 'armed observer' in patrol cars in Philadelphia – and perhaps that degree of involvement has helped to produce what will surely become a classic. His *City Police* is an insider's view of backstage police behaviour which affirms the essential role of observation. For in microscopic detail, Rubinstein takes us into the policeman's world of body cues, symbolic assailants, selective inattention, implicit meanings, perceptions of space and situated 'normality'. Although he never directly spells out his own involvement in encounters – did he ever draw or use his gun? did he ever have to fight? did he assist in arrests? – he clearly got inside the skins of the patrolmen. The information he collected on violence and corruption could only have been gained by a trained observer who was accepted by the policemen. The complete observer role is a fiction because he or she is always part of the situation and because distancing oneself from the police role – say by explaining at each encounter to the citizen the reason for an academic's presence – may destroy precisely what one wishes to observe. Ineluctably, the researcher is drawn into some participation and must decide for himself where the border of legitimacy lies. Cain (1973: 199) reports being tested out by the policemen before she was initiated into 'easing' behaviour, which included drinking beer in a cupboard. She considers that the rapport built up during the observation period was essential to the success of her interviews with policemen and she admits that her qualitative material has possibly more validity than the quantitative data.

But, in general, the dilemmas of observational research with the police are likely to display considerable correspondence with qualitative studies employing immersion in field-work in other areas (Johnson, 1975; McCall and Simmons, 1969). To a certain extent there is an advantage in single-person research with the police because, as Manning argued at Leuven, this often entails easy access, a less threatening profile, low intrusiveness in the organization, and a high capacity for personalized relationships (Punch, 1976a: 25). This 'lone maverick' approach, however, does depend on the nature of the research problem, funding, and the sorts of data to be collected.

3. Field-Work: On Patrol in the Warmoesstraat

The station selected for my research was Bureau Warmoesstraat (Punch, 1976b), in the heart of the red-light district, which had been receiving adverse publicity about alleged mistreatment of Surinamers from the former Dutch colony in the West Indies (Bagley, 1973). Fris had chosen a group (of about fifteen men) who were not too 'fanatical' or idle, thus he hoped middle-of-the-roaders in terms of their attitude to police work, and a young, self-confident policeman, whom I shall call Willem, to take me under his wing. I had asked to be assigned to one shift in order to avoid meeting a large number of people on different shifts with whom it would be difficult to build up a relationship (Veendrick and Jongman, 1976: 13, worked with 84 policemen in a period of two months). There was a brief meeting with the station chief, where acquaintance was made with key personnel, and I was ready to begin my field-work.

I could speak and understand Dutch. My command of the language was fairly elementary but I could pick up the meaning of most conversations (incidentally the immersion in field-work dramatically improved my Dutch). This proved vital on a number of levels. Communication with the policemen was much easier than if they had been forced to speak in English. More importantly, interaction with the public was comprehensible and, while it was often necessary to clarify situations afterwards (with the danger of getting a one-sided account), I could follow radio messages, conversations between policemen, and verbal exchanges during incidents. Additionally I could read the extensive documentary material in the station – telegrams, the station diary, reports, charge-sheets, complaints, 'wanted' notices, telex messages, etc.

The first few patrols took place in day-time and much of the activity was routine – stopping and checking the papers of cars, dealing with harmless drunks, and giving information to the public. In the day-time it was pleasant to stroll – although adjusting to the patrolmen's measured tread took some time – around Amsterdam in the sunshine, yet I still felt strange on the streets. Policemen always attract interest and I began to feel that everyone was looking at me too. Gradually, instead of avoiding eye-contact, I began to return stares, forcing people to look away. It was noticeable that, when the policemen interacted with the public, the people concerned seemed naturally to accept my presence as if assuming that I was a policeman in plain clothes. In fact my presence with the police scarcely ever raised comment in six months of field-work. Occasionally the men referred to me as a detective for the public's benefit:

> Riding in a patrol-car along the Zeedijk, Tom noticed a battered Simca parked near a club for Surinamers with a scruffy youth sitting in the passenger's seat. 'Heroin birds', he said and parked further down the street. The driver returned and the car passed us, moving out into the Prins Hendrikkade. We overtook them outside Central Station and forced them to stop. The two policemen each took a door and hauled out the two youths. Tom pushed his suspect up against a bus-shelter and began to search him. In a detached and almost bemused way the young man said immediately, 'I bought a shot in — but otherwise I don't have any stuff on me and I'm not armed, honest, I'll take it easy, don't worry.' Tom wanted to move the cars which were blocking the narrow and busy street in front of the station, and said sternly to the suspect, but with a smile at me behind his back. 'You stay here with your hands up and don't try anything because this detective here [pointing at me] is keeping an eye on you.' I frowned authoritatively. (field notes)

In deciding to work with one group, I also decided to do exactly the same duties as they did. There are shifts, such as the late-evening shift (6 p.m. to 2 p.m.) at weekends, where action is practically guaranteed and it would have been easy to select attractive shifts and avoid dreary shifts (like 7 a.m. until 3 p.m. on Sundays). But my introductory story was that I wanted to observe general police work, without the frills and without selection of particular problems or offences. To share their experience I went on night duty, weekend duty, day duty, and so on. I went on foot patrol, in weather from drenching rain to humid heat, and in cars. During my second period of research (January to March 1975) there were some bitterly cold nights and I went out on patrol wearing two pairs of socks, wool pyjamas inside my trousers, two pullovers, scarf, gloves, and a woollen cap pulled over my ears. I prayed that we would not have to rescue someone from a canal! When the chance arose I showed willingness to help. Sometimes this meant clearing up in the canteen, making coffee, helping with English-speaking suspects or 'customers' asking about something at the counter, giving a hand to load a damaged motor-bike into a van, sweeping glass off the road after an accident, searching a house, helping to lift a drunk off the street, and fetching take-away meals. I began with the notion that my role should be passive but, for a number of reasons, this became more and more difficult.

However, my willingness to adopt precisely the same work hours as the policemen paid dividends in terms of acceptance. In the first place, almost all officers and specialized police services, including most of the detectives, work office hours and the patrolmen are left to themselves in the evenings and at night. This accentuates their ideology that they bear the brunt of the work, on a twenty-four-hour basis, while the bosses are at home watching television or relaxing. The appearance of someone who was prepared to share their life of constantly changing shifts, which causes a number of domestic problems, and of sometimes dreary routine, in all sorts of weather, elicited a positive response. I was seen as willing to experience police life 'where it's at', on the streets, at times when the patrolman was abandoned by his own superiors. I also learnt to distance myself with disparaging remarks from the effete, bohemian image of radical intellectuals. It was not difficult to give vent to my love–hate relationship with academia, but, perceiving the warm response of policemen to a tirade about the idle, shiftless, ideologically blinkered, sexually promiscuous world of sociologists, I began to use this litany to puncture the initial defences of new acquaintances within the police. It always worked.

After my initial month in August 1974 I returned to England, wrote a report analysing the contacts which I had observed on the street between the police and the public (and sent copies to strategically placed people within the Amsterdam Police) and requested a further three months in the following year, which was promptly granted. During that month I had always been accompanied by Willem. Willem was twenty-six, had been a sailor, was unmarried, and was active in sports – namely parachute jumping, boxing, judo and karate (in which he was an instructor, having received advanced training in Japan). The son of a policeman, he was a 'hardliner' interested chiefly in catching criminals and was highly disparaging about other duties. He believed in tough enforcement and hard work. The appearance of a large American-style car in the red-light district would invariably arouse his attention and he would step in its path, hold up an authoritative hand, and politely but firmly ask for the driver's papers. His major interests were finding weapons or drugs.

When I returned to Amsterdam in January 1975, Willem had left for detective training. But the fact that I was prepared to return to the same group for a further three months greatly accelerated my general acceptance. Most of the men soon began to use my Christian name. Also they began to tell me that Willem was a 'fanatic', that he went out of his way to look for work, and that most of them were more easy-going. Indeed, I became worried about the low number of police–public contacts which I was recording until I realized that those of the previous period had been inflated by Willem's 'control everything' philosophy. My analysis of these contacts was really a.. analysis of the work of a 'rate-buster' rather than an indicator of a general picture of police–public relations. It is also fair to add, however, that police work in Amsterdam has a seasonal element responding to the ebb and flow of tourism, and the winter months are the off-season whereas in the full season the days are long and the streets crowded. However, my acceptance seemed to be complete when 'Jan' ostentatiously lifted his buttocks from the seat of the patrol car and broke wind with aplomb. It was the turning point of the research and I felt like Whyte (1955: 318) stumbling on the informal social structure of Cornerville.

I soon found that some policemen were more sympathetic to me than others, some were more fun to be with, and some always seemed to be getting interesting cases. I now had a floating role free from a mentor, where I could more or less choose with whom I patrolled. I could go to the roster and select a car or a foot patrol and ask the sergeant if it was all right. More and more I went out in cars, not simply because I was lazy or to get out of the cold, but because they were linked by radio with headquarters and tended to get the most interesting calls. The foot patrols were in radio contact with the station but were limited by their beat area and their restricted mobility. More and more I went out with a select half of the group and tried to avoid the dull or uncommunicative other half. I got to know these men well and one of them, 'Hans', almost filled a 'Doc' role (Whyte, 1955: 291, was adopted by Doc in Cornerville) because he was so perceptive and articulate.

By now we had shared many incidents together and my regular appearance had led to me being as familiar as a piece of furniture. Hans, for example, would come and get me if something interesting was happening such as plain-clothes duties. Working on tips or with a specific goal, these occasions usually produced results and were much sought after by the men who welcomed the break from uniform and the chance to do some 'real' police work. Once Hans rushed into the canteen and beckoned to me. Three men in plain clothes were to move in on a suspected drugs deal in a hotel. On arrival at the hotel the suspects had just left for the train to

Switzerland. We rushed off and arrived at the station with minutes to spare and delayed the train. I noticed a young man and woman in a compartment but Tom said we were looking for three people, not two. I insisted on asking for their passports because I felt intuitively that they might be the suspects. They were, and we started to search the compartment. The train could not wait for more than a few minutes. Suddenly Hans pulled out a small packet of white powder from behind the central heating and shouted 'Bingo!' 'What's that?' asked the youth. 'Sugar?' said Hans, contemptuously slapping the man's face with the packet. Handcuffed, they were hauled off to the station. The pleasure at being right was an indicator that by now I had a strong identification with the work of the patrolmen. I considered them my colleagues, felt a unity with the group, and was prepared to defend them in case of physical (or intellectual) attack (Punch, 1977).

At the same time some of the men began to treat me almost as a colleague (I say 'almost' because collegiality is highly prized among policemen), and would give me the portable radio to carry or ask me to hold a suspect's arm. Once I was handcuffed to a suspect to prevent him running away and on another occasion a policeman asked me to hold his pistol while he handcuffed a suspect. I felt somewhat foolish as I stood gingerly holding a pistol in the middle of the street while onlookers stared dumbly at the arrest. But more and more I became involved in a participant role. I chased people, searched people, searched cars, searched houses, held people, and even shouted at people who abused my 'colleagues'. Fortunately I was never placed in a situation where I had to decide whether or not to fight on behalf of the policemen. In the few violent occasions that occurred I found that my reactions were so slow and my inability to decide what to do so chronic that the incident was over before I could weigh in. As if I believed in the cool voice of academic reason, I used to rush around the combatants futilely imploring them to calm down.

In fact, during the research, nobody aimed a fist or a gun at me. Sometimes I would stand between two squabbling drunks to show the patrolmen that I was not frightened. But, in fact, I always felt fortified by the presence of two policemen (normally I am a physical and moral coward). There was frequently an element of danger and yet it never seemed very real. On numerous occasions we went into buildings with drawn pistols or arrested people who were thought to be armed. But I never had to lead the charge and could simply stay to one side or stand behind a pillar. Probably there was more danger in a high-speed chase through the narrow, cobbled streets, but some element of danger attends all observation with the police. There were frequent raids, for example, on clubs frequented by Surinamers, and their hostility to the police, based on claims of racial prejudice and mistreatment, made these potentially explosive occasions. Normally, raids would consist of at least six or eight men and yet if a real fight had developed then we would have been in trouble and hopelessly outnumbered. Normally I stayed by the door because I was told that to walk unarmed in plain clothes through a densely crowded club was asking for a knife in your back. Such situations were probably the most stressful that I encountered – as opposed to confronting victims injured in assaults or accidents – because of the intense hostility directed at me on the assumption that I was a policeman.

As with observation on some deviant and criminal groups, there arose the ethical question as to the observer's reaction to witnessing misbehaviour on the part of the policemen. The literature on the police alerts one to widespread and deeply engrained malpractices such as corruption, mistreatment of suspects, racial prejudice, and denial of legal rights to suspects (Humphry, 1972; Walker Report, 1968; Sherman, 1974). Initially I came to the conclusion that these abuses, amply documented in English and American material, were largely absent in Amsterdam policing. In six months graft and corruption were scarcely mentioned, not even jokingly or on informal occasions out of duty, and revelations of such practices in the papers were almost nonexistent.

In the summer of 1976 my contacts with the Warmoesstraat had tailed off as I had become more and more involved in writing. Around that time there were rumours internally of dubious police practices related to the Chinese gambling and drugs world. One evening I went to Hans's flat for a celebration and several policemen began talking excitedly about corruption. I learnt more in that evening, thanks to the liberating effects of alcohol, than in all my field-work. It was not so much a series of shocking personal revelations – indeed, the whole tenor of the discussion emphasized the honesty of the men present (one could hardly expect it to be otherwise) – but more that a subterranean police culture which had largely escaped me suddenly emerged. There was talk of policemen sleeping with prostitutes, accepting bribes, keeping an extra round from the range to use in case of a hasty shot which the constable did not want to report, covering up for colleagues in delicate situations, and running messages for members of the Chinese underworld. Hans and Tom explained, 'How much do you think you found out when you were with us? You wrote somewhere that you thought we were open-hearted. Well, we only let you see what we wanted you to see. You only saw about fifty per cent. We showed you only a half of the story.' Bert then said that as far as he was concerned I had seen ninety per cent. Tom had had a young constable in tow for three weeks and he turned to him and said, 'How long have we been working together? Three weeks? Well, I haven't let you see a thing. Not a thing'.

It would almost require another book to go into the intricacies of that corruption scandal, which did not really touch the uniformed patrolmen but was focused on plain-clothes men in vice and drugs, and Hans almost deserves a book to himself. He would have made a good sociologist. But I cannot go into detail because I identify the station where I worked and individuals would be easily recognizable. To capture the stories behind the stories it would probably be necessary to write a novel, as Wambaugh (1970, 1972, 1975) has successfully done for police work in Los Angeles. However, it is worth noting that my favourable field impressions were based on a partial picture and that keeping in contact with my informants proved invaluable during the writing-up phase. The field-work may have been essential in gaining the trust of these men, but it is probably true that I have learned far more about the police since I stopped observation, and am still learning.

After the research period in early 1975, there followed two more months in July and August when I also carried out a number of interviews (Punch, 1976). I interviewed policemen of all ranks from commissioner to constable as well as a number of people outside the force. The interviews were carried out after I had developed rapport with the policemen and were informed by my practical experiences on the street. There was no attempt at a random sample and I simply selected people I knew or who occupied important organizational positions. In the closed social world of a police force, interviewing strangers can be a futile and frustrating business, and interviews with constables not in my group were not very successful. For police–citizen encounters on the street I had a check-list, based on Reiss's (1971) research, which enabled me to generalize about the sorts of people with whom the police interact. Thus, I could call on documentary and internal statistical evidence, interviews and accounts, and statistical data on suspects and other groups (for example, using age, sex, nationality, attitudes to the police, and police attitudes to the public) based on observations from police work on the street.

In the meantime I had taken up a teaching appointment in The Netherlands. Initially I suffered withdrawal symptoms and hankered after the atmosphere of the station and the friends I had made among the policemen. The university seemed a pedantic and unreal world and I had considerable difficulty in readjusting.

Fortunately, I more or less had 'carte blanche' to return to the station. This proved less and less satisfying, as the group gradually split up when people applied to forces in other towns or were selected for the detectives. But the good old days had gone, and my appearances gradually tailed off, although I remained in informal contact with some officers and some men. But as Polsky (1971: 145) says, field-work is fun. To a certain extent it is a 'holiday' from academic rituals and it provides an opportunity to get away from books, papers, essays, seminars, and sedentary pontificating on the ills of the world. Working with the police takes you out of the university and into the entrails of society, where you witness incidents from sudden birth to sudden death. And basically all you have to do is watch and listen. The patrolmen, for instance, cannot escape the paperwork surrounding modern policing, but all such onerous tasks I could avoid. I could enter extreme situations yet without being responsible for settling them. In the car, I could lean back and watch pretty girls on the streets while the men kept their eyes open for incidents (as well as the girls). In the car you feel connected with the rising and falling rhythm of the city. Amsterdam is a beautiful city, marred in day-time by teeming streets, clogged with traffic. We, however, could drive through empty streets at night and cruise effortlessly alongside the canals watching the first rays of sunrise break over the artistic gables of the house tops. In effect, we saw Amsterdam at its best, and also at its worst.

4. Comment

In this final section I shall endeavour to generalize about my field experiences with the Amsterdam Police. Basically the problems encountered in researching the police overlap to a considerable extent with the dilemmas found in most observational studies (McCall and Simmons, 1969). There are some specific aspects peculiar to the police – such as danger, shift-work, the visibility of uniforms (and hence the visibility of the accompanying researcher), the ethical ambivalences of police work, etc. – and there now exist enough studies for someone to think of collecting reports of field-work with the police in order to draw up an analytical balance-sheet as to the parallels with, and divergences from, the standard accounts of qualitative and observational research. My research was given an added dimension by the fact that I was working in another culture and in a foreign language, unlike the majority of police studies to date. Of course the Amsterdam Police does not, to my knowledge, practise cannibalism, and popping over the North Sea is not like Evans-Pritchard setting off stoically into the bush. But, at times, the backwardness of Dutch sociology and its reluctance to enter the field made me feel like a lone anthropologist, addicted to his 'tribe' and resentful of the lack of understanding about it in the wider society (Clarke, 1975).

A favourable aspect of working with the police is that it is a routinized, bureaucratic organization. With exceptions, you know when a shift begins and ends. And if you want to interview 'Constable Van der Linden' for two hours beginning at six o'clock, then the sergeant arranges for him to be free. The bureaucracy will work for you and organize things for you and that can greatly facilitate field-work. It avoids some of the aimless, diffuse aspects of field-work with deviant groups where the researcher is dependent on the mood and behaviour of the group and where prior planning of research activities proves almost impossible. There was at my disposal a room for interviewing, a photocopying machine for documentary material, a telephone for making appointments, and transport to bring me to incidents or to bring me home (once I was brought home in a patrol-car when I was ill and once to collect a cheque-book in order to get some money out of the bank). I even had a police bicycle lent to me because I had no car for getting home when the public transport stopped running. For much of the research I had no effective institutional base in The Netherlands so that these facilities greatly assisted the research.

Otherwise, the dilemmas and pitfalls of participant observation with the police are little different from those of studying other groups. There is an element of danger, but that is also true of research with certain deviant groups – Yablonsky (1973: 94) was threatened during his communes research, and Hunter Thompson (1967: 283) was beaten up by Hell's Angels. It may be necessary to absolve the police from responsibility in case of accident and sign a document stating that the researcher patrols at his own risk. This was not necessary in my case, but I did take out special insurance coverage.

There is, too, always the question-mark surrounding the extent to which individuals modify their behaviour in the presence of the observer. My feeling echoes that of Becker (1970: 46) in believing that people do not keep up such an act for long and that what they are engaged in is often more important to them than the fact that an outsider is present. A policeman may speak more politely to a citizen because a researcher is at his elbow, but in many situations he does not have time to think but must react instantly. In any event, my appearances were so commonplace that after a while I do not believe people noticed me during routine cases. However, the more I was accepted the more they expected me to act *as a colleague.* In my willingness to be accepted by the policemen I over-identified perhaps too readily and this doubtless endangered my research role. For the patrol group is a cohesive social unit and the policeman's world is full of seductive interests so that it is all too easy to 'go native'.

There also exists a potential dilemma of witnessing crimes either on the part of suspects, or, indeed, on the part of the policemen. Would it infringe the research role to appear as a witness against a suspect? Would one feel obliged to testify against a policeman who had been observed in violation of the law? The sociologist has no right to privileged information and may have to be prepared to suffer for protecting his respondents. Fortunately, this problem did not arise in my study. There is, however, a more general ethical issue as raised by Becker's (1967) query, 'Whose side are we on?' Frequently, research studies have emphasized the exposure of pernicious practices within control institutions and have tended to identify with those groups who suffer from such practices (Bianchi *et al.*, 1975). In researching the police I was conscious that many academic colleagues have a critical, if not hostile, perspective on the police and this made me somewhat defensive about my research. Some radical criminologists, for example, had advised me to infiltrate the police organization (they emphasized the advantage I enjoyed in being trusted by the police), to collect damaging material and to photocopy documents, and then to expose the police in the most embarrassing light possible. I rejected this espionage model of research, but there remained one's personal feelings about people who come into contact with the police.

During my study I have often shared the back seat of the patrol-car with a handcuffed suspect who had just been deprived of his freedom. Naturally this first-hand observation of suspects raises a number of moral questions about the nature and effects of law and crime and about the law-enforcement process. My own feelings were to have little sympathy for individuals concerned in crimes of violence and in dealing in hard drugs. It was difficult to get worked up about many of the minor offences, such as shoplifting, and the suspects were often either stupid, in drawing attention to themselves, or else just unlucky at being caught. But to a large extent I accepted police work as an enterprise and 'morally' approved of most of its activities. This feeling was accentuated by the fact that the predatory underworld of Amsterdam holds little romantic appeal for me. Quite frankly, the procession of pickpockets, ponces, prostitutes, dealers, muggers, car thieves, drunken drivers, burglars, bouncers, army deserters, shoplifters, delinquents and suspects accused of violence with knife or gun, were simply not the sort of people that, face to face, have a Damon Runyon appeal. And if the eye and ear are important for collecting data, then why not the nose? Some of these people literally stink. Perhaps that tells the reader more about me than about criminals, but I have seen, and smelt, enough suspects to raise severe doubts as to my ability of identifying with them. The role of drugs in criminality in Amsterdam can mean that suspects are in a very poor physical and hygienic state, while the city-centre world of bars and vice attracts a species of over-weight, over-dressed, loud-mouthed café-dwellers who seem willing to beat someone up at the slightest excuse. For a number of reasons, then, I reservedly accepted the side I was on.

There is often no definite end-point to a field study. I was restricted by teaching obligations and half of the research was carried out in time that was technically vacation. In total I spent about six months on patrol. This seems to be the acceptable *minimum* and compares unfavourably with classical anthropological studies, with Whyte's (1955) four years in Cornerville, and Suttles' (1968) three years in the Near West Side of Chicago. But, finally, I should like to re-endorse my earlier remarks that observation is essential to penetrating the police culture. Immersion in the field also provides a degree of life experience that is lacking in most academic environments. The police force is an institution concerned minutely with regulating everyday behaviour and with applying societal norms. Its work is intrinsically interesting on a human level and its performance socially important in terms of providing data about a largely closed social world. Policemen work at the nerve-edge of society, where control is exercised, where sanctions are applied, and where crises are resolved. They inhabit profane areas of society, where good citizens fear to tread, and face situations where the buck can no longer be passed on. Encounters become instant morality plays with the abstract values of our civilization – justice, liberty, equality before the law, etc. – being daily redefined in unedifying and irresolute conflicts accompanied by blood, blasphemy and violence. The magic and the mundane, the routine and the ritual, the sacred and the profane mingle in police work into a blend irresistible to the hackneyed plots of television serials and, less conspicuously, into rich and fruitful material for the study of social interaction. Participant observation enables one to go behind the public front of a conspicuous service bureaucracy to witness 'backstage' behaviour when the actors are off-stage, not performing to a public, and not peddling stereotyped scripts for the benefit of bystanders. In essence, the appeal of field-work is that it is concerned with

real people and that confrontation with people, in all their baffling
complexity, is a fruitful antidote to a positivist methodology and
a natural science model for the social sciences.

References

Bagley, C. (1973) 'Holland's red niggers', *Race Today*, March: 6–7.
Becker, H.S. (1967) 'Whose side are we on?', *Social Problems*, 239–47.
Becker, H.S. (1970) *Sociological Work*. London: Allen Lane.
Bianchi, H., Simondi, M. and Taylor, I. (eds) (1975) *Deviance and Control in Europe*. London: Wiley.
Bittner, E. (1967) 'The police on skid row: a study of peace-keeping', *American Sociological Review*, 32 (5): 699–715.
Brunt, L. (1975) 'Anthropological fieldwork in The Netherlands', in P. Kloos and H.T.M. Claessen (eds), *Current Anthropology in The Netherlands*. The Hague: Government Publishing Office.
Buckner, H.T. (1967) 'The police: the culture of a social control agency', PhD thesis, University of California at Berkeley.
Cain, M. (1973) *Society and the Policeman's Role*. London: Routledge & Kegan Paul.
Clarke, M. (1975) 'Survival in the field: implications of personal experience in fieldwork', *Theory and Society*, 2 (1): 95–123.
Faris, R.E.L. (1970) *Chicago Sociology*. Chicago: University of Chicago Press.
Fox, J.C. and Lundman, R.J. (1974) 'Problems and strategies in gaining research access in police organizations', *Criminology*, 12 (1): 52–69.
Goffman, E. (1959) *The Presentation of Self in Everyday Life*. Harmondsworth: Penguin.
Goffman, E. (1972) *Interaction Ritual*. Harmondsworth: Penguin.
Humphry, D. (1972) *Police Power and Black People*. London: Panther.
Johnson, J.M. (1975) *Doing Field Research*. New York: Free Press.
Kirkham, G.L. (1974) 'From professor to patrolman', *Journal of Police Science and Administration*, 2 (2): 127–37.
Kirkham, G.L. (1976) *Signal Zero*. Philadelphia: Lippincott.
Maanen, J. van (1975) 'Police socialisation', *Administrative Science Quarterly*, 20: 207–28.
McCall, G. and Simmons, J.L. (eds) (1969) *Issues in Participant Observation*. Reading, MA: Addison-Wesley.
Manning, P.K. (1972) 'Observing the police', in J.D. Douglas (ed.), *Research on Deviance*. New York: Random House.
Manning, P.K. (1974a) 'Police lying', *Urban Life and Culture*, 3 (3): 283–305.
Manning, P.K. (1974b) 'Dramatic aspects of policing: selected propositions', *Sociology and Social Research*, 59 (1): 21–9.
Phillips, D. (1973) *Abandoning Method*. London: Jossey-Bass.
Polsky, N. (1971) *Hustlers, Beats, and Others*. Harmondsworth: Penguin.
Punch, M. (1974a) 'The policeman's role in the community: a field note', *Nederlands Tijdschrift voor Criminologie*, 16: 59–70.
Punch, M. (1974b) 'Area bobbies, Rotterdam style', *Police*, 6 (8): 14–15.
Punch, M. (1976a) 'Report on workshop: police action and the public', in L. van Outrive and S. Rizkalla (eds), 'Final Report: International Seminar on Police Research', Catholic University of Leuven and University of Montreal.

Punch, M. (1976b): 'Front-line Amsterdam: policework in the inner city', *British Journal of Law and Society*, 3 (2): 218–32.

Punch, M. (1976c): *Fout is Fout: Gesprekken met de Politie in de Binnenstad van Amsterdam*. Meppel: Boom.

Punch, M. (1977) 'Warmoesstraat: einde afschuifsysteem', *Vrij Nederland*, 25 June.

Punch, M. and Naylor, T. (1973) 'The police: a social service', *New Society*, 24 (554): 358–61.

Quinney, R. (1970) *The Social Reality of Crime*. Boston: Little, Brown.

Reiss, A.J. Jr (1971) *The Police and the Public*. New Haven, CT: Yale University Press.

Rubinstein, J. (1973) *City Police*. New York: Ballantine.

Sherman, L.W. (1974) *Police Corruption*. New York: Anchor.

Skolnick, J.H. (1975): *Justice Without Trial*, 2nd edn. New York: Wiley.

Suttles, G. (1968) *The Social Order of the Slum*. Chicago: Chicago University Press.

Thompson, H. (1967) *Hell's Angels*. Harmondsworth: Penguin.

Toebosch, J. (1975) 'Politie en wetenschap', *Rijks Politie Magazine*, 16 (9): 5–7.

Veendrick, L. and Jongman, R. (1976) *Met de Politie op Pad*. Groningen: Kriminologisch Instituut.

Walker Report (1968) *Rights in Conflict*. New York: Bantam.

Wambaugh, J. (1970) *The New Centurions*. Boston, MA: Little, Brown.

Wambaugh, J. (1972) *The Blue Knight*. Boston, MA: Little, Brown.

Wambaugh, J. (1975) *The Choirboys*. New York: Delacorte Press.

Westley, W.A. (1970) *Violence and the Police: A Sociological Study of Law, Custom and Morality*. Cambridge, MA: MIT Press.

Whyte, W.F. (1955) *Street Corner Society*, 2nd edn. Chicago: Chicago University Press.

Yablonsky, L. (1973) *Hippy Trip*. Harmondsworth: Penguin.

16

Increasing the Generalizability
of Qualitative Research

Janet Ward Schofield

Traditional Views of Generalizability

Campbell and Stanley (1963) laid the groundwork for much current thinking on the issue of generalizability just over twenty-five years ago in a groundbreaking chapter in the *Handbook of Research on Teaching*. They wrote, '*External validity* asks the question of *generalizability*: To what populations, settings, treatment variables, and measurement variables can the effect be generalized?' (1963: 175). They then went on to list four specific threats to external validity: the interaction of testing and the experimental treatment, the interaction of selection and treatment, reactive arrangements, and the interference of multiple treatments with one another. Although Campbell and Stanley specifically included populations, settings, treatments, and measurement variables as dimensions relevant to the concept of external validity, the aspect of external validity that has typically received the lion's share of attention in textbook and other treatments of the concept is generalizing to and across populations. This may well be due to the fact that, because of advances in sampling theory in survey research, it is possible to draw samples from even a very large and heterogeneous population and then to generalize to that population using the logic of probability statistics.

Campbell and Stanley (1963), as well as many others in the quantitative tradition, see the attempt to design research so that abstract generalizations can be drawn as a worthy effort, although issues connected with internal validity are typically given even higher priority. Thus researchers in the quantitative tradition have devoted considerable thought to the question of how the generalizability of experimental and quasi-experimental studies can be enhanced. Such efforts are consistent with the fact that many

From E.W. Eisner and A. Peshkin (eds), *Qualitative Inquiry in Education: The Continuing Debate*, Teachers College Press, New York, 1989, pp. 201–32.

quantitatively oriented researchers would agree with Smith (1975: 88) that 'the goal of science is to be able to generalize findings to diverse populations and times'.

In contrast to the interest shown in external validity among quantitatively oriented researchers, the methodological literature on qualitative research has paid little attention to this issue, at least until quite recently. For example, Dobbert's (1982) text on qualitative research methods devotes an entire chapter to issues of validity and reliability but does no more than mention the issue of generalizability in passing on one or two pages. Two even more recent books, Kirk and Miller's *Reliability and Validity in Qualitative Research* (1986) and Berg's *Qualitative Research Methods for the Social Sciences* (1989), ignore the issue of external validity completely. The major factor contributing to the disregard of the issue of generalizability in the qualitative methodological literature appears to be a widely shared view that it is unimportant, unachievable, or both.

Many qualitative researchers actively reject generalizability as a goal. For example, Denzin writes:

> The interpretivist rejects generalization as a goal and never aims to draw randomly selected samp'es of human experience. For the interpretivist every instance of social interaction, if thickly described (Geertz, 1973), represents a slice from the life world that is the proper subject matter for interpretive inquiry. . . . Every topic . . . must be seen as carrying its own logic, sense of order, structure, and meaning. (1983: 133–4)

Although not all researchers in the qualitative tradition reject generalization so strongly, many give it very low priority or see it as essentially irrelevant to their goals. One factor contributing to qualitative researchers' historical tendency to regard the issue of external validity as irrelevant and hence to disregard it is that this research tradition has been closely linked to cultural anthropology, with its emphasis on the study of exotic cultures. This work is often valued for its intrinsic interest, for showing the rich variety and possible range of human behavior, and for serving a historical function by describing traditional cultures before they change in an increasingly interconnected and homogeneous world. For researchers doing work of this sort, the goal is to describe a specific group in fine detail and to explain the patterns that exist, certainly not to discover general laws of human behavior.

Practically speaking, no matter what one's philosophical stance on the importance of generalizability, it is clear that numerous characteristics that typify the qualitative approach are not consistent with achieving external validity as it has generally been conceptualized.

For example, the traditional focus on single-case studies in qualitative research is obviously inconsistent with the requirements of statistical sampling procedures, which are usually seen as fundamental to generalizing from the data gathered in a study to some larger population. This fact is often cited as a major weakness of the case study approach (Bolgar, 1965; Shaughnessy and Zechmeister, 1985).

However, the incompatibility between classical conceptions of external validity and fundamental aspects of the qualitative approach goes well beyond this. To give just one example, the experimental tradition emphasizes replicability of results, as is apparent in Krathwohl's statement: 'The heart of external validity is replicability. Would the results be reproducible in those target instances to which one intends to generalize – the population, situation, time, treatment form or format, measures, study designs and procedures?' (1985: 123). Yet at the heart of the qualitative approach is the assumption that a piece of qualitative research is very much influenced by the researcher's individual attributes and perspectives. The goal is *not* to produce a standardized set of results that any other careful researcher in the same situation or studying the same issues would have produced. Rather it is to produce a coherent and illuminating description of and perspective on a situation that is based on and consistent with detailed study of that situation. Qualitative researchers have to question seriously the *internal* validity of their work if other researchers reading their field notes feel the evidence does not support the way in which they have depicted the situation. However, they do not expect other researchers in a similar or even the same situation to replicate their findings in the sense of independently coming up with a precisely similar conceptualization. As long as the other researchers' conclusions are not inconsistent with the original account, differences in the reports would not generally raise serious questions related to validity or generalizability.

In fact, I would argue that, except perhaps in multisite qualitative studies, which will be discussed later in this paper, it is impractical to make precise replication a criterion of generalizability in qualitative work. Qualitative research is so arduous that it is unlikely that high-quality researchers could be located to engage in the relatively unexciting task of conducting a study designed specifically to replicate a previous one. Yet studies not designed specifically for replication are unlikely to be conducted in a way that allows good assessment of the replicability issue. Of course it is possible, even likely, that specific ideas or conclusions from a piece of qualitative work can stimulate further research of a qualitative or quantitative nature that provides information on the replicability of that one aspect of a study. However, any piece of qualitative research is likely to contain so many individual descriptive and conceptual components that replicating it on a piece-by-piece basis would be a major undertaking.

The Increasing Interest in Generalizability in the Qualitative Tradition

In the past decade, interest in the issue of generalizability has increased markedly for qualitative researchers involved in the study of education. Books by Patton (1980), Guba and Lincoln (1981), and Noblit and Hare (1988), as well as papers by Stake (1978), Kennedy (1979), and others, have all dealt with this issue in more than a cursory fashion. Two factors seem to be important in accounting for this increase in attention to the issue of generalizability. First, the uses of qualitative research have shifted quite markedly in the past decade or two. In the area of education, qualitative research is not an approach used primarily to study exotic foreign or deviant local cultures. Rather it has become an approach used widely in both evaluation research and basic research on educational issues in our own society. The issue of generalizability assumes real importance in both kinds of work.

The shift in the uses of qualitative work that occurred during the 1970s was rapid and striking. The most obvious part of this shift was the inclusion of major qualitative components in large-scale evaluation research efforts, which had previously been almost exclusively quantitative in nature (Fetterman, 1982; Firestone and Herriott, 1984). The acceptance of qualitative research as a valid and potentially rich approach to evaluation progressed to the point that Wolcott wrote, with only some exaggeration, 'By the late 1970s the term "ethnography" . . . had become synonymous with "evaluation" in the minds of many educators' (1982: 82). Evaluations are expensive and time-consuming undertakings. Although formative evaluations are usually site-specific, the worth of a summative evaluation is greatly enhanced to the extent it can inform program and policy decisions relating to other sites. In fact, as Cronbach (1982) points out, when summative evaluations are reported, no more than a fraction of the audience is interested primarily in the specific program and setting that was the object of the study. Even at the study site itself, by the time the evaluation is completed, changes may well have occurred that have important consequences for program functioning and goal achievement. Thus the question of whether an evaluation's findings can usefully be generalized to a later point in time at the site at which the evaluation was conducted is an issue that, although often ignored, requires real consideration.

The issue of generalizability is also salient for more basic qualitative research on educational issues in this country. Funding agencies providing resources for qualitative studies of educational issues are presumably interested in shedding light on these issues generally, not just as they are experienced at one site. For example, I am currently directing a qualitative study of computer usage in an urban high school. It is clear that the impetus for the funding of this study by the Office of Naval Research derived from concerns about the Navy's own computer-based education and training efforts, not from concerns about the public schools. Quite apart from the goals of funding agencies, many qualitative researchers themselves hope to accomplish more than describing the culture of the specific school or classroom that they have chosen to study. For example, Peshkin writes of his study of school and community in a small town in Illinois, 'I hoped . . . to explicate some reality which was not merely confined to other places just like Mansfield' (1982: 63), a hope tellingly reflected in the title of his book, *Growing Up American* (1978), as opposed to 'Growing Up in Illinois' or 'Growing Up in Mansfield'. This desire to have one's work be broadly useful is no doubt often stimulated by concern over the state of education in our country today. It is also clearly reinforced by the fact that, unlike most readers of ethnographic reports of exotic cultures, most readers of qualitative reports on American education have had considerable exposure during their own school years to at least one version of the culture described. Thus, unless the researcher chooses a very atypical site or presents an unusually insightful analysis of what is happening, the purely descriptive value of the study may be undercut or discounted.

So far I have argued that qualitative research's shift in both purpose and locale in the last decade or two has contributed to an increased interest in generalizability among qualitative researchers. There is yet one other factor contributing to this trend – the striking rapprochement between qualitative and quantitative methodologies that has occurred in the last decade (Cronbach *et al.*, 1980; Filstead, 1979; Reichardt and Cook, 1979; Spindler, 1982). Exemplifying this trend is the shift in the position of Donald Campbell. Campbell and Stanley at one point contended that the 'one-shot case study', which is one way of describing much qualitative research, has 'such a total absence of control as to be of almost no scientific value' (1963: 176). However, more recently

Campbell wrote a paper to 'correct some of [his] own prior excesses in describing the case study approach' (1979: 52) in which he takes the, for many, rather startling position that when qualitative and quantitative results conflict, 'the quantitative results should be regarded as suspect until the reasons for the discrepancy are well understood' (1979: 52).

One result of the rapprochement that has occurred is that qualitative and quantitative researchers are more in contact with each other's traditions than had typically been the case heretofore. As is often the case when a dominant tradition makes contact with a minority one, the culture and standards of the dominant group make a significant impact on the members of the minority group. This trend has most likely been reinforced by the fact that a great deal of the qualitative research on education conducted in the past fifteen years has been embedded within multimethod evaluation projects undertaken by private research firms that have traditionally specialized in quantitative research. Thus the concept of external validity and the associated issue of generalizability have been made salient for qualitative researchers, whose own tradition has not predisposed them to have given the issue a great deal of thought.

Reconceptualizing Generalizability

Although many qualitative researchers have begun to recognize the importance of dealing with the issue of generalizability, it is clear that the classical view of external validity is of little help to qualitative researchers interested in finding ways of enhancing the likelihood that their work will speak to situations beyond the one immediately studied – that is, that it will be to some extent generalizable. The idea of sampling from a population of sites in order to generalize to the larger population is simply and obviously unworkable in all but the rarest situations for qualitative researchers, who often take several years to produce an intensive case study of one or a very small number of sites. Thus most of the work on generalizability by qualitative researchers in this decade has dealt with developing a *conception* of generalizability that is useful and appropriate for qualitative work.

A second approach to the issue of generalizability in qualitative research has been very different. A number of individuals have worked on ways of gaining generality through the synthesis of pre-existing qualitative studies. For example, Noblit and Hare (1988) have recently published a slim volume on meta-ethnography. Substantially earlier, Lucas (1974) and Yin and Heald (1975) had developed what they call the 'case survey method'. Ragin (1987) has presented yet another way of synthesizing qualitative studies, one that employs Boolean algebra. I will discuss these approaches to generalizing from qualitative case studies briefly at the end of this chapter. [This discussion is omitted here.] At the moment, I would like to focus on issues connected with the first approach – that is, with transforming and adapting the classical conception of external validity such that it is suitable for qualitative work.

Important and frequently cited discussions of conceptions of generalizability appropriate in qualitative work can be found in Guba and Lincoln (1981, 1982), Goetz and LeCompte (1984), and Stake (1978). Guba and Lincoln's stance on the issue of generalizability is aptly summarized in two excerpts of their own words. Guba and Lincoln write:

> It is virtually impossible to imagine any human behavior that is not heavily mediated by the context in which it occurs. One can easily conclude that generalizations that are intended to be context free will have little that is useful to say about human behavior. (1981: 62)

They go on to say:

> The aim of (naturalistic) inquiry is to develop an idiographic body of knowledge. This knowledge is best encapsulated in a series of 'working hypotheses' that describe the individual case. Generalizations are impossible since phenomena are neither time- nor context-free (although some transferability of these hypotheses may be possible from situation to situation, depending on the degree of temporal and contextual similarity). (1982: 238)

Given these views, Guba and Lincoln call for replacing the concept of generalizability with that of 'fittingness'. Specifically, they argue that the concept of 'fittingness', with its emphasis on analyzing the degree to which the situation studied matches other situations in which one is interested, provides a more realistic and workable way of thinking about the generalizability of research results than do more classical approaches. A logical consequence of this approach is an emphasis on supplying a substantial amount of information about the entity studied and the setting in which that entity was found. Without such information, it is impossible to make an informed judgment about whether the conclusions drawn from the study of any particular site are useful in understanding other sites.

Goetz and LeCompte (1984) place a similar emphasis on the importance of clear and detailed description as a means of allowing decisions about the extent to which findings from one study are applicable to other situations. Specifically, they argue that qualitative studies gain their potential for applicability to other situations by providing what they call 'comparability' and 'translatability'. The former term

> refers to the degree to which components of a study – including the units of analysis, concepts generated, population characteristics, and settings – are sufficiently well described and defined that other researchers can use the results of the study as a basis for comparison. (1984: 228)

Translatability is similar but refers to a clear description of one's theoretical stance and research techniques.

Stake (1978) starts out by agreeing with many critics of qualitative methods that one cannot confidently generalize from a single case to a target population of which that case is a member, since single members often poorly represent whole populations. However, he then goes on to argue that it is possible to use a process he calls 'naturalistic generalization' to take the findings from one study and apply them to understanding another *similar* situation. He argues that through experience individuals come to be able to use both explicit comparisons between situations and tacit knowledge of those same situations to form useful naturalistic generalizations.

Several major themes can be found in the work of qualitative researchers who have written recently on the concept of generalizability. Whether it is Guba and Lincoln (1981, 1982) writing of fittingness, Goetz and LeCompte (1984) writing of translatability and comparability, or Stake (1978) discussing naturalistic generalizations, the emerging view shared by many qualitative researchers appears to involve several areas of consensus. First of all, there is broad agreement that generalizability in the sense of producing laws that apply universally is not a useful standard or goal for qualitative research. In fact, most qualitative researchers would join Cronbach (1982) in arguing that this is not a useful or obtainable goal for any kind of research in the social sciences. Second, most researchers writing on generalizability in the qualitative tradition agree that their rejection of generalizability as a search for broadly applicable laws is not a rejection of the idea that studies in one situation can be used to speak to or to help form a judgment about other situations. Third, as should be readily apparent from the preceding discussion, current thinking on generalizability argues that thick descriptions (Ryle, cited in Geertz, 1973) are vital. Such descriptions of both the site in which the studies are conducted and of the site to which one wishes to generalize are crucial in allowing one to search for the similarities and differences between the situations. As Kennedy (1979) points out, analysis of these similarities and differences then makes it possible to make a reasoned judgment about the extent to which we can use the findings from one study as a 'working hypothesis', to use Cronbach's (1982) term, about what might occur in the other situation. Of course, the generally unstated assumption underlying this view is that our knowledge of the phenomena under study is sufficient to direct attention to important rather than superficial similarities and differences. To the extent that our understanding is flawed, important similarities or differences may inadvertently be disregarded.

Three Targets of Generalization

Given the growing emphasis on generalizability in qualitative research and the emerging consensus about how the concept of generalizability might most usefully be viewed by qualitative researchers, two questions present themselves:

To what do we want to generalize?
How can we design qualitative studies in a way that maximizes their generalizability?

It is to these two questions that I will devote the majority of the rest of this chapter. Although I will use the term *generalize* here and elsewhere, it is important that the reader recognize that I am not talking about generalization in the classical sense. Rather, I use it to refer to the process as conceptualized by those qualitative researchers to whose work I have just referred.

I believe that it is useful for qualitative researchers interested in the study of educational processes and institutions to try to generalize to three domains: to *what is*, to *what may be*, and to *what could be*. I will deal with these possibilities one at a time, providing the rationale for striving to generalize to each of these kinds of situations and then suggesting some ideas on how studies can actually be designed to do this.

Studying What Is

From one perspective the study of any ongoing social situation, no matter how idiosyncratic or bizarre, is studying *what is*. But when I use the phrase *studying what is*, I mean to refer to studying the typical, the common, or the ordinary. The goal of describing and understanding cultures or institutions as they typically are is an appropriate aim for much current qualitative research on educational institutions and processes. If policy-makers need to decide how to change a program or whether to continue it, one very obvious and useful kind of information is information on how the program usually functions, what is usually achieved, and the like. Thus the goal of studying *what is* is one important aim for many kinds of summative evaluations. It is also appropriate outside of the area of evaluation for researchers hoping to provide a picture of the current educational scene that can be used for understanding or reflecting on it and possibly improving it. Classic works of this type that focus primarily on *what is* are Wolcott's *The Man in the Principal's Office* (1973) and Jackson's *Life in Classrooms* (1968). If one accepts the goal of designing research to maximize the fit between the research site and *what is* more broadly in society, an obvious question that arises is how this can be accomplished within the context of the qualitative tradition.

Studying the Typical   One approach sometimes used is to study the typical (Bogdan and Biklen, 1981; Goetz and LeCompte, 1984; Patton, 1980; Whyte, 1984). Specifically, I would argue that choosing sites on the basis of their fit with a typical situation is far preferable to choosing on the basis of convenience, a practice that is still quite common.

The suggestion that typicality be weighed heavily in site selection is an idea that needs to be taken both more and less seriously than it currently is. When I say that it needs to be taken more seriously than it currently is, I am suggesting that researchers contemplating selecting a site on the basis of convenience or ease of access need to think more carefully about that decision and to weigh very carefully the possibility of choosing on the basis of some other criterion, such as typicality. When I say that the strategy of selecting a typical site needs to be taken less seriously than it may sometimes be, I intend to point out that choosing a typical site is not a 'quick fix' for the issue of generalizability, because what is typical on one dimension may not be typical on another. For example, Wolcott (1973) chose to focus his ethnographic study of a principal on an individual who was typical of other principals in gender, marital status, age, and so forth. This choice most likely substantially enhanced the range of applicability or generalizability of his study. Yet such a typical principal operating in an atypical school or an atypical system or even an atypical community might well behave very differently from a typical principal in a typical school in a typical system. The solution to this dilemma cannot be found in choosing typicality on every dimension. First of all, not too many typical principals operate in environments that are typical in every way. So this strategy gains less in the realm of generalizability or fittingness than it might appear to at first glance. More important, even if one could achieve typicality in all major dimensions that seem relevant, it is nonetheless clearly true that there would be enough idiosyncracy in any particular situation studied so that one could not transfer findings in an unthinking way from one typical situation to another.

Carried to extremes or taken too seriously, the idea of choosing on the basis of typicality becomes impossible, even absurd. However, as a guiding principle designed to increase the potential applicability of research, it is, I believe, useful. This is especially true if the search for typicality is combined with, rather than seen as a replacement for, a reliance on the kind of thick description emphasized by Guba and Lincoln (1981, 1982), Goetz and LeCompte (1984) and Stake (1978). Selection on the basis of typicality provides the potential for a good 'fit' with many other situations. Thick description provides the information necessary to make informed judgments about the degree and extent of that fit in particular cases of interest.

In arguing that qualitative researchers would do well to seek to study the typical, I am not suggesting that we study the typical defined solely by national norms. Research that followed this prescription would greatly increase our knowledge of typical situations, but in a nation as diverse as the United States, it would provide too restricted, pallid, and homogeneous a view of our educational system. My emphasis on typicality implies that the researcher who has decided on the kind of institution or situation he or she wants to study – an urban ghetto school, a rural consolidated school, or a private Montessori school – should try to select an instance of this kind of situation that is, to the extent possible, typical of its kind. Such an approach suggests, for example, that a researcher interested in studying mathematics teaching choose to observe classrooms that use a popular text and generally accepted modes of instruction, rather than falling for convenience's sake into the study of classrooms that may well do neither of these. Furthermore, to the extent preliminary investigation of possible sites suggests that some or all are atypical in certain regards, careful thought about the possible implications of this atypicality for the topic under study may help to aid in site selection.

In sum, the point of my argument here is that choosing a site for research on the basis of typicality is far more likely to enhance the potential generalizability of one's study than choosing on the basis of convenience or ease of access – criteria that often weigh more heavily than they should. However, even if one chooses on the basis of typicality, one is in no way relieved of the necessity for thick description, for it is foolhardy to think that a typical example will be typical in all important regards. Thus thick description is necessary to allow individuals to ask about the degree of fit between the case studied and the case to which they wish to generalize, even when the fit on some of the basic dimensions looks fairly close.

Performing Multisite Studies   An alternate approach to increasing the generalizability of qualitative research was evident in the sudden proliferation in the 1970s of multisite qualitative studies. Such studies were almost always part of federally funded evaluation efforts focusing on the same issue in a number of settings, using similar data collection and analysis procedures in each place. Well-known examples of this approach include the Study of Dissemination Efforts Supporting School Improvement (Crandall *et al.*, 1983; Huberman and Miles, 1984) and the study of Parental Involvement in Federal Educational Programs (Smith and Robbins, 1984). One of the primary purposes of conducting such multisite studies is to escape what Firestone and Herriott (1984) have called the 'radical particularism' of many case studies and hence to provide a firmer basis for generalization.

The multisite studies conducted in the 1970s were extremely varied, although they were all quite expensive and tended to take several years to complete. At least two kinds of variation have special implications for the extent to which this approach actually seems likely to produce results that are a good basis for generalization to many other situations. The first of these is the number of sites studied. Firestone and Herriott's (1984) survey of twenty-five multisite case study efforts found major variation on this dimension, with one study including as few as three sites and another covering sixty. All other things being equal, a finding emerging repeatedly in the study of numerous sites would appear to be more likely to be a good working hypothesis about some as yet unstudied site than a finding emerging from just one or two sites.

A second dimension on which multisite studies vary, which is also likely to affect the degree of fit between these studies and situations to which one might want to generalize, concerns the heterogeneity of the sites chosen for study. Generally speaking, a finding emerging from the study of several very heterogeneous sites would be more robust and thus more likely to be useful in understanding various other sites than one emerging from the study of several very similar sites (Kennedy, 1979). Heterogeneity can be obtained by searching out sites that will provide maximal variation or by planned comparisons along certain potentially important dimensions. An example of the second strategy can be found in the parental-involvement study previously mentioned. The sites chosen for study were selected to allow comparison between urban and rural settings, between those with high and low reported degrees of involvement, and so forth (Smith and Robbins, 1984). This comparative strategy is potentially quite powerful, especially if there is heterogeneity among cases within each of the categories of interest. For example, if several rather different rural cases all share certain similarities that are not found in a heterogeneous group of urban cases, one has some reasonable basis for generalizing about likely differences between the two settings. Although the most obvious comparative strategy is to select cases that initially differ on some variable of interest as part of the research design, it is also possible to group cases in an *ex post facto* way on the basis of information gathered during the fieldwork. For example, if one were studying numerous very different classrooms and found that student achievement gains were quite high in some and quite low in others, one could compare these two sets of classrooms as a strategy for trying to suggest factors that contribute to high or low gains.

In sum, the possibility of studying numerous heterogeneous sites makes multisite studies one potentially useful approach to increasing the generalizability of qualitative work to *what is*. Yet I am very hesitant to see this approach as the only or even the best solution to the problem. First, such studies can be quite expensive, and the current lull in their funding highlights the extent to which such research is dependent on federal dollars that may or may not be forthcoming. Second, as Firestone and Herriott (1984) point out, budget constraints make it likely that studies including very large numbers of sites are less likely than studies of a relatively small number of sites to be able to devote intensive and prolonged care to studying the details of each site. Thus there is typically a trade-off to be made between the increased potential for generalizability flowing from studying a large number of sites and the increased depth and breadth of description and understanding made possible by a focus on a small number of sites. In suggesting that an increased number of sites leads to increased generalizability, I am assuming that enough attention is paid to each site to ensure that problems of internal validity do not arise. To the extent such problems do arise, generalizability is obviously threatened, since one cannot speak meaningfully of the generalizability of invalid data. The fact that roughly forty percent of the multisite studies surveyed by Firestone and Herriott (1984) involved just one or two short visits to the research site raises serious questions about whether such studies can appropriately be categorized as qualitative research in the usual sense of that term. The term *qualitative research*, and more especially the word *ethnography*, usually implies an intensive, ongoing involvement with individuals functioning in their everyday settings that is akin to, if not always identical with, the degree of immersion in a culture attained by anthropologists, who live in the society they study over a period of one or more years (Dobbert, 1982; Spindler, 1982; Wolcott, 1975). Thus it is conceivable, though not logically necessary, that attempts to gain generalizability through studying large numbers of sites undercut the depth of understanding of individual sites, which is the hallmark of the qualitative approach as it has come to be understood.

Studying What May Be
The goal of portraying typical schools – or, for that matter, typical instances of federal educational programs as they now exist – is, I believe, worthwhile. Yet accepting this as our only or even primary goal implies too narrow and limited a vision of what qualitative research can do. I would like to suggest that we want to generalize not only to *what is* but also to *what may be*. Let me explain. Here I am proposing that we think about what current social and educational trends suggest about likely educational issues for the future and design our research to illuminate such issues to the extent possible. Let me use some of my own current research to illustrate this possibility, without implying that it is the best or only example of such an approach.

One very obvious and potentially important trend in education recently has been the increasing utilization of microcomputers in instruction. In fact, microcomputers are being adopted in schools at an almost frantic pace (Becker, 1986) in spite of tight educational budgets and a generally acknowledged tendency on the part of educational institutions to resist rapid change. There is a clear division of opinion about the likely consequences of this trend. At one extreme are those who see computers as having the capability to revolutionize education in absolutely fundamental ways. Proponents of this school of thought make the rather startling claim that 'the potential of computers for improving education is greater than that of any prior invention, including books and writing' (Walker, 1984: 3). Others take quite a different stance, emphasizing the inherent conservativism of the teaching profession with regard to pedagogical change and the failure of other highly touted educational innovations to bring about far-reaching changes. Thus it seemed important to me to design a research project focused on understanding the impact of computer usage on students and classrooms (Schofield and Evans-Rhodes, 1989; Schofield and Verban, 1988). One could approach this issue with an emphasis on what is. For example, it would be possible to choose a school that is presently typical in terms of the uses it makes of computers in instruction. But this strategy encounters an immediate problem if one's goal is to speak to what may be. Changes in both microcomputer technology and in individuals' level of experience with computers have been so rapid in the past decade that a study of what is today could arguably be a study of primarily historical interest by the time it gets conducted, written, and published. In hopes of not just documenting the present, which is rapidly becoming the past, but of speaking to the future, I have made a number of methodological decisions that, in their abstract form, may be of use to others interested in making their work applicable to what may be.

Studying the 'Leading Edge' of Change   First, since it is hard to know what kinds of computer usage will become most typical or popular in the future, I have made a point of studying a broad array of uses rather than just one particular kind. More important, I have not looked only for heterogeneity of usage but for types of usage that are now in their infancy but that many informed observers see as likely to be common in the future. Thus I consciously chose to study a school that not only uses computers as they are currently employed around the country to teach computer programming and word processing in fairly typical ways but that also was the field test site for the kind of artificially intelligent computer-based tutor that researchers in a number of centers around the country are currently developing for classroom use (Feigenbaum and McCorduck, 1983; Lawler and Yazdani, 1987). I see this choice as a step in the direction of increasing the chances that this work will 'fit' or be generalizable to the educational issues important at the time the work is published. But this is only a mere first step.

Probing Factors Likely to Differentiate the Present from the Future   One of the big problems in trying to make one's work applicable to even the fairly near future is, as Cronbach (1975) has so eloquently argued, that people and institutions change. Thus it is logically impossible to see the future even when studying futuristic uses of artificial intelligence, because one is studying that future technology in the context of a present-day institution peopled with individuals who are shaped by the era in which they live.

There is no completely satisfactory solution to this situation, but a partial one emerged as I grappled with the issue. It is to think through how the present and the future are likely to differ. Then the research can be structured in a way that explicitly probes the impact of things that are likely to change over time. Of course, if the analysis of the likely differences between present and future is wrong, this approach will not be particularly useful. But if the analysis is accurate, this strategy has the potential to enhance greatly the usefulness of the study.

Let me illustrate in concrete terms how I have done this. Given the rapidity with which computers are being adopted for use in widely varying arenas of life, especially in schools, it seems a reasonable expectation that one major difference between now and five to ten years in the future is what might be called the 'novelty factor'. Specifically, many of today's high school students are having their first real introduction to the computer, or at least to its use for educational purposes, in their high school classrooms. However, in ten years it is rather unlikely that high school students will be having their first exposure to educational computing in the tenth or eleventh grade. I have used this assumption, which is, I think, relatively uncontroversial, to influence the shape of my study in a way that will allow it to speak more adequately to the future. For example, in interviews students were specifically asked about the impact of novelty on their reactions to the computer and its importance in shaping their feelings about computer usage. Similarly, observers in the study carefully looked for reactions that appeared to be influenced by students' unfamiliarity with the computers. Moreover, I have been careful to find out which students have had prior computer experience and what kind of experience this has been in order to see as clearly as possible whether these students differ from those for whom computer use is a completely novel experience. The fact that students were observed during the full course of the school year allowed assessment of whether any initial differences in students' reactions due to prior experience were transitory or relatively long-lasting. To the extent that novelty is crucial in shaping students' reactions, I will be forced to conclude that my study may not help us understand the future as well as it might otherwise. To the extent that students' reactions appear to be more heavily influenced by things that are unlikely to change in the near future, such as adolescents' striving for independence from adult control, the likely applicability of the findings of the study to the near future is clearly increased.

Considering the Life Cycle of a Phenomenon   The preceding discussion of the possible impact of novelty on students' reactions to educational computing brings up an important point regarding qualitative work and the issue of generalizability. The ethnographic habit of looking at a phenomenon over substantial time periods allows assessment of one aspect of generalizability that quantitative research usually does not – of where a particular phenomenon is in its life cycle and what the implications of this are for what is happening. Qualitative research, when studying a dynamic phenomenon, is like a movie. It starts with one image and then moves on to others that show how things evolve over time. Quantitative research, in contrast, is more typically like a snapshot, often taken and used without great regard for whether that photograph happened to catch one looking one's best or looking unusually disheveled. This point can be illustrated more substantively by briefly discussing a study that I carried out in a desegregated school during its first four years of existence (Schofield, 1989). The study tracked changes in the school by following two different groups of students from the first day they entered the school to graduation from that school three years later. Important changes occurred in race relations over the life of the institution and over the course of students' careers in the school. Such findings suggest that in asking about what happens in desegregated schools and what the impact of such schools is on students, it is important to know where both the students and the institution are in their experience with desegregation. Yet virtually all quantitative studies of desegregation, including, I must admit, some of my own, tend to ignore these issues completely. In fact, as I discovered in reviewing the desegregation literature (Schofield and Sagar, 1983), many do not even supply bare descriptive information on the life-cycle issue. Paying attention to where a phenomenon is in its life cycle does not guarantee that one can confidently predict how it will evolve. However, at a minimum, sensitivity to this issue makes it less likely that conclusions formed on the basis of a study conducted at one point in time will be unthinkingly and perhaps mistakenly generalized to other later points in time to which they may not apply.

Studying What Could Be
As mentioned previously, I would like to argue that qualitative research on education can be used not only to study *what is* and *what may be* but also to explore possible visions of *what could be*. By studying what could be, I mean locating situations that we know or expect to be ideal or exceptional on some *a priori* basis and then studying them to see what is actually going on there.

Selecting a Site that Sheds Light on What Could Be When studying what could be, site selection is not based on criteria such as typicality or heterogeneity. Rather it is based on information about either the *outcomes* achieved in the particular site studied or on the *conditions* obtaining there. Perhaps the best-known example of site selection based on outcomes is choosing to study classrooms or schools in which students show unusual intellectual gains, as has been done in the voluminous literature on effective schools (Bickel, 1983; Dwyer *et al.*, 1982; Phi Delta Kappan, 1980; Rutter *et al.*, 1979; Weber, 1971). For an example of site selection based on the conditions obtaining at the site, a less common approach, I will again make reference to my own work on school desegregation.

When thinking about where to locate the extended study of a desegregated school mentioned previously, I decided not to study a typical desegregated school. First, given the tremendous variation in situations characterized as desegregated, it is not clear that such an entity could be found. Second, there is a body of theory and research that gives us some basis for expecting different kinds of social processes and outcomes in different kinds of interracial schools. In fact, in the same year in which the *Brown* v. *Board of Education* decision laid the legal basis for desegregating educational institutions, Gordon Allport (1954) published a classic analysis of racial prejudice in which he argued that interracial contact can either increase or decrease hostility and stereotyping, depending on the kind of conditions under which it occurs. Specifically, he argued that in order to ameliorate relations between groups such as blacks and whites three conditions are especially important: equal status for members of both groups within the contact situation, a cooperative rather than a competitive goal structure, and support for positive relations from those in authority. A substantial amount of empirical and theoretical work stemming from Allport's basic insight has been carried out in the past three and a half decades, most of which supports his emphasis on the crucial importance of the specific conditions under which intergroup contact occurs (Amir, 1969; Aronson and Osherow, 1980; Cook, 1978; Pettigrew, 1967, 1969; Schofield, 1979; Schofield and Sagar, 1977; Slavin, 1980; Stephan, 1985).

It is clear that desegregating school systems often take little if any heed of the available theory and research on how to structure desegregated schools in a way likely to promote positive intergroup relations, perhaps at least partly because much of this work is laboratory based and hence may seem of questionable use in everyday situations. Thus selecting a site for study on the basis of typicality might be expected to yield a site potentially rich in sources of insight about the problems of desegregated education but weak in shedding light on what can be accomplished in a serious and sophisticated effort to structure an environment conducive to fostering positive relations between students. Since both scholars in the area of intergroup relations and the public are well aware of the potential for difficulties in desegregated schools, the task of seeing whether and how such difficulties can be overcome seems potentially more informative and useful than that of documenting the existence of such difficulties. Thus I chose to study a site that at least approximated a theoretical ideal. My goal was not to generalize to desegregated schools as a class. Rather it was to see what happens under conditions that might be expected to foster relatively positive outcomes. If serious problems were encountered at such a site, there would be reason to think that problems would be encountered in most places or, alternatively, to revise or reject the theory that led to the site selection. However, if things went well at such a site, the study would then provide an opportunity to gain some insight into how and why they go well and into what the still-intractable problems are.

Of course, the strategy of choosing a site based on some *a priori* theoretical viewpoint or, for that matter, any seriously held expectation about it raises a difficult problem. If one is unduly committed to that viewpoint, one's analysis of both what happens and why may be heavily influenced by it, and one may not ask whether other more fruitful perspectives might emerge from a more dispassionate approach to studying the situation. This is the very danger that has led to the development of such elaborate safeguards in the quantitative tradition as the double-blind experiment. Although such procedures are rarely used in the qualitative tradition, a substantial literature on the issue of internal validity in qualitative research offers assistance with this problem to the researcher who pays it close heed (Becker, 1958; Bogdan and Biklen, 1981; Glaser and Strauss, 1967; Goetz and LeCompte, 1984; Guba, 1981; Guba and Lincoln, 1981; Kirk and Miller, 1986; Miles and Huberman, 1984a 1984b; Patton, 1980; Strauss, 1987). Furthermore, if one's purpose is not to support or reject a specific *a priori* theory but to discover, using an approach that is as open as possible, what is actually happening in a site that was chosen with the assistance of a particular theory, problems related to internal validity are somewhat mitigated. For example, the fact that I chose to study a school that theory suggested might be conducive to positive relations did not keep me from exploring in considerable depth problems that occurred there (Sagar and Schofield, 1980; Schofield, 1981, 1989).

One characteristic of the school chosen for the study was especially helpful in assessing the degree to which the theory on which the site was chosen was useful. Specifically, for various reasons, conditions in two of the three grades in this school came much closer than conditions in the remaining grade to meeting those that theory suggests are conducive to producing positive relations. Thus it was possible to assess intergroup relations as the children went from one kind of environment to another within the school (Schofield, 1979, 1989; Schofield and Sagar, 1977). This suggests one very useful strategy for studying what may be – selecting an 'ideal' case and a comparative case that contrasts sharply on the relevant dimensions.

Generalizing from an Unusual Site to More Typical Ones
Although I indicated above that my goal was to learn about the possibilities and problems associated with a *certain kind* of desegregated education, I would like to argue that studying a site chosen for its special characteristics does not necessarily restrict the application of the study's findings to other very similar sites. The degree to which this is the case depends on the degree to which the findings appear to be linked to the special characteristics of the situation. Some of the findings from the study I have been discussing were clearly linked to unusual aspects of the school and hence have very limited generalizability to other situations, although they may none the less be important in demonstrating what is possible, even if not what is generally likely. For example, I found very low levels of overt racial conflict in the school studied (Schofield and Francis, 1982). It would obviously be misguided to conclude on the basis of this study that intergroup conflict is unlikely in all desegregated schools, since the school's emphasis on co-operation, equal status, and the like did actually appear to play a marked role in reducing the likelihood of conflict.

However, other findings that emerged from the study and were also related to atypical aspects of the situation may have a greater degree of applicability or generalizability than the finding discussed above. For example, I found the development of a color-blind perspective and of an almost complete taboo against the mention of race in the school studied (Schofield, 1986, 1989). Since the emergence of the color-blind perspective and the accompanying taboo appeared to be linked to special characteristics of the school, I would not posit them as phenomena likely to occur in most desegregated schools. But I feel free to argue that *when* they do develop, certain consequences may well follow because these consequences are the logical outcomes of the phenomena. For example, with regard to the taboo against racial reference, if one cannot mention race, one cannot deal with resegregation in a straightforward way as a policy issue. Similarly, if one cannot mention race, there is likely to be little or no effort to create or utilize multicultural curricular materials. Thus, although the taboo against racial reference may not occur in a high proportion of desegregated schools, when it does occur the study I carried out gives a potentially useful indication of problems that are likely to develop.

I would now like to turn to a third finding of the study, one so unrelated to the atypical aspects of the situation studied that it is a reasonable working hypothesis that this phenomenon is widespread. After I observed extensively in varied areas of the school and interviewed a large number of students, it became apparent that the white children perceived blacks as something of a threat to their physical selves. Specifically, they complained about what they perceived as black roughness or aggressiveness (Schofield, 1981, 1989). In contrast, the black students perceived whites as a threat to their social selves. They complained about being ignored, avoided, and being treated as inferior by whites, whom they perceived to be stuck-up and prejudiced (Schofield, 1989). Such findings appear to me to be linked to the black and white students' situation in the larger society and to powerful historical and economic forces, not to special aspects of the school. The consequences of these rather asymmetrical concerns may well play themselves out differently in different kinds of schools, but the existence of these rather different but deeply held concerns may well be widespread.

I have gone into some detail with these examples because I think they raise a crucial point for judging the applicability or generalizability of qualitative work. One cannot just look at a study and say that it is similar or dissimilar to another situation of concern. A much finer-grained analysis is necessary. One must ask what aspects of the situation are similar or different and to what aspects of the findings these are connected.

[. . .]

Summary and Conclusions

Although qualitative researchers have traditionally paid scant attention to the issue of attaining generalizability in research, sometimes even disdaining such a goal, this situation has changed noticeably in the past ten to fifteen years. Several trends, including the growing use of qualitative studies in evaluation and policy-oriented research, have led to an increased awareness of the importance of structuring qualitative studies in a way that enhances their implications for the understanding of other situations.

Much of the attention given to the issue of generalizability in recent years on the part of qualitative researchers has focused on redefining the concept in a way that is useful and meaningful for those engaged in qualitative work. A consensus appears to be emerging that for qualitative researchers generalizability is best thought of as a matter of the 'fit' between the situation studied and others to which one might be interested in applying the concepts and conclusions of that study. This conceptualization makes thick descriptions crucial, since without them one does not have the information necessary for an informed judgment about the issue of fit.

This paper argues that three useful targets for generalization are *what is*, *what may be*, and *what could be* and provides some examples of how qualitative research can be designed in a way that increases its ability to fit with each of these situations. Studying *what is* refers to studying the typical, the common, and the ordinary. Techniques suggested for studying *what is* include choosing study sites on the basis of typicality and conducting multisite studies. Studying *what may be* refers to designing studies so that their fit with future trends and issues is maximized. Techniques suggested for studying *what may be* include seeking out sites in which one can study situations likely to become more common with the passage of time and paying close attention to how such present instances of future practices are likely to differ from their future realizations. Studying *what could be* refers to locating situations that we know or expect to be ideal or exceptional on some *a priori* basis and studying them to see what is actually going on there. Crucial here is an openness to having one's expectations about the phenomena disconfirmed.

[. . .]

Note

Much of the research on which this paper is based was funded by the Office of Naval Research, Contract Number N00 14-85-K-0664. Other research utilized in this paper was funded by Grant Number NIE-G-78-0126 from the National Institute of Education. However, all opinions expressed herein are solely those of the author, and no endorsement by ONR or NIE is implied or intended. My sincere thanks go to Bill Firestone and Matthew Miles for their constructive comments on an earlier draft of this paper.

References

Allport, G.W. (1954) *The Nature of Prejudice*. Cambridge: Cambridge University Press.

Amir, Y. (1969) 'Contact hypothesis in ethnic relations', *Psychological Bulletin*, 71: 319–42.

Aronson, E. and Osherow, N. (1980) 'Cooperation, prosocial behavior, and academic performance: experiments in the desegregated classroom', in L. Bickman (ed.), *Applied Social Psychology Annual*, Vol. 1. Beverly Hills, CA: Sage, pp. 163–96.

Becker, H.J. (1986) 'Instructional uses of school computers', *Reports from the 1985 National Survey*. 1: 1–9. Baltimore, MD: Center for Social Organization of Schools, Johns Hopkins University, pp. 1–9.

Becker, H.S. (1958) 'Problems of inference and proof in participant observation', *American Sociological Review*, 23: 652–9.

Berg, B.L. (1989) *Qualitative Research Methods for the Social Sciences*. Boston: Allyn & Bacon.

Bickel, W.E. (1983) 'Effective schools: knowledge, dissemination, inquiry', *Educational Researcher*, 12 (4): 3–5.

Bogdan, R.C. and Biklen, S.K. (1981) *Qualitative Research for Education: An Introduction to Theory and Methods*. Boston: Allyn & Bacon.

Bolgar, H. (1965) 'The case study method', in B.B. Wolman (ed.), *Handbook of Clinical Psychology*. New York: McGraw-Hill, pp. 28–39.

Brown v. *Board of Education* (1954) 347 US 483.

Campbell, D.T. (1979) 'Degrees of freedom and the case study', in T.D. Cook and C.S. Reichardt (eds), *Qualitative and Quantitative Methods in Evaluation Research*. Beverly Hills, CA: Sage, pp. 49–67.

Campbell, D. and Stanley, J. (1963) 'Experimental and quasi-experimental designs for research on teaching', in N. Gage (ed.), *Handbook of Research on Teaching*. Chicago: Rand McNally, pp. 171–246.

Collins, T. and Noblit, G. (1978) *Stratification and Resegregation: the Case of Crossover High School*. Final report of NIE contract 400-76-009.

Cook, S.W. (1978) 'Interpersonal and attitudinal outcomes in cooperating interracial groups', *Journal of Research and Development in Education*, 12: 97–113.

Crandall, D.P. *et al.* (1983) *People, Policies and Practices: Examining the Chain of School Improvement*, Vols 1–10. Andover, MA: Network.

Cronbach, L.J. (1975) 'Beyond the two disciplines of scientific psychology', *American Psychologist*, 30: 116–27.

Cronbach, L.J. (1982) *Designing Evaluations of Educational and Social Programs*. San Francisco: Jossey-Bass.

Cronbach, L.J., Ambron, S.R., Dornbusch, S.M., Hess, R.D., Hornik, R.C. Phillips, D.C., Walker, D.F. and Weiner, S.S. (1980) *Toward Reform of Program Evaluation*. San Francisco: Jossey-Bass.

Denzin, N.K. (1983) 'Interpretive interactionism', in G. Morgan (ed.), *Beyond Method: Strategies for Social Research*. Beverly Hills, CA: Sage, pp. 129–46.

Dobbert, M.L. (1982) *Ethnographic Research: Theory and Application for Modern Schools and Societies*. New York: Praeger.

Dwyer, D.C., Lee, G.V., Rowan, B. and Bossert, S.T. (1982) 'The Principal's Role in Instructional Management: Five Participant Observation Studies of Principals in Action.' Unpublished manuscript, Far West Laboratory for Educational Research and Development, San Francisco.

Feigenbaum, E.A. and McCorduck, P. (1983) *The Fifth Generation: Artificial Intelligence and Japan's Computer Challenge to the World*. Reading, MA: Addison-Wesley.

Fetterman, D.M. (1982) 'Ethnography in educational research: the Dynamics of diffusion', in D.M. Fetterman (ed.), *Ethnography in Educational Evaluation*. Beverly Hills, CA: Sage, pp. 21–35.

Filstead, W.J. (1979) 'Qualitative methods: a needed perspective in evaluation research', in T.D. Cook and C.S. Reichardt (eds), *Qualitative and Quantitative Methods in Evaluation Research*. Beverly Hills, CA: Sage, pp. 33–48.

Firestone, W.A. and Herriott, R.E (1984) 'Multisite qualitative policy research: Some design and implementation issues', in D.M. Fetterman (ed.), *Ethnography in Educational Evaluation*. Beverly Hills, CA: Sage, pp. 63–88.

Geertz, C. (1973) 'Thick description: toward an interpretive theory of culture', in C. Geertz (ed.), *The Interpretation of Cultures*. New York: Basic Books, pp. 3–30.

Glaser, B. and Strauss, A. (1967) *The Discovery of Grounded Theory*. Chicago: Aldine Publishing.

Goetz, J.P. and LeCompte, M.D. (1984) *Ethnography and Qualitative Design in Educational Research*. Orlando, FL: Academic Press.

Guba, E. (1981) 'Criteria for assessing the trustworthiness of naturalistic inquiry', *Educational Communication and Technology Journal*, 29: 79–92.

Guba, E.G. and Lincoln, Y.S. (1981) *Effective Evaluation: Improving the Usefulness of Evaluation Results through Responsive and Naturalistic Approaches*. San Francisco: Jossey-Bass.

Guba, E.G. and Lincoln, Y.S. (1982) 'Epistemological and methodological bases of naturalistic inquiry', *Educational Communication and Technology Journal*, 30: 233–52.

Huberman, A.M. and Miles, M.B. (1984) *Innovation Up Close: How School Improvement Works*. New York: Plenum Press.

Jackson, P.W. (1968) *Life in Classrooms*. New York: Holt, Rinehard & Winston.

Kennedy, M.M. (1979) 'Generalizing from single case studies', *Evaluation Quarterly*, 3 (4): 661–78.

Kirk, J. and Miller, M.L. (1986) *Reliability and Validity in Qualitative Research*. Beverly Hills, CA: Sage.

Krathwohl, D.R. (1985) *Social and Behavioral Science Research: New Framework for Conceptualizing, Implementing, and Evaluating Research Studies*. San Francisco: Jossey-Bass.

Lawler, R.W. and Yazdani, M. (eds) (1987) *Artificial Intelligence and Education: Learning Environments and Tutoring Systems*, Vol. 1. Norwood, NJ: Ablex Publishing.

Lucas, W. (1974) *The Case Survey Method: Aggregating Case Experience*. Santa Monica, CA: Rand.

Miles, M. and Huberman, A. (1984a) 'Drawing valid meaning from qualitative data: toward a shared craft', *Educational Researcher*, 13: 20–30.

Miles, M. and Huberman, A. (1984b) *Qualitative Data Analysis: Sourcebook of New Methods*. Newbury Park, CA: Sage.

Noblit, G.W. and Hare, R.D. (1988) *Meta-Ethnography: Synthesizing Qualitative Studies*. Beverly Hills, CA: Sage.

Patton, M.Q. (1980) *Qualitative Evaluation Methods*. Beverly Hills, CA: Sage.

Peshkin, A. (1978) *Growing up American: Schooling and the Survival of Community*. Chicago: University of Chicago Press.

Peshkin, A. (1982) 'The researcher and subjectivity: reflections on an ethnography of school and community', in G. Spindler (ed.), *Doing the Ethnography of Schooling: Educational Anthropology in Action*. New York: Holt, Rinehart & Winston, pp. 48–67.

Pettigrew, T. (1967) 'Social evaluation theory: convergences and applications', in D. Levine (ed.), *Nebraska Symposium on Motivation*, Vol. 5. Lincoln, NE: University of Nebraska Press.

Pettigrew, T. (1969) 'Racially separate or together', *Journal of Social Issues*, 25: 43–69.

Phi Delta Kappan (1980) *Why Do Some Urban Schools Succeed? The Phi Delta Kappa Study of Exceptional Urban Elementary Schools*. Bloomington, IN: Phi Delta Kappa and Indiana University.

Ragin, C.C. (1987) *The Comparative Method: Moving beyond Qualitative and Quantitative Strategies*. Berkeley, CA: University of California Press.

Reichardt, C.S. and Cook, T.D. (1979) 'Beyond qualitative *versus* quantitative methods', in T.D. Cook and C.S. Reichardt (eds), *Qualitative and Quantitative Methods in Evaluation Research*. Beverly Hills, CA: Sage, pp. 1–33.

Rutter, M., Maughan, B., Mortimore, P., Ouston, J. and Smith, A. (1979) *Fifteen Thousand Hours: Secondary Schools and Their Effects on Children*. Cambridge, MA: Harvard University Press.

Sagar, H.A. and Schofield, J.W. (1980) 'Racial and behavioral cues in black and white children's perceptions of ambiguously aggressive acts'. *Journal of Personality and Social Psychology*, 39: 590–8.

Schofield, J.W. (1979) 'The impact of positively structured contact on intergroup behavior: Does it last under adverse conditions?' *Social Psychology Quarterly*, 42: 280–4.

Schofield, J.W. (1981) 'Competitive and complementary identities: images and interaction in an interracial school', in S. Asher and J. Gottman (eds), *The Development of Children's Friendship*. New York: Cambridge University Press.

Schofield, J.W. (1986) 'Causes and consequences of the colorblind perspective', in S. Gaertner and J. Dovidio (eds), *Prejudice Discrimination and Racism: Theory and Practice*. New York: Academic Press, pp. 231–53.

Schofield, J.W. (1989) *Black and White in School: Trust, Tension, or Tolerance?* New York: Teachers College Press. (Original work published 1982.)

Schofield, J.W. and Evans-Rhodes, D. (1989) 'Artificial intelligence in the classroom: the impact of a computer-based tutor on teachers and students', paper presented at the 4th International Conference on Artificial Intelligence in Education, Amsterdam, The Netherlands, May.

Schofield, J.W. and Francis, W.D. (1982) 'An observational study of peer interaction in racially-mixed "accelerated" classrooms', *Journal of Educational Psychology*, 74: 722–32.

Schofield, J.W. and Sagar, H.A. (1977) 'Peer interaction patterns in an integrated middle school', *Sociometry*, 40: 130–8.

Schofield, J.W. and Sagar, H.A. (1983) 'Desegregation, school practices and student race relations', in C. Rossell and W. Hawley (eds), *The Consequences of School Desegregation*. Philadelphia, PA: Temple University Press, pp. 58–102.

Schofield, J.W. and Verban, D. (1988) 'Computer usage in the teaching of mathematics: Issues which need answers', in D. Grouws and T. Cooney (eds), *Effective Mathematics Teaching*. Hillsdale, NJ: Erlbaum, pp. 169–93.

Shaughnessy, J.J. and Zechmeister, E.B. (1985) *Research Methods in Psychology*. New York: Knopf.

Slavin, R.E. (1980) 'Cooperative learning', *Review of Educational Research*, 50: 315–42.

Smith, A.G. and Robbins, A.E. (1984) 'Multimethod policy research: a case study of structure and flexibility', in D.M. Fetterman (ed.), *Ethnography in Educational Evaluation*. Beverly Hills, CA: Sage, pp. 115–32.

Smith, H.W. (1975) *Strategies of Social Research: the Methodological Imagination*. Englewood Cliffs, NJ: Prentice-Hall.

Spindler, G. (1982) 'General introduction', in G. Spindler (ed.), *Doing the Ethnography of Schooling: Educational Anthropology in Action*. New York: Holt, Rinehart & Winston, pp. 1–13.

Stake, R.E. (1978) 'The case-study method in social inquiry', *Educational Researcher*, 7: 5–8.

Stephan, W.J. (1985) 'Intergroup relations', in G. Lindzey and F. Aronson (eds), *The Handbook of Social Psychology*, Vol. 2. New York: Random House, pp. 599–658.

Strauss, A.L. (1987) *Qualitative Analysis for Social Scientists*. Cambridge: Cambridge University Press.

Walker, D.F. (1984) 'Promise, potential and pragmatism: computers in high school', *Institute for Research in Educational Finance and Governance Policy Notes*, 5: 3–4.

Weber, G. (1971) *Inner-City Children Can Be Taught to Read: Four Successful Schools*. Washington, DC: Council for Basic Education.

Whyte, W.F. (1984) *Learning from the Field: A Guide from Experience*. Beverly Hills, CA: Sage.

Wolcott, H.F. (1973) *The Man in the Principal's Office: an Ethnography*. New York: Holt, Rinehart & Winston.

Wolcott, H.G. (1975) 'Criteria for an ethnographic approach to research in schools', *Human Organization*, 34: 111–27.

Wolcott, H.F. (1982) 'Mirrors, models, and monitors: educator adaptations of the ethnographic innovation', in G. Spindler (ed.), *Doing the Ethnography of Schooling: Educational Anthropology in Action*. New York: Holt, Rinehart & Winston, pp. 68–95.

Yin, R.K. (1981) 'The case study crisis: some answers', *Administrative Science Quarterly*, 26: 58–64.

Yin, R.K. (1984) *Case Study Research: Design and Methods*. Beverly Hills, CA: Sage.

Yin, R.K. and Heald, K.A. (1975) 'Using the case survey method to analyze policy studies', *Administrative Science Quarterly*, 20: 371–81.

Yin, R.K. and Yates, D. (1975) *Street-Level Governments: Assessing Decentralization and Urban Services*. Lexington, MA: D.C. Heath.

17

The Obviousness of Social and Educational Research Results

N.L. Gage

Is what we find out in social and educational research old hat, stale, platitudinous? Are the results of such research mere truisms that any intelligent person might know without going to the trouble of doing social or educational research?

The Importance of the Obviousness Question

The obviousness question has important ramifications. It can influence the motivation of any person who is thinking about doing social or educational research. Why do research if you are not going to find anything new, anything not already known? Obviousness also relates to the justification of social science departments and schools of education in expecting or requiring their faculties and graduate students to do social and educational research. It also concerns government funding policies, such as those of the National Science Foundation and the National Institute of Mental Health that support social research, and those of the US Department of Education, particularly the Office of Educational Research and Improvement, that support educational research. Foundations, school boards, state legislatures, and Congressional committees need to be convinced, before they put up the money, that social and educational research will produce something that any intelligent adult might not already know.

So, the issue of obviousness, apart from piquing our intellectual curiosity, has tremendous practical importance. Unless social and educational researchers face that issue, they may lack motivation to do research and lose societal support expressed in dollars.

The Charge of Obviousness

Does anyone really hold that social and educational research yields

From *Educational Researcher*, 20 (1), 1991, pp. 10–16.

only the obvious? I begin with an old joke attributed to James T. Farrell, the novelist who became famous in the 1930s for *Studs Lonigan*. Farrell was quoted in those days as having defined a sociologist as someone who will spend $10,000 to discover the location of the nearest house of ill fame. He actually used a less polite term, and nowadays he would have said a quarter of a million dollars. I also remember a fellow graduate student who could always get a laugh by referring to the content of some of his textbooks as 'unctuous elaborations of the obvious'.

Schlesinger's Critique

The first serious piece of writing that I know of that made the same charge appeared in 1949 in the *Partisan Review*. It was in a review by Arthur Schlesinger, Jr, of the two volumes of *The American Soldier*, which had just been published. *The American Soldier* was written by a group led by Samuel. A. Stouffer, who later became a professor of sociology at Harvard. It reported on the work done by sociologists and other social scientists in surveying, with questionnaires and interviews, the attitudes of American soldiers during World War II. The first volume, subtitled 'Adjustment during Army Life', dealt with soldiers' attitudes during training, and the second, subtitled 'Combat and its Aftermath', dealt with soldiers' attitudes while they were engaged with the enemy and risking their lives. As a young assistant professor, I found the two books impressive for their methodological thoroughness, sophisticated interpretation, and theoretical formulations of such concepts as 'relative deprivation'.

So I was taken aback after some months when I discovered a review of those two volumes by Arthur Schlesinger, Jr, the distinguished historian. Then a young professor at Harvard University, Schlesinger had just won a Pulitzer Prize for his *Age of Jackson*. Witty and vituperative, Schlesinger's review also denounced what he considered the pretensions of social scientists. Schlesinger wrote:

> Does this kind of research yield anything new? . . . [T]he answer . . . is easy. Most of the *American Soldier* is a ponderous demonstration in Newspeak of such facts as these: New recruits do not like noncoms; front-line troops resent rear-echelon troops; combat men manifest a high level of anxiety as compared to other soldiers; married privates are more likely than single privates to worry about their families back home. Indeed, one can find little in the 1,200 pages of text and the innumerable surveys which is not described more vividly and compactly, and with far greater psychological insight, in a small book entitled *Up Front* by Bill Mauldin. What Mauldin may have missed will turn up in the pages of Ernie Pyle. (1949: 854)

Lazarsfeld's Examples

At about the same time as Schlesinger, Paul Lazarsfeld, a professor of sociology at Columbia University, also reviewed *The American Soldier*. Lazarsfeld (1949) was clearly aware of the same problem of obviousness. He wrote:

> [I]t is hard to find a form of human behavior that has not already been observed somewhere. Consequently, if a study reports a prevailing regularity, many readers respond to it by thinking 'of course, that is the way things are'. Thus, from time to time, the argument is advanced that surveys only put into complicated form observations which are already obvious to everyone.
>
> Understanding the origin of this point of view is of importance far beyond the limits of the present discussion. The reader may be helped in recognizing this attitude if he looks over a few statements which are typical of many survey findings and carefully observes his own reaction. A short list of these, with brief interpretive comments, will be given here in order to bring into sharper focus probable reactions of many readers.
>
> 1.   Better educated men showed more psychoneurotic symptoms than those with less education. (The mental instability of the intellectual as compared to the more impassive psychology of the man-in-the-street has often been commented on.)
> 2.   Men from rural backgrounds were usually in better spirits during their Army life than soldiers from city backgrounds. (After all, they are more accustomed to hardships.)
> 3.   Southern soldiers were better able to stand the climate in the hot South Sea Islands than Northern soldiers. (Of course. Southerners are more accustomed to hot weather.)
> 4.   White privates were more eager to become noncoms than Negroes. ([Because of their having been deprived of opportunity for so many years], the lack of ambition among Negroes was [quite understandable].)
> 5.   Southern Negroes preferred Southern to Northern white officers [because Southerners were much more experienced in having interpersonal interactions with Negroes than Northern officers were].
> 6.   As long as the fighting continued, men were more eager to be returned to the States than they were after the Germans surrendered [because during the fighting, soldiers were in danger of getting killed, but after the surrender there was no such danger]. (1949: 379–80)

Keppel's Position

For a later sample of the worry about obviousness, we can turn to an essay by Frank Keppel, titled 'The Education of Teachers', which appeared in 1962 in a volume of talks on American education by American scholars that had been broadcast by radio to foreign audiences. Keppel had left the deanship of the Harvard Graduate School of Education to serve as US Commissioner of Education under President Kennedy. As Commissioner he led the movement that resulted in the Elementary and Secondary Education Act of 1965, the first major effort in the US to improve the education of children from low-income families. In his article, Keppel indicated that some people question the principles that have emerged from psychological studies of teaching and learning. Without committing himself as to whether he agreed, he summed up the critics' arguments this way:

> The efforts to use scientific methods to study human behavior seem to them [the critics] ridiculous if not impious. The result is a ponderous, pseudo-scientific language which takes ten pages to explain the obvious or to dilute the wisdom long ago learned in humanistic studies. . . . To build an art of teaching on the basis of the 'behavioral sciences', they suggest, is to build on sand. (1962: 91)

Conant's Position

The very next year obviousness was mentioned again, by another prestigious educator, namely, James Bryant Conant, who had been president of Harvard University for 20 years, and then the US High Commissioner (and eventually the US ambassador) in West Germany. During World War II, he had been a member of the highest scientific advisory committees, including the one that led to the production of the atom bomb. When he returned from Germany, he devoted himself almost exclusively to educational problems. In 1963, he published a book titled *The Education of American Teachers*, in which he reported on his studies of teacher education programs and schools – studies made through much interviewing, reading, and visiting. His book gained extremely wide and respectful attention. Yet, when I looked into it, as an educational psychologist, I couldn't help being dismayed by Conant's assertion that educational psychology largely gives us merely common-sense generalizations about human nature – generalizations that are 'for the most part highly limited and unsystematized generalizations, which are the stock in trade of every day life for all sane people' (1963: 133).

Phillips's Critique

These references to obviousness take us only into the 1960s. Did the attacks disappear after that? Or are there more recent statements on the obviousness of educational and social research results? In 1985, a volume of papers appeared on the subject of instructional time, which had been central in a variety of formulations, such as John

B. Carroll's model of school learning, Benjamin Bloom's mastery approach to teaching, and the concept of academic engaged time developed by Charles Fisher and David Berliner. All of these writers seemed to agree that the more time students spent in studying, practicing, and being engaged with the content or skills to be learned, the greater the related learning they achieved. The correlations between academic engaged time and achievement were not perfect, of course, because outside of the laboratory, correlations are never perfect, even in the natural sciences and certainly not in the social and behavioral sciences.

The subject of instructional time thus received a lot of attention in many articles and several books, including the edited volume, *Perspectives on Instructional Time*, to which the philosopher of the social sciences, Denis Phillips, contributed a chapter entitled 'The Uses and Abuses of Truisms' (1985). Here Phillips first cited Hamlyn, also a philosopher, who had criticized the work of Piaget. Hamlyn had asked his readers to try to imagine a world in which Piaget's main ideas were untrue:

> a world where children mastered abstract and complex tasks before concrete and simple ones, for example. Such a world would differ crazily from our own, and one gets the sense that many of Piaget's views are unsurprisingly and necessarily (if not trivially) true. (Phillips, 1985: 311)

Phillips then raised the same kind of question about the research on instructional time: 'What sort of world would it be if children learned more the *less* time they spent on a subject? If achievement were not related to the time spent engaged on a topic?' (1985: 311). So, just as with Piaget's major findings, 'one gets the sense that these findings [about instructional time] are almost necessarily (and perhaps even trivially) true' (1985: 311). 'Indeed, it suddenly seems strange to dress up these truisms as "findings"' (1985: 312).

Phillips then went on to make a distinction between truisms and statements that are trivially true. '[T]he latter are, in effect, a subgroup of the former. A truism is a statement the truth of which is self-evident or obvious . . . whereas a trivially true statement is one that is true by virtue of the meaning of the terms involved (for example, "All colored objects are colored" or "All bachelors are unmarried")' (1985: 312). He went on to say that '"It is easier to keep a small group of children working on a task than it is a large group" is a truism, for it is obviously true, but it is not true by virtue of the meanings of the terms involved' (1985: 312). Phillips also pointed out that:

> truisms and statements that are trivially true are not thereby *trivial*. The

terms *truism* and *trivially true* refer to the patentness of the truth of statements, whereas *trivial* refers to their degree of value or usefulness. The two do not automatically go together; many a statement the truth of which is far from obvious is of no practical use ... and many truisms are vitally important and even theoretically significant ('The sky is dark at night' [this truism bears on the theory of the expanding universe]). (1985: 313)

Furthermore,

truisms uncovered by researchers, then, are not necessarily trivial. But on the other hand *truisms do not require research in order to be uncovered.* Agencies would be wasting money if they awarded grants to researchers who wanted to determine if all bachelors in the United States were unmarried, or if the sky is dark at night, or if small groups are easier to control than large groups. (1985: 313; emphasis added)

In Short

Let me summarize the argument so far. I have presented a series of opinions quite damaging to the notion that social and educational research yields results that would not already be known to any intelligent and thoughtful citizen. These opinions are hard to ignore. Extremely estimable people – Farrell, Schlesinger, Keppel, Conant, Lazarsfeld, and Phillips – all have made statements that might well give pause to any sensible person considering the pursuit of social and educational research or any organization being asked to part with money to support such research. I have presented these statements in chronological order extending from novelist James T. Farrell in the mid-1930s to philosopher Denis Phillips in the mid-1980s.

Empirical Examination of Obviousness

One noteworthy characteristic of all of these criticisms is that they were what might be called nonempirical or, at least, not systematically and formally empirical. Informal and personal, the appraisals were not made with any great specificity, detail, explicitness, or exactitude. Presumably, Schlesinger had not actually compared the statements of results reported in *The American Soldier* with statements made by Bill Mauldin or Ernie Pyle. He did not perform a content analysis of the two kinds of reports about soldiers to show in any literal way that the sociologists' statements of results had been anticipated by the insights of the cartoonist and the journalist. The same point can be made about what was said by Keppel and Conant: They did not go into any detail, or become at all specific, to support their allegations. However, the sociologist Lazarsfeld did go into detail and referred to specific results, namely, soldiers' attitudes of various kinds. Phillips referred to specific findings about instructional time, or time on task, and also findings about size of group or class size.

Rice's Studies

Now I should like to go back and look at some empirical efforts that seem to me to bear upon the whole issue of obviousness. I begin with what may be the first process-outcome study in the history of research on teaching. The results of this investigation were published by Joseph Mayer Rice (1913) under the title 'The Futility of the Spelling Grind'. Rice reported, after studying tests on 33,000 school children, that there was no correlation worth noticing between amount of time devoted to spelling homework and classwork and competence in spelling.

Rice's evidence is still being cited in support of the argument that spelling competence results from 'incidental' learning, rather than from any 'systematic' teaching; that is, spelling is 'caught' rather than 'taught'. So far as instructional time or 'academic engaged time' is concerned, the issue does not appear to be the open-and-shut case implied by Phillips when he asked. 'What kind of world would it be if achievement were not related to the time spent engaged on a topic?' (1985: 311). As Rice put it,

> concerning the amount of time devoted to spelling . . . an increase of time . . . is not rewarded by better results. . . . The results obtained by forty or fifty minutes' daily instruction were not better than those obtained where not more than ten or fifteen minutes had been devoted to the subject. (1913: 86–7)

Apparently, showing a relationship between time on task and achievement was not as easy as falling off a log, as it should have been if the relationship between time-on-task and achievement were necessarily true, that is, a truism. At least in one subject matter, namely, spelling, the relationship between time-on-task and achievement was fragile, perhaps even nonexistent. So perhaps the relationship depended on the subject matter. Perhaps other factors also made a difference. Things may be more complicated than we should expect if the relationship were a truism.

Similarly, if smaller groups were always easier to control, a relationship that Phillips assumed to be a truism, then they should show higher time-on-task and thus higher achievement. However, the trickiness of the relationship between class size and achievement is by now well established. Reducing class size from 40 to 20 does not improve achievement with any consistency at all. Glass

(1987) reported that it required an 'exhaustive and quantitative integration of the research' to refute well-nigh unanimous older assessments (for example, Goodlad, 1960) that class size made no difference in achievement, student attention, and discipline. Even then Glass found that the relationship of class size to achievement appeared only probabilistically (in 111 of 160 instances, or 69 percent) when classes of approximately 18 and 28 pupils were compared. Moreover, the duration of the instruction made a big difference: the relationship was stronger in studies of pupils taught for more than 100 hours. In addition, the class size had to be reduced dramatically to make a major improvement: 'Bringing about even a 10 percentile rank improvement in the average pupil's achievement . . . may entail cutting class size (and, hence, increasing schooling costs) by a third to a half' (1987: 544).

Alleging that a relationship (for example, the size-of-group relationship to the ease of control) is a truism implies that it should always be found and that no exceptions should occur. Thus, all bachelors without exception are unmarried, all colored objects without exception are colored. By the same reasoning, if the group size-controllability relationship were a truism, all smaller groups should be easier to control than all larger groups. If the age-reasoning ability relationship were a truism, all older children should be capable of more abstract and valid reasoning than all younger children. But, of course, the last two examples are untrue. If a truism is 'an undoubted or self-evident truth, especially one too obvious or unimportant for mention' (*Webster's New Collegiate Dictionary*, 1979), then these relationships are not truisms because they are not always 'undoubted' or 'self-evident'.

Suppose we change the 'truism' to a probabilistic statement (for example, children *tend* to learn more, the more time they spend on a subject; time on task is positively but *imperfectly* correlated with achievement). Now the research aims to determine the strength of the tendency, or the magnitude of the positive correlation. Does the r equal .05, .25, .45, .65, or .85? It seems to be a truism that the size of the time on task versus achievement correlation depends on many factors: the reliability of the achievement measure, the variabilities of the two variables, perhaps the subject matter, and so on. Is the research to answer these important and specific practical questions still unnecessary?

Here may lie one key to the problem: to enhance the truism with the specifics that make it have value for theory and practice, the research does become necessary. Even if the broad generalization is a truism, the specifics of its actualization in human affairs – to determine the magnitude of the probability and the factors that affect that magnitude – require research. Even if 'smaller groups tend to be more easily controlled' were a truism, we would ask, how much difference in group size is needed to produce a given difference in controllability? How do other factors – age and gender of group members, task difficulty, and the like – affect the difference in controllability resulting from changes in group size? Similar questions would apply to all the other seemingly truistic findings. Even if intelligent people could always (without any research) predict the direction (positive or negative) of a relationship between two variables, they could not predict its size and its contingencies without research-based knowledge.

Lazarsfeld's Examples

Let us go back now to Lazarsfeld's examples of obvious results from the World War II studies of *The American Soldier*. Recall his examples of the 'obvious' conclusions from that study: better educated men showed more psychoneurotic symptoms; men from rural backgrounds were usually in better spirits than those from cities; Southern soldiers were better able than Northerners to stand the climate in the South Sea Islands; White privates were more eager to become noncoms than Black privates were; Southern Negroes preferred Southern to Northern White officers; and men were more eager to be returned to the States during the fighting than they were after the Germans surrendered.

Lazarsfeld asked, 'Why, since they are so obvious, is so much money given to establish such findings?' However, he then revealed that

> *Everyone of these statements is the direct opposite of what was actually found.* Poorly educated soldiers were more neurotic than those with high educations; Southerners showed no greater ability than Northerners to adjust to a tropical climate; Negroes were more eager for promotion than whites, and so on. . . . If we had mentioned the actual results of the investigation first, the reader would have labelled these 'obvious' also. Obviously something is wrong with the entire argument of obviousness. It should really be turned on its head. Since every kind of human reaction is conceivable, it is of great importance to know which reactions actually occur most frequently and under what conditions . . . (1949: 380)

Lazarsfeld's rhetorical ploy has always impressed me as fairly unsettling for those who make the allegations of obviousness, but its force depends on whether we are willing to grant him his assumption that we accepted the first version of the research results as valid, so that he could then startle us with his second presentation, which gave the true findings: the results that were actually obtained. It might be argued that Lazarsfeld's assumption was unwarranted and that most of us would not have believed that first set of statements that he later revealed were spurious.

The Mischels' Study

So I took notice when I heard about investigations that made no assumptions of the kind that Lazarsfeld's exercise required. The first of these (Mischel, 1981; Mischel and Mischel, 1979) consisted of giving fourth- and sixth-grade children (Ns = 38 and 49, respectively) items presenting psychological principles stated in both their actual form and the opposite of the actual forms. For example, the first item dealt with the finding by Solomon Asch that college students would respond contrarily to the evidence of their senses about which of three lines had the same length as a comparison line when the students first heard four other students (confederates of the investigator) misidentify the same-length line. The second item concerned Harry Helson's finding that the same water temperature feels cooler on a hot day than on a cool day. In all, there were 17 such items, some of which were presented to only one of the two grade-level groups. The children circled the one of the two to four choices that they thought described what would happen in each situation.

Of the 29 opportunities for either the fourth graders or the sixth graders to select the actual research result to a statistically significant degree, the groups did so on 19, or 66 percent. One group or the other was wrong to a statistically significant degree on five opportunities, and there was no statistically significant correctness or incorrectness on five opportunities. Clearly, the children had substantial success, but far from the perfect record that would support the allegation of almost universal obviousness.

But these were only children. What about college students and adults? And what happens when the research results are presented as flat statements rather than as multiple-choice items requiring the selection of the actual result from two or more alternatives?

Baratz's Study

Baratz (1983) selected 16 social research findings from various studies, and then did an experiment. She manipulated, for each of the findings, whether the statement concerning that finding was the true finding or the opposite of the true finding. She also presented each finding, either the true one or the opposite one, with or without an explanation of the finding. That second manipulation was intended to 'explore the possibility that adding explanations to the findings may render the findings more obvious' (1983: 20).

Thus, each of her subjects – 85 male and female undergraduates enrolled in introductory psychology at Stanford University – evaluated 16 findings: four statements with a true finding plus explanation, four statements with the opposite finding plus explanation, four statements with a true finding without explanation, and four statements of an opposite finding without an explanation. Each finding was presented in the same format: first, the question addressed by the study, such as 'a study sought to determine whether people spend a larger proportion of their income during *prosperous* times or during a *recession*'. And for this study the reported finding was 'In prosperous times people spend a larger proportion of their income than during a recession.' The statement of the opposite finding differed from that of the true finding only in the order of the critical terms, and half of the findings were followed at the time by a short explanation, which was presented as the 'explanation given by our subject'.

Here are two sample pairs of the true and opposite findings used by Baratz in her experiment: 'People who go to church regularly tend to have more children than people who go to church infrequently' versus 'People who go to church infrequently tend to have more children than people who go to church regularly' and 'Single women express more distress over their unmarried status than single men do' versus 'Single men express more distress over their unmarried status than single women do.'

For each of the 16 findings presented to each student, the students were asked how readily predictable or obvious the finding was and were instructed to choose one of the responses on the following four-point scale:

1. I am *certain* that I would have predicted the result obtained rather than the opposite result.
2. I *think* that I would have predicted the result obtained rather than the opposite result, but I am *not certain*.
3. I *think* that I would have predicted the opposite to the obtained result, but I am *not certain*.
4 I am *certain* that I would have predicted the *opposite* to the obtained result.

The subjects were asked to express their 'initial impressions of the relevant findings, i.e. the kind of impression that you might form if you read a brief article about the research in your daily newspaper' (1983: 25).

In a summary table, Baratz presented the mean percentage of subjects who marked either 'I am *certain* that I would have predicted the reported outcome', or 'I *think* I would have predicted the reported outcome' for pairs of opposite findings. When the reported outcome was 'A', 80 percent of her students claimed they would have predicted that outcome. When the reported outcome was 'B', 66 percent of her subjects claimed they would have predicted that outcome. Thus, as Baratz put it, 'It is clear that findings that contradict each other were both retrospectively judged "obvious". . . . These results show clearly that reading a result made that result appear obvious. No matter which result was presented, the majority of the subjects thought that they would have predicted it' (1983: 26).

I considered Baratz's experiment and her findings to be persuasive. They seemed to provide evidence against the argument that social research yields only obvious findings. Her results indicated that intelligent people, namely, Stanford undergraduates, tend to regard any result they read, whether it is the true one or the opposite of the true one, as obvious. This tendency to say results are obvious was, of course, only a tendency; not all of her subjects followed that tendency, but it was a majority tendency. [. . .]

So the allegation of obviousness may now be countered with the research result that people tend to regard even contradictory research results as obvious. Perhaps even that result will henceforth be regarded as obvious.

References

Baratz, D. (1983) 'How justified is the "obvious" reaction', *Dissertation Abstracts International*, 44/02B, 644B. University Microfilms No. DA 8314435.

Conant, J.B. (1963) *The Education of American Teachers*. New York: McGraw-Hill.

Glass, G.V. (1987) 'Class size', in M.J. Dunkin (ed.), *The International Encyclopedia of Teaching and Teacher Education*. Oxford: Pergamon, pp. 540–5.

Goodlad, J.I. (1960) 'Classroom organization', in C.W. Harris (ed.), *Encyclopedia of Educational Research*, 3rd edn. New York: Macmillan, p. 224.

Keppel, F. (1962) 'The education of teachers', in H. Chauncey (ed.), *Talks on American Education: A Series of Broadcasts to Foreign Audiences by American Scholars*. New York: Teachers College, Columbia University, pp. 83–94.

Lazarsfeld, P.F. (1949) '*The American Soldier* – an expository review', *Public Opinion Quarterly*. 13: 377–404.

Mischel, W. (1981) 'Metacognition and the rules of delay', in J.H. Flavell and L. Ross (eds), *Social Cognitive Development: Frontiers and Possible Futures*. New York: Cambridge University Press.

Mischel, W. and Mischel, H. (1979) 'Children's Knowledge of Psychological Principles', unpublished manuscript.

Phillips, D.C. (1985) 'The uses and abuses of truisms', in C.W. Fisher and D.C. Berliner (eds), *Perspectives on Instructional Time*. New York: Longman, pp. 306–16.

Rice, J.M. (1913) *Scientific Management in Education*. New York: Hinds, Noble & Eldredge. (Original work published 1897.)

Schlesinger, Jr, A. (1949) 'The statistical soldier', *Partisan Review*, 16: 852–6.

Index